HOW TO BECOME A BILLIONAIRE BY SELLING

NOTHING

HOW TO BECOME A BILLIONAIRE BY SELLING

NOTHING

Aditya Magal

EBURY PRESS

An imprint of Penguin Random House

EBURY PRESS

USA | Canada | UK | Ireland | Australia
New Zealand | India | South Africa | China

Ebury Press is part of the Penguin Random House group of companies whose addresses can be found at global.penguinrandomhouse.com

Published by Penguin Random House India Pvt. Ltd
4th Floor, Capital Tower 1, MG Road,
Gurugram 122 002, Haryana, India

Penguin
Random House
India

First published by Random House India 2014

10 9 8 7 6 5 4 3 2

ISBN 9788184004342

Typeset in Adobe Garamond by Saanvi Graphics, Noida

Printed at Repro India Limited

www.penguin.co.in

The Family—many times shy and good for it

The Reader—thank you

CONTENTS

THE MAN WHO SOLD NOTHING

I am the greatest person in the world. This isn't random boasting; it's an honest, down-to-earth, and humble self-review. It is a conclusion that I have arrived at after years of jaw-dropping, outrageously awe-inspiring fantasticness. If I were a film critic and my awesome life were turned into a movie, I would rate it a 100 million stars out of 10. I'm a whole freakin' universe with more stars than 10 million Milky Way, Andromeda, and M61 galaxies combined.

Greatness radiates off me like light radiates off the sun. I am bathed in it. Clothed in it. Made from it. I am the superintendent of awesomeness. The badshah of badass, the shahenshah of the masses, the pharoah of the stock markets, the ultimate chick magnet, physical specimen par excellence (I have muscles on muscles on muscles. I have muscles in places most people don't even have places), beer drinker among beer drinkers, and the championest player of Super Mario, among other things.

Matter is made of teeny-tiny atoms and electrons. I am made of GREATOMS and GREATONS. They bear the seeds of my greatness. Heck, God particles blast out of my fingers like lightning bolts. If you are a friend, you are welcome to bask in them. If you are a foe, you shall burn in my light.

All the letters in all the words in all the sentences of all the paragraphs in all the pages of all the books ever written and then adapted into all the screenplays turned into Hollywood films subsequently ripped off into Bollywood films simply fail to address the exorbitant greatness I exude.

Yet, despite my overwhelming talent and humongous greatness, I am best known for being humble. I invented humility.

I realize that I am merely the humble vessel through which awesomeness flows.

As with all great men, my greatness too is tested from time to time. This is the story of the time it was tested the most.

Within these pages lie the sordid, epic adventure of a hero battling evil of an unimaginable scale. If you still haven't figured it out, the hero is me. This is a bloodstained saga of discombobulated bodies, eviscerated abdomens, broken bones, shattered hearts, infected minds, and burnt souls—all bound by the unforgiving hand of fate. There will be dragons, orcs, and goblins the kind of which will make Hannibal Lecter, Mogambo, and Gabbar Singh piss in their pants. Little babies will be sacrificed, women will be made slaves, and leaders will be made bonded labourers doing menial chores.

Welcome, o noble reader, to *How to Become a Billionaire by Selling Nothing.*

Let us begin.

I was sitting in my 15th floor office one fine evening watching the world's largest television (so big it makes a blue whale look like a Bluetooth earpiece) custom-made for me by Samsung Electronics. Did I mention that along with being the greatest, I am also the richest man in the world? I can well afford to have flatscreen TVs the size of freakin' billboards hung up on my office walls like swimsuit calendars.

I operate out of more offices and work stations than the President of the United States. Also, my plane is bigger than his.

The head office of the Jhunjhunwala empire is a posh piece of real estate in the heart of India's financial capital—Mumbai. Behind Dalal Street stands a tall, white skyscraper with giant bull horns drilled into its apex. This, my friends, is my temple. On its 15th floor is my sanctum. The building is called Jhunjhunwala Chambers. It is located on Nariman Point—it used to be called 'Nariman' till I pointed towards it one day, and since then it's been called Nariman Point—adjacent to the Arabian sea, a few metres from the state legislature building and more importantly, a stone's throw away from the financial cauldron of India's money market—the Bombay Stock Exchange.

Dalal Street and I are father and son. I was raised by Dalal Street. This is where I started my career as a stock picker 25 years ago. Today, I watch over it like a dutiful son does his ageing dad.

These days, everyone from the Queen of England to the King of Qatar wait in line to kiss my billionaire bottom. My left butt cheek alone is worth ten times more than Australia's Gross Domestic Product.

As I watched TV, marvelling at the interplay of pixels on the HD 4D LED platinum encased screen, I heard a quick knock on my door. I swivelled the chair to find the 23-year-old office-boy Nitin gently peeking his head like a tortoise through the crevice of the door.

'Kya hai bhai?' I asked.

'Sir, koi aapse milne aaya hai. Ramakant Shastri.'

'Theek hai. Bhej do andar,' I ordered as Nitin withdrew his tortoise head. Soon he popped inside head and all, holding the door ajar.

A scrawny man, with grey hair at the temples, a moustache drawn across his upper lip, and a slim laptop bag slung across his shoulder, hobbled in nervously trying to crack a smile.

I told the fellow to sit down and instructed Nitin to fetch the guest a glass of ice-cold water.

'What can I do for you?' I asked as the man seated himself on the bright red couch adjacent to the TV. Quickly I kicked the floor and flashed across towards him. He seemed startled at the speed of my chair. Having turned the TV off, I gazed intently at him with the breathtaking stare of a zen-master.

'My name is Ramakant Shastri. I am an entrepreneur.'

'I'm Jhunjhunwala. I have no surname—just like GOD. I Rock \m/.'

'Of course I know, Sir. Everyone knows who you are! Aap toh aadmi nahin bhagwan hain! Aapki charcha prithvi se lekar devlok tak ki jaati hai! Kuber bhagwan bhi aapse hi home loan lete hain!!'

Impressed with this very sincere and accurate appraisal of my great self, peppered with words most commonly used in an episode of 'Mahabharat' (and an HDFC bank ad), I smiled. 'Very nice. So why are you here?'

'I am the founder of a company called Notco and I am here to seek investment for my company.'

'What does Notco make?' I asked with interest.

Ramakant Shastri sipped the glass of cold water Nitin had silently brought in while we were conversing. Slowly setting it down and looking as refreshed as a heroine in a bathing scene, he smiled widely and spoke fervently, 'We've introduced a revolutionary new product called…WAIT…FOR..IT…WAIT FOR IT…Hold your breath…are you holding your breath, Sir?'

'Yes. I have paused the process of respiration. Now please tell me about the product before I blow up like a cycle tube. My face is turning beet red and holding my breath makes my voice squeaky! With this voice I am sure I will be cast as Theodore, the voice of the second Chipmunk, in *Alvin and the Chipmunks* dubbed in Hindi as *Alvin aur Rang Birangi Nachne Wale Gilheriyan.* On a side note, I am amazed at the amount of words I am able to manufacture while holding my breath! I must add this to my repertoire of skills,' I screamed squeakily.

'Oh! I'm sorry Sir. Without further ado, let me introduce you to…THE FUTURE.

'Notco's

'Revolutionary,

'New,

'Fantastic,

'Imaginative,

'Jaw-dropping,

'Mind-blowing,

'Attention-grabbing,

'Diaphragm-shattering,

'Electrifying,

'World-beating,

'Time and space warping,

'Supercalifragilisticexpialidociousing Product:

NOTHING.'

'Excuse me?!' I exclaimed, flabbergasted. My gast had never been this badly flabbered till today.

Steely and calm, the fellow answered, 'It's called NOTHING, Sir. It's Notco's new invention. We would like you to invest in my company so that I can make NOTHING.'

Confused and wondering if this was a joke, I asked squeamishly, trying to recover my breath from the Chipmunk squeaking and the subsequent gast flabbering, 'Err…is Nothing the name of the product?'

'Yes Sir, Nothing is the name of the product.'

'Okay, but what *is* the product?'

'It's Nothing, Sir.'

'It's nothing… Meaning?'

'It's Nothing.'

Even more confused and beginning to get unsettled, wondering if I was indeed hearing right or if the sound waves had changed somewhere in my ear canal into an audio signal my brain had misinterpreted to be heard as 'nothing', I prodded vehemently, 'No, No…hold on, what exactly is the product?'

'It's Nothing, Sir. I am committed to making the finest Nothing in the world. *I have a dream and that dream is to make Nothing affordable for everyone.*'

Before I could open my mouth, he yammered away, 'As an entrepreneur, I shall develop the best Nothing, then put it in tiny sachets, small packets, medium-sized packages, big cartons, large trunks, extra-large shipping containers, extra-extra-large cargo jets…

'I will put Nothing on T-shirts, caps, and trousers. I want people of all colours and all collars—blue, white, and everything in between—to buy Nothing.

'NOTHING is for men, women, the living, the dead. If Science proves the existence of ghosts tomorrow, even they will use Nothing.

'NOTHING is the future, and I as an entrepreneur request you—the world's greatest investor—to help me make my dream of making Nothing a reality.'

'Is this a joke?!' I thundered.

'No Sir! I am dead serious. I honestly and sincerely believe in Nothing and I want to make it with your money.'

'Let me just get this clear one more time—You want me, the world's greatest investor, the world's most awesome person, the world's richest man, an individual with a very impressive lung capacity which allows him to manufacture an inordinate amount of words even when he isn't breathing, to finance a company which makes nothing?'

'Exactly Sir! I need your help in making Nothing.'

'Eh! What shit is this? How do you even make this…what is it called…nothing?'

'I'm glad you asked me that question, Sir,' Ramakant beamed as he took another sip. The ice within the glass was quickly liquefying. I felt the same thing happening to my brain.

'The secret to making Nothing is funnels,' Ramakant proclaimed, placing the glass on the table with a thud and proceeding to open his arms.

'Funnels????!'

'Funnels. You know those triangular things with hollow tubes at their tips. They guide stuff into stuff which usually holds stuff.'

'Yes you idiot, I know what a funnel is. My question is how the hell can you make nothing with funnels?'

'See Sir, the thing is that *something* comes from *somewhere*. All of this around us, you, me, cars, animals, computers, newspapers, diapers, dandruff…well…is basically something and is found somewhere. Likewise *Nothing* comes from *nowhere.*' Ramakant beamed again and paused for a reaction.

'Ah…'

'You must have come across characters in novels and movies saying 'I'm in the middle of nowhere'. This always piqued my interest. I mean where is nowhere? After years of painful research, I have discovered that *nowhere* is where something is *not.*'

Scratching my head I blurted, "Whaa?!'

He continued, 'We beings live in these bits of *somewhere* called cities and countries. We even describe these places as *'Somewhere here'* or *'Somewhere there'*. This is where we build our homes, offices, schools…in short, our entire lives.

'Nowhere is the exact opposite of somewhere.

'Nowhere is where there's none of this stuff. No people, no trees, no animals, no habitation, no civilization. Just Nothing… in all its glory.

'Nothing is found nowhere.

'The deeper we venture into nowhere, the better the quality of Nothing we will find! And that's what the middle of nowhere actually means—the purest and rarest Nothing is found bang in the middle of nowhere.

'We must therefore go to the middle of nowhere to obtain nothing.'

'I am astounded by the sheer bizzarity of this!' I yelled.

'Actually Sir, it's not that uncommon. History shows that almost all ancient civilizations knew about Nothing and used to harness its power.

'Take a look at the Egyptians for instance. Thousands of years ago they built Pyramids out in the middle of nowhere. Why?' asked Ramakant tracing over his moustache with his finger.

'To bury their pharaohs? How the hell should I know?'

'My research indicates that all Pyramids are basically industrial storehouses of Nothing!

'All this garbage about kings ascending to the afterlife is just government propaganda to hide the truth.

'In reality, all these Pyramids were actually upside-down funnels used to suck Nothing from nowhere. That's why they built these things in the desert because a place like that was a classic and naturally occurring expanse of Nothing!'

'But the Pyramids don't look like funnels!'

'That's because the governments that came into power later didn't like the shape of the upturned pyramids. They thought that the funnel tubes looked like giant erections. Obviously aap agar triangle cheezon pe khamba staphit karenge toh government bhi Censor board wala kam hi karega na.'

'What the hell!'

'Yes Sir. Bloody narrow-minded governments! At that time, erections were classified as the devil's deeds, so they destroyed all the funnel tubes and constructed this story of pharaohs and the afterlife. Frankly speaking, I don't blame them. They would have looked like triangular stone dicks. That's just vulgar and obscene!

'That's why Pyramids these days look the way they do—like Bingo Mad Angles—though they were actually built as funnels to suck and store Nothing from nowhere. I mean if you look at the Sphinx, for instance, the evidence is just there! That nose of the Sphinx. It was a funnel tube as well, but the government bastards lopped it off!'

'I guess the Sphinx was getting a bit nosy…right?'

'Yes Sir. I'm glad I'm getting through to you.'

I further reclined back in my chair and peered steadily at the scrawny man sitting across from me. Clad in a striped shirt and a pair of dull grey khaki pants, he smiled sheepishly at me. I was unsure if all he had just said was a prank—nothing, nowhere, pyramids, sphinxes, erections. This is not what you expect from an entrepreneur. Perhaps, sensing my doubt, he quickly pressed his lips. His smile vanished and a more serious looking Ramakant opened his black bag and pulled out a laptop.

Trying to look casual, he continued puncturing the silence with 'Now Sir, what I want to do is basically go to all the nowheres in the world. I've made a map containing all the sites of nowhere I have discovered so far.

'Antarctica,

'The Kalahari Desert,

'Valleys in the Amazon Rainforest,

'Underwater Caverns in the Australian Great Barrier Reef,

'Siberia,

'Here in India, the biggest nowhere is in West Bengal—the Sundarbans Mangroves. In the middle of all those marshes lies in solitude—the untapped Nothing.

'There are no living things there. Just acres and acres of natural nowhere. Mother Earth's gift to us all!

'This is where I will setup a giant Nothing-manufacturing unit.'

'Let me get this straight once and for all. You want to go nowhere and make nothing?' I asked, now fully convinced this guy was either high on dope or an escaped mental patient or a prankster. There was no other explanation for it.

'Yes. I intend to build a factory in the nowhere, and then install giant funnels. Those funnels are connected to motors whose fans rotate and suck Nothing from the atmosphere!

'And once we capture Nothing, we process it and sell it. What do you think?'

Taken aback at the sudden question, I bellowed a very confused 'uhhh'.

As if spurred on by it, he quickly clicked the mouse on his laptop and seconds later turned the screen towards me.

'Our key to success lies in being able to:

'Develop the necessary infrastructure to suck out Nothing. The more we suck and the better we suck, the more profitable our venture becomes.

'Find the best nowhere. The better the nowhere, the better the Nothing.

'And this is why I need your money so that I can start installing funnels in factories located nowhere to make Nothing.'

Irritated and slightly angered by the fact that the prank had carried on for far too long I barked, *'Mr Shastri, Have you gone mad?'*

'No Sir! I am a genius like Nikola Tesla. In his time, people called him mad too, but today everyone recognizes what a genius he was.'

'There's a famous saying in the stock market', I raged pointing my finger at him, 'Don't ever write a cheque with your mouth you can't cash with your ass.' In Hindi it means mooh se dhanadesh mat likho joh pichwade se bharna pade. Do you realize you don't even have a product?'

Taken aback he said, 'Sir, I think I have failed to make you understand the power of Nothing. My bad. I'll give it one more try. Everybody else makes money selling something. That's what the world is made of. *I will be the one guy who makes money selling NOTHING.'*

'Alright. So tell me, who will buy nothing?'

'Sir, in life, everyone wants to have everything and EVERYTHING is SOMETHING + NOTHING.'

'Others sell something. I sell nothing because life without Nothing is incomplete. That way everyone can have something and Nothing, thus end up with everything.'

'This is absurd logic. How much do you want me to invest?' I asked out of curiosity. '5000 crores,' he answered coolly.

I stared at him aghast, gulped some dry air, and reclined once again in my chair. Fully convinced by then that this was a joke, I let out a sarcastic grin of amusement. Sensing my state of mind, he tried to salvage the situation.

'Essentially Nothing is an extremely versatile product. It's easy to manufacture, ridiculously easy to store, and so malleable that you can use it in anything! Isn't that amazing? To be able to use NOTHING in Anything?' he smiled expansively.

'Err...'

'It's got cross industry appeal...'

I cut him off and readied to leave. 'Okay listen Rajnikant...I mean...Ramakant. I don't understand your product. Call me old-fashioned or whatever, but I am the World's greatest investor and I did not become one by investing in companies and products I don't understand. So, it's been nice talking to you and I wish you the best of luck with...Nothing. But I have other important things to do, so goodbye!'

Like a kid in a toy store, he pleaded, 'Sir! Just hold on please. I know it's a hard idea to grasp essentially because it's in a space which is yet to develop.'

'And what space is that?'

'What I mean is it's an abstract product as of now. It's not so much a product as an idea and frankly people will pay to own the idea. That's what it is. Nothing is abstract. Not concrete but formless and expressive.

'ALL WE NEED TO DO IS CREATE A MARKET FOR NOTHING. THEN PEOPLE WILL BUY NOTHING.'

'Mr Shastri, I am not going to invest in non-existent products.' I sternly declared.

Shastri counter-argued, 'But don't you see Sir? That's where the opportunity lies. Nothing has a lot of potential.

'My company is creating a new market for non-existent products because people are sick, tired, and unhappy with existing, existent products. It's time for non-existent products to enter the market, and with your help I am confident India will become a world leader in the manufacture of non-existent products.'

In that moment, I felt that the easiest and most effective method of getting rid of Ramakant Shastri was to punch him in the face and knock him out. But before I could swerve a right hook, he flashed the one thing I hate to see the most from entrepreneurs...a PPT presentation. It was a loaded gun ready to shoot a smoking barrel right at my brain.

'As you can see Sir, in the first of my 79,871-slide PPT presentation, I discuss the value of Nothing and how it will be the world's next mega product. Nothing will be bigger than any product ever made by anyone who makes something.

'Just take a look, Sir!

'Do you see, Sir? Nothing is the future and I hope Nothing makes sense to you now.'

Bored and weary, eager to move on and away from this individual who I was now convinced was a lunatic, I grunted as I raised myself up to leave, 'Like I said Mr Ramakant... I don't understand your...errr...non-existent...abstract...whatever it is you're calling it...product...So I'm going to pass.

'Wish you good luck. I have to go now. I've made 12,000 million dollars trading stocks today and I am hungry. Also, I have to take my wife out to dinner. I hope you understand Mr Shastri.'

'Of course! Of course! You are exceptional. You make time to spend with your family. I must learn from you, Sir. I have been so busy trying to make and sell Nothing that I have not seen my wife's face for the past three months.'

'Oh, well I think your wife is very lucky to have such a hard-working and creative husband who spends all of his time in nothing.'

Do you see, Sir? Nothing is the future and I hope Nothing makes sense to you now.

'Thank you, Sir! Thank you so much. I will tell her you said this when I meet her next week. It's her birthday or our anniversary or something. I am sure it's important but I am not sure what...'

As he tried to remember what was important, I tried to make a quick getaway. 'Okay dude...I've gotta go. So see you...'

With soft, childlike eyes, the man gawked desperately. His hopes clung to his eyes. 'One minute, Sir! Just one minute. I am sorry for holding you back from your family duties, but can you please consider my idea just one more time?'

With enraged eyes, I howled 'Ramakant Shastri, let me ask you one more time. Are you serious about this or are you trying to pull my leg? Mujhe fasane ke liye sting operation toh nahin kar rahe ho? '

Wiping the sweat off his brow and packing the laptop, he searched for an answer as I continued, 'I am dumbfounded that you even ask me to invest in such a non-existent idea about a literally non-existent product.'

'Sir! Sir! It's non-existent definitely but it's abstract! Please help me Sir. You are the first man I've come to with this idea and your guidance and expertise will go a long way in helping our small little company. So please help me!'

'Oh, You definitely need help. Lots and lots of help. Professional help.'

'I do Sir. I am an entrepreneur who wants to make his dream a reality. I want to sell a world-class product to the world but to be able to do that, I need funding. You are the patron saint of the world's most profitable companies. The God of the stock markets. The king of kings and the superstar, superhero, megastar, awesome, greatest investor of all time!'

'Hmm... The praise is justified. I have decided something. I will help you. Hold on.'

'What Sir?' he asked a tad bit excited.

I was so eager to get rid of this fellow that I would have carried this buffoon on my gigantically well-built herculean shoulders and dropped him like an anvil right from the balcony of my office. But the thought of my wife and kids at home stopped me. He'd have to change his name from Ramakant Shastri to SPLAT! after hitting the road below.

But I was hungry and a dead body on the ground below would cause a traffic jam. I could easily avoid the jam by flying home in my helicopter. Maybe I could hover past Mukesh Ambani's house and tell Nita to do more ab crunches (she practices yoga around this time only everyday).

I remembered that all my helicopters were being upgraded with afterburners so they were in the chop shop. So I decided to take the Bentley instead. I cancelled my homicide plans and rang in my Secretary.

Twenty seconds later, she pushed her head in just like Nitin had a few minutes back.

'Ah! Secretary, well, well, well, we meet again. I've been expecting you,' I said as I turned my gaze from Shastri to the Secretary glancing around like an evil James Bond villain.

'Umm…yes Sir…you called me in.'

'Please get me my cheque book. I have decided to give Mr Ramakant Shastri here some of my money. Also, give him the number of that celebrity psychologist doctor I was telling you about. The same one who helps Junior Ambani deal with the insecurities he feels for being worth only 14 billion dollars as compared to his brother Senior Ambani who is worth 19 billion.'

'Yes Sir,' she said and hastened to discharge the duties I had just assigned her. One more turtle head bob later, I received my cheque book (my favorite book).

'Here you go, Ramakant. I am signing a pristine leaf from my cheque book. Treasure it for this is the greatest gift you will ever receive—my money. Countless people crave for this gift, but here I am gifting it to you, for I am benevolent.'

I signed my golden name in golden ink from a golden pen. I gave the cheque to Ramakant and spoke these golden words:

'This is a cheque for one lakh rupees. It's a little less than 5000 crores, but it will be helpful. Collect the psychologist's number on your way out, please.'

'But why are you giving me these, Sir?' a fidgety Ramakant, by now on his feet, asked.

'Any person who earnestly believes in nothing and wants to sell nothing and wants my money to make and sell nothing, seriously needs to have his head examined. So take this cheque, cash it in, and then use the money to pay the head doctor. If anything is left, then feel free to buy yourself a novelty item like a T-shirt or a watch. But if you do buy a watch, buy a Titan watch because Titan is a company I hold a huge stake in. Your purchase would help in increasing sales revenue and consequently impact the share price. In fact buy two titans. Bang them together and watch a clash of the titans. HAHAHAHA!'

As I laughed away to glory holding my sexy paunch, blown away by the genius play of puns, the perplexed man said, 'This is all very sudden Sir, but I understand. I think this is a personality evaluation test which I must pass to obtain an investment from your esteemed self.'

'Yeah…something like that I guess. You can discuss this with the psychologist. I shall take your leave now and you shall take my leave now. We shall take each other's leave now.'

'Goodbye, Mr Shastri!'

'Bye Sir! Thank you for everything.'

'Sure. Thanks for nothing.'

'Ah! Ah…I get it, Sir! Hahahaha! You have a terrific sense of humour, Sir! HAHAHA! Thanks for nothing.'

'Remember to see the doctor.'

'I will Sir! I will.'

AWESOMENESS IS HAZARDOUS TO HEALTH

'I'm sorry to inform you, Mr Jhunjhunwala, that you're suffering from a very dangerous disease called awesomitis,' a dreary, bespectacled gentleman in a doctor's coat spoke as I opened my droopy eyes and sat up.

Trying to fathom what I had just been told, I tried to remember how I had arrived at the present juncture. I asked, concerned, 'Oh no! Will I die, doctor? Will the world be robbed of my awesome awesomeness? That's just so unfair...especially to the world!'

'For the moment you are safe, but we had to perform emergency surgery on you.'

'Surgery! Holy crap. Did you cut me open without my permission? I feel so violated! This is a breach of my sovereignty and integrity. It is a grievous defilement of my personal space! Did my enemies put you upto this? I bet you harvest human organs and sell it on the black market. How could you surgecilize me? HOW? I demand an explanation and free ice cream.'

The doctor was taken aback that I had discovered his nefarious design, and tried to calm me down. 'Well actually, you were brought in here by your wife and home staff a few hours back. We did an emergency scan of your body and realized that you were just overflowing with awesomeness. That's why we had to cut your awesomix out.'

'Huh? How can I be sure you haven't stolen my kidneys or something? How can I be sure you have not kidnapped me and arranged to sell me to a dance bar? I know my gorgeous man-curves and sexy figure are titillating, but kidnapping me is not the right way to go about things.'

'Please relax Mr Jhunjhunwala. We haven't kidnapped you. Perhaps you are still hazy from the morphine. Anyway, please relax. You might rupture your stitches. As I said earlier, we had to remove your awesomix.'

'Awesomix? What's that?' I asked looking suspiciously at the organ pimp.

'The awesomix, Mr Jhunjhunwala, is a little fleshy gland in your abdomen, just above your intestinal area. It's very small…may be an inch long. Really tiny, maybe a little bigger than Digvijay Singh's brain, but no more.'

'Oh! You mean Digvijay Singh, the politician?'

'Uhh…let's just say, he is the owner of Costa Rica's finest chain of Punjabi dhabas.'

'Achha, yes, I know him. He is definitely a real person. Daler Mehndi ki shaadi mein usne hi catering ki thi. He was paid in CDs of Tunak Tunak Tun.'

'The awesomix is like a thermometer-cum-safety valve which measures and limits people's awesomeness. Now in people who are partially awesome, it's a little bigger than an inch. In people who are very awesome, it's maybe a few inches long but in people who are just magnificently, stupendously, gigantically just overflowing with cauldrons of awesomeness, it becomes enlarged. Like really, really huge! As huge as a car battery,' the doctor elaborated moving his hands fervently all the while.

Seized with wonder at the level to which my health had deteriorated, I exclaimed 'Wow! My awesomix must have been as big as an Exide car battery then.'

'No,' he said stoically.

'An Amaron battery then?' I prodded.

'Well, to tell you the truth, your awesomix was way bigger. It was not just bigger than a car battery, but an entire truck engine itself!'

'Oh! Thank Ganesha, you removed it when you did or else it would have become bigger than a plane battery,' I sighed with relief.

'I don't think planes have batteries. Luckily we were able to get you here in time for the surgery.'

'I never thought my awesomeness would be so life-threatening!'

The grave looking, 30-something doctor, raised himself up on his toes playfully. 'Oh but it most definitely is. Yes. You are truly truly awesome. A magnificent specimen of life-blistering awesomeness. Even now, despite having your awesomix removed, you are just reeking of awesomeness. I've never seen anything like it. This level of awesomeness is so fatal, it could endanger the lives of ordinary folk. That's why we've quarantined you here in a special awesomeness ward.'

'Oh! I'm so sorry my awesomeness has caused this much trouble, doctor. Can I at least see my family?'

'Please don't apologize,' the doctor said trying his best not to cause me to panic. 'Our tests showed that your family is somehow used to your level of greaton radiation. Being exposed to your awesomeness, they seem to have developed some type of anti-body defence mechanism. They can be allowed near you for short periods. Would you like me to fetch them?'

'Yes please!'

'Ok. I'm going on my rounds. I'll be back soon. My colleagues will help you if you need anything. Just summon the staff for any assistance. I'll let them know they can visit now. It's good you are awake. I'm the deputy in the team of doctors monitoring you. My name is Dr Iyengar.'

'Nice to meet you, doctor Iyengar,' I said feeling partially indebted that this man had put his life at risk to save me from my own awesomeness, yet not entirely confident he wasn't running an organ plus human trafficking racket.

'Anytime,' he said and walked out of the door with a sense of pride.

I found myself on a king-size hospital bed as I lay underneath a vibrant blue bed sheet with pink petals printed on. I made a mental note to buy shares of Bombay Dyeing the moment I left this place.

It was a large room. The VIP suite as the doctor/organ smuggler had mentioned. There was a 50-inch plasma screen TV on the wall, a myriad of coloured glass portraits, a teak wood bookshelf, and a cappuccino maker as well in the room.

I remarked to myself I should fall ill more often. This was 8-star treatment. Even the alarm which fetched the nurse was a digital blinking icon on a touchscreen remote labeled 'Interactive health pad'. I clicked a few icons and found that it doubled up as a room service call-up device and tripled up as an instant, multiplayer gamepad for the *Batman: Arkham Asylum* video game. Sweet!

Next to me was a drip plugged into my arm with the polythene bag inverted from a rosewood beanpole. A handwritten note on the right side-table next to a basket of Swiss chocolates read: *'Dear Mr Jhunjhunwala, wishing you a very wonderful stay at JK Hospital. Our courteous staff and administrators are ever present and very happy to assist you to a full and hearty medical recovery. Your Chief Healthcare Professional, Dr Rajesh Rana'.*

JK was the hospital of choice for the affluent. It's a 20 floor, 20 acre, futuristic hospital built on a small islet a few nautical miles from the Bombay High oilfield and is equipped with every medical tool and wonder drug imaginable. The infirmary is stocked with pharmaceuticals years ahead of today's time.

I tapped the remote as the TV flickered on.

'30 newborns die as incubator short circuits at government hospital. Angry parents and relatives protest outside the hospital as the Government of West Bengal offers 50,000 as compensation and sets up a committee to probe the cause of the short circuit which literally

fried these infants to death,' an anchor with a deadpan, unflinching expression, blared on a news channel.

Here I was in a palatial dwelling rife with every amenity and luxury achievable with cash. Created by the rich just for the rich so that they wouldn't have to go through the grind of the sick common man. Meanwhile, somewhere else, newborns were being herded like lab rats, tucked neatly into rooms one-fourth the size of this ward, and kept alive by flimsy incubators. In this case, the journey from life to death for these little ones had been painfully short. Short circuited literally.

Bummed with the news, I angrily switched the TV off and rang for the nurse. Pushing away at the keypad, the alarm icon blinked repeatedly as a young nurse and a younger steward walked in.

Both were dressed in white with JK imprinted profoundly on the uniform's chest pocket.

'Good evening Sir, how can we help you. We are your personal healthcare attendants. I'm Garima and this is Rajesh,' the nurse said warmly as she introduced herself and the boy standing beside her.

This was the first time I had been sick to a level which required hospitalization and it was also my first trip to JK.

A flicker of pain sparked across my abdomen as I withdrew my hand from the gauze. Irritated and uncomfortable, I whined, 'I want to see my wife! Where is she? That doctor said he'd fetch her! I don't trust that organ stealer! I bet he's run off with my pancreas! I know what this is, you people have kidnapped me! I'm too much of an awesome genius and you want to dissect my brain and find out what makes my neurons tick. Aaaaaaah!'

'Please relax, Sir,' Rajesh pleaded as he continued to smile. 'We aren't kidnapping you. Your wife has been contacted. She is currently at the hospital spa. Poor madam! All the stress of watching you being hospitalized has left her very stressed. She'll be here in a short while, hopefully much more relaxed, with exfoliated skin and smelling of olive oil.'

'Oye! Don't talk to me about how my wife smells,' I thundered.

'Sorry Sir, just trying to comfort you,' Rajesh smiled and looked at Garima who nodded in approval.

I tugged at my gown. 'And what the hell is this?! I hate this bloody gown. It's short and uncomfortable. I can't even remove this bloody bed sheet because if I did, this bloody gown being so short would allow you folks generous access to...strategic areas.'

'I'm again very sorry dear Sir. You see our standard issue hospital gowns didn't fit you so we had to improvize.'

'Well, what did you do?'

'We had to take three or four gowns meant for the pregnant women down in the maternity ward and stitch them together for you to...err...accommodate your extended body girth,' Rajesh explained.

'OYE! Are you calling me fat? You better not be calling me fat! I will buy this hospital so fast and transfer you so quickly to the pathology lab, you'll spend the rest of your life analyzing stool samples, got it!'

Rajesh quickly apologized. 'Oh...oh...oh! I'm sorry Sir. Very sorry. I meant no insult. Please don't put me in pathology. Brrr. That place gives me the chills! I merely meant to say that the hospital does not have the gowns fit for a man of your dimensions. We don't have gowns in size XXXXXXXXXXXXXXXXXXXXXXXL...'

'Nonetheless, please do not worry,' Garima said intent on also not being stuck in pathology. 'This will never happen again. We have already placed an order with a truck cover maker to manufacture gowns for plus-size people like yourself.'

'ARE YOU CALLING ME FAT AGAIN?!'

Rajesh answered 'No! Of course not, Sir. All we are saying is...'

I cut him short. 'Bah! Whatever. Bring me my wife. I feel violated in this gown. I hate this place, God dammit!'

'I'm so sorry, Sir! Is there anything we could do to alleviate your misery and ensure a speedy recovery?' Garima asked, intent on not pissing me off further.

'Sure.' I replied readily. 'I'd like a bottle of whiskey.'

'To drink?'

'You could say it's an experiment where I try to study the effects of alcohol on myself. I will make observations, draw inferences, and put down my findings in my research thesis.'

'Err... I don't understand, Sir!'

'Of course to drink!' I explained looking at Garima. 'Hamein tight hona hai. Daaru kahaan se milega?'

'I'm sorry Sir, but you are a patient.' Rajesh interjected. 'You've been advised complete bed-rest to recover from surgery and are on a special food programme. So I'm deeply sorry, but no alcohol or smoking for you.'

'God dammit! I hate this place. You two go and get my wife and I'd like to talk to the surgeon who cut me open as well. Fetch them both. NOW!' I ordered.

'Yes Sir!' Garima said and furiously scampered away with Rajesh. Both were glad they were being dispatched without being transferred to Pathology.

I saw a quick opportunity and pressed the pad again. Another steward came rushing in.

'Good evening, Sir!' he said. 'My name is Ramkumar. I'll be your attendant in Rajesh's absence. How may I assist you?'

Wasting no time I said, 'If you get me a bottle of whiskey right now, I will give you 1000 rupees.'

'Err... Let me just look at your chart,' he said looking at the chart hanging at the foot of the bed.

'No, please. That's not necessary. Look, I'll give you 1500 rupees. That's a fifty percent increase in bribe if you get me that bottle of whiskey. I'll also give you 100 crores if you wear iron boots and kick that organ-stealing doctor in between his legs.

Ramkumar blinked.

I continued, 'Think about it. Moreover, I've been misdiagnosed. I'm suffering from awesomitis. The only way to cure that is alcohol. When Dr Rana gets here, I'll explain my condition to him and he'll gladly prescribe scotch. Now be a good fellow and get me some whiskey. My tongue is dryer than a bedouin's hands.'

'Bedou…what? I don't think I am allowed to do that, Sir. I'm sorry,' he said sternly.

'Look…Ramkumar…I will give you 2000 rupees, okay? Yeh toh poori bottle whiskey se bhi zyaada hai. Just get me some. I promise I won't divulge how I received the whiskey. Moreover, you are my attendant, right?'

'Yes.'

'So it's your duty to do what I tell you to do. It is your dharma to smuggle in whiskey for me. *Your dharma*!' I repeated making a strong case for getting tight.

Ramkumar looked immersed in thought. It was a lucrative offer—whiskey for me and money and silence for him.

After a minute, he stammered hesitantly, 'Okay…'

'That's good,' I smiled, glad I had brought him over to the dark side. 'Now go and hurry back before anyone sees you!'

Ramkumar ran off as I waited patiently. I was bored and spent the next few minutes playing on the gamepad. Soon I heard the rushed patter of running feet. It was Ramkumar. Pushing the door ajar, the skinny lad hurried towards me and conjured up a paper bag with a small 500 ml bottle of whiskey.

I screamed in delight. 'Atta boy! That's the spirit.'

Nervously, Ramkumar looked back to see if he had shut the doors properly and asked, 'Should I get you a glass, Sir or will you drink from the bottle itself?'

'Oh don't bother,' I said pointing at the beanpole. 'You see this glucose drip hooked to my vein?'

'Yes.'

'Just empty the liquid in the drip bag and refill it with the whiskey.'

The boy looked perplexed and exclaimed after a few seconds of silence. 'You cannot be serious!'

'You see this glucose drip hooked to my vein? Just empty the liquid in the drip bag and refill it with the whisky.'

'I am dead serious,' I said wondering why he was doubting me. 'I never joke about whiskey. Now hurry up. I want at least half the bottle within me before I meet the doc or before those two fetch my wife. Hurry!'

Nervousness turned into bedazzlement as Ramkumar moved fast. Striking like lightning, the 20-year-old removed the bag from the beanpole, emptied the liquid into a glass, and proceeded to unscrew the whiskey bottle and started filling up the bag. After every pour, he looked at me like a bartender asking if I'd had enough. I gestured him to fill it up!

'There. It's done, Sir. Khatam ho gaya,' he said emptying the last few drops into the bag as I smiled in approval.

'Very good! Thank you Ramkumar. Now hurry along. Also dispose off the bottle. If anyone asks, tell them it's whiskey shampoo...like beer shampoo, except its whiskey shampoo.'

'Sure Sir,' Ramkumar obliged tucking the empty bottle into his pyjamas. 'But will you be okay? I mean this is desi daaru, not imported scotch like you are used to. It's just something I picked up from a fellow attendant's stash downstairs.'

'Don't worry yaar,' I said glad that someone at this hospital was finally asking the right questions about my health. 'Desi ho ya vilayati, jab hona hai tight toh koi bhi tharra se kaam chalega.'

'Hehe! Theek hai Sir. Cheers!' an amused Ramkumar said as he slid out through the door.

I nestled my head in the soft, white pillow and felt the cold whiskey enter my veins. I was starting to feel better already. Slowly I closed my eyes and wandered away.

'Dude! What the hell is wrong with you?' a shrill voice screamed as I awoke into the land of the un-intoxicated. 'You just had your appendix removed and you're already drinking? And how the hell did you manage to smuggle whiskey into this place?!' Opening my hazy eyes, I looked at the screaming figure. It was an irate Ramesh screaming his head off. Garima and Rajesh quivered behind him.

Ramesh is my best friend. He's about 3 years elder to me and while obviously not as good looking, smart, sexy, or rich as me, he does make up with a strong sense of loyalty, compassion, honour, and judgement. Ramesh is one of the few people who've known me even before I became a billionaire.

Both he and I started out on the Bombay Stock Exchange back in the late 80s with a few bucks and fewer dreams. Two and a half decades later, we still remain the best of friends, often bouncing ideas off one another. Even today, we chill out on Dalal Street eating pani-puri and tooty-frooty ice cream from the street vendors as we discuss everything under the sun, most notably the ozone layer.

While I am a billionaire, Ramesh hasn't done too badly either. He's a millionaire and more importantly, he's a great friend.

The short, stocky, Humpty Dumpty-like Ramesh with traces of a once hairy civilization on his scalp, was now looking at me with his pointy eyes and broad nose. The wavy, bushy moustache on his lip growled as he yelled.

'Do you have any idea how sick you've been? On top of that, you hook up a whiskey drip to your arms! Are you freakin' crazy!'

I had been awakened from my whiskey-induced stupor by Garima. Ramesh had come to visit and when she was waking me up, she had noticed the whiskey droplets falling into my bloodstream. Quite naturally, I was at the end of a verbal beating from my best friend.

Pleading my innocence I hit back, 'I haven't done anything wrong yaar! The doctor said I have to be on a liquid diet.'

'THAT DOESN'T MEAN YOU START DRINKING! You have no regard for yourself or your health. Look how fat you've become! As it is, you're diabetic. You eat so much we have to weigh you in tons not kilos! Your BP is super high and your heart beats faster than a snare drummer in a heavy metal band! AND NOW

YOU'RE DRINKING IN THE FREAKIN' HOSPITAL! Your cholesterol level is off the charts and you don't do any exercise! And before you say it…NO! Playing Angry Birds on your cellphone is not exercise!'

'OYE! I'M NOT FAT. I'm just extra fleshy and I do exercise—I work out at McDonalds at least 5 or 6 times a week! Don't you get it! I am the victim here! On top of all this, I've just recovered from awesomitis. You shouldn't yell at poor old sick me!' I implored.

Ramesh paused for a moment and looked at me, strangely amused. 'Did you just say awesomitis?'

'Yeah,' I replied. 'The doctor…err…healthcare professional… said I have awesomitis because my awesomix got swollen.'

Ramesh paused again, grabbed the chart and glanced over it. Quietly raising his head he asked outraged, 'DUDE! HOW BLOODY DRUNK ARE YOU? It's not awesomitis you moron, its *appendicitis*! You had your *appendix* removed.'

'Are you sure? I mean I heard the doctor say I had my awesomix removed.'

'Jesus! Did you imagine yet another conversation, O awesomely narcissistic fat one!'

'No man! I swear. You're mistaken. I had my awesomix removed because I'm way too awesome and I have awesomitis.'

'Shut up!' Ramesh riled on as Garima and Rajesh watched silently. 'I brought you here after you fainted in your office. We flew you by an air ambulance. You keeled over in pain and passed out. We brought you here and informed your wife. I'm bloody well not mistaken!'

'I don't believe you. I think you're drunk!' I said convinced my best friend was inebriated. 'You're just jealous my awesomeness has now reached a level where it is medically recognized. Hmmmpf!'

Ramesh began to stare at me like a violent psychopath. I braced myself for a vicious explosion of advice, angry instruction, and a scolding of epic proportions, when a rapid knock on the door distracted us.

'Saved for now,' I said to myself grinning at Ramesh with the satisfaction of an escaped convict. Ramesh looked at me with an expression of 'dekh loonga tujhe' as he mumbled something and turned towards the door. Rajesh rushed over and pulled the door open.

A 40-something gentleman in a stiff white coat walked in followed by the organ black marketeer from before. A few more younger looking folks numbering around 10–12 followed him towards my bed. Garima and Rajesh stepped aside and nodded their heads as the doctor halted at the foot of my bed and smiled.

'Good evening, Mr Jhunjhunwala! I'm Dr Rajesh Rana, Head of Surgery here at JK. You've already met my deputy Dr Iyengar here,' he said as the latter smiled from behind him.

'Who are these people? Your team?' asked Ramesh wandering his eyes at the group which stood around the doctor, still unhappy that the interrupting doctor had prevented him from discharging his discourse on disease to me.

'Yes. They are from the JK medical college,' he said waving his arms about, excited he was leading an entourage of knowledge seekers. 'They are here to learn about the various diseases which affect rich people like yourself, Sir Sri Jhunjhunwala. Many of them observed from the viewing room, the surgery we performed to remove your appendix.'

'Very nice, you all have my permission to worship me. You can break coconuts on the floor, garland me, and wave your agarbattis around in clockwise direction around my face,' I said, generously granting access to the bevy of admirers.

Ramesh interrupted, 'SHUT UP!' and then switched to look at the doctor and complained loudly, 'He has no regard for his health. He's been drinking whiskey by hooking the IV Drip into his veins!'

Dr Rana nodded disapprovingly. 'What is this, Mr Jhunjhunwala! What is this?! This is very bad. You must take care of your health. You are more than 50 now and you must take care of yourself, especially when you are recovering from surgery! You cannot drink whiskey like this just a few hours after surgery!'

'Should I drink rum then?'

'No! You should drink only what we give you to drink.'

'What about Glucon-D?'

'Well, yes you can drink that.'

'Accha. Can I drink Bagpiper-W?'

'What is that?'

'It's also like Glucon-D, but more effective'

'Sure, you can drink any health drink which helps maintain the electrolyte balance in your body.'

Ramesh moved towards the head of the bed and flicked me over the forehead as the interns laughed. 'OWW! Why'd you do that? Don't you know I am sick? Doctor! Take this man away. He is physically assaulting me!' I said rubbing my forehead.

Ramesh fumed. 'Don't believe him, doctor! Bagpiper W is Bagpiper Whiskey. Even now he's talking about drinking!'

The doctor, embarrassed that he didn't know that, looked at Ramesh and quickly shot off question after question as the interns and I looked on.

'Does he smoke?'

'Of course, like a chimney,' said Ramesh staring at me angrily as the doctor continued, 'How much does he drink?'

'He drinks like a fish. Minimum 2 per day.'

'Glasses?'

'Bottles.'

'Hmm. What about food?'

'He eats like a pig,' said Ramesh as I glanced at a couple of the interns furiously taking down notes.

Dr Rana sighed and surmised, 'This is not Good Mr Jhunjhunwala. You smoke like a chimney, drink like a fish, and eat like a pig. You don't exercise and it says here in your chart that you are also addicted to Gutkha. No wonder the stress of it all made your appendix blow up like a helium balloon.'

Hurt by the diagnosis, I protested, 'But Doctor! Your junior doctor said my Awesomix was as big as a battery. Balloon kab se ban gaya?'

'Appendix',' retorted Dr Iyengar.

Disregarding my protestations, Dr Rana asked, 'What does your diet currently consist of?'

'Well, I'm currently on a well-balanced and nutritious high cholestrol, high alcohol diet,' I replied sheepishly hoping to avoid eye contact with Ramesh as I was sure his eyes were turning a violent red.

The doctor nodded furiously 'You cannot take your health lightly Mr Jhunjhunwala. This is wrong! You have to switch immediately to a low carb, NO alcohol, NO Gutkha, NO smoking diet with lots of exercise.'

'NO WAY! I'd rather die!' I screamed in agony.

'I am serious Mr Jhunjhunwala! You need to watch your health and eat plenty of leafy green vegetables and fresh fruits. This will help in controlling your cholesterol and reduce your diabetes.'

'I don't mind eating vegetables and fruits. Can I deep fry them in oil or cheese or beer?'

Ramesh moved over and flicked me even harder.

'OWW! Stop hitting me!' I cried twitching in pain.

The doctor disregarding Ramesh's continuous assaults rigidly tried to hammer the point home. 'As it is you are overweight Mr Jhunjhunwala. You are not only *Over* the weight limit but also *over the overweight limit*. You've become very fat.'

'DON'T CALL ME FAT DOCTOR! I'M NOT FAT! I'VE JUST BEEN BLESSED GENEROUSLY WITH NATURAL BULK! IF I WERE A WRESTLER THEY'D CALL ME BULK HOGAN!'

'Mr Jhunjhunwala, please! Please understand what I am saying. You are obese. Being this fat is not good for you!'

'I'M NOT FAT! I'M BIG! I'm so big that when I stand in front of the sun, I cause an eclipse!'

The doctor looked frustrated and huddled with his team into an obfuscated cloud. A couple of minutes later he walked over as the rest of the team left the room.

'I suggest you take a vacation, Mr Jhunjhunwala.'

'Huh? Why?' I asked as though he had asked me to go to jail.

'Think of it as a health retreat. Your recovery will be faster if you can relax in a stress-free environment and take care of your diet and exercise. All your health parameters are over the limit. You need to de-stress. This will help you recover from your surgery as well.'

'Hmm,' I said realizing I hadn't taken a vacation in a long time.

Echoing my thought, Ramesh looked at the doctor and said, 'He hasn't taken a vacation in the last 10 years.'

'Well, you better go and relax Mr Jhunjhunwala. You need it,' the doctor repeated convincing me like a travel agent.

I kept quiet and tugged on my ear as Ramesh reassured the doctor, 'Don't worry, doctor. I'll make sure he goes even if I have to air-drop him like a food relief package onto a beach somewhere.'

The doctor looked at me unsurely as another wooden knock thumped the door.

Unable to see who it was, as the doctor was blocking my view, I tried to squirm into a better viewing position.

'Don't worry doctor. He'll go on vacation. *SHE* will make sure of that,' Ramesh hollered with a tinge of excitement.

The doctor moved back and I saw my wife walking towards us. I smiled happily.

For the next four weeks, I recuperated on an archipelago in the South China Sea. I had no choice as Ramesh and Dr Rana had ~~brainwashed~~ convinced my darling wife that this vacation was good for me. Reluctant as I was to leave the empire unguarded, I had been dragged by a concerned wife to a coral reef resort designed only for billionaires. It's so exclusive, they don't even tell you its name unless you show them a copy of your bank balance attested by the Finance Minister. Along with it, is a signed undertaking from the Prime Minister that that if anything happens to the said person while on the resort, then the country's entire armed forces will declare war and destroy any elements responsible for such happenings.

Upon this resort, I slaved away much against my will, jet-skiing, parasailing, hovercrafting, and getting massaged with saffron-induced hot oil by French therapists. I was subjected to many tortures like spa sessions, scuba diving, bowling, water polo, lacrosse, horse racing, and various other unpleasant tasks intended to rejuvenate my body and life force into a state of stress-free living.

This apart, the wife force fed me heaps of cabbage, carrots, beans, and every other vegetable under the sun to cut down my diabetes. I even lost a kilo. Oh, the horror! My sexy curves had been ruined! I had never been treated this badly my entire life!

I was scheduled to return only after 2 more weeks. My wounds had healed and the scars of the surgery had been erased by the plastic surgery department of the resort's in-house hospital.

I had woken up that day at around 7 in the morning. The wife had gone for a jog and I lazed around watching the waves soaking the white sandy beach from the porch of my 35-bedroom beach-side mansion. Giant Rock Canyons loomed in the horizon as I basked in the glow on a lazyboy beach recliner.

Warren Buffett was in the cottage to my left while George Soros, out partying all night, had passed out in the cottage to my right.

A few Sports Illustrated Swimsuit models frolicked about in their bikinis. Oh! The sacrifices one has to make for the sake of good health. This was hell! As I sipped some finely ground filter coffee and pondered how best to spend yet another day on this archipelago of misery, my phone rang. It was Ramesh.

'Hello!' I greeted.

His voice was fuzzy and distorted 'Hi Jhun, sorry for calling so early though in India its pretty late.'

'What? You want a kitty at eight?'

'I said LATE.'

'You like Fish Bait?'

'I SAID LATE! I SAID I'M CALLING LATE!'

'YOU WANT ME TO FIND YOU A DATE?'

'LATE DAMMIT! LATE!'

'HUH! I CAN'T HEAR YOU VERY WELL MAN. DID YOU JUST SAY YOU WANT TO GO TO KUWAIT?'

'LATE! LATE!'

'YOU WANT TO CHECK YOUR PROSTATE?'

'ABEY GENDE! APPENDIX KE SAATH SAATH KAAN BHI KHARAB HO GAYA KYA?!!!!'

The line was clearer now (pun intended). Pulling my ears I replied 'Sorry dude, line wasn't very clear. I'm telling you telecom companies these days carry signals the same bloody way a housefly carries malaria.'

Ramesh grunted 'So Jhun, how are you doing?'

'Bah…don't ask. I'm fighting with Warren Buffett next door. He tried to steal guavas from the tree in the courtyard but I prevented him and we got into a snowball fight.'

'Snowball fight?! I thought you were on a beach.'

'I am on a beach. This island is so fancy that you can choose your own weather. Press a button and it starts snowing. Press another and a giant volcano props out of the ground and starts throwing out hot lava. Last night Buffett tried to scamper towards the guava tree in the snow. I caught his tracks and fired snowballs at him.'

'But why was Warren Buffett stealing your guavas?'

'I don't know man! I'm a victim of a hate crime!' I pointed out as Ramesh listened intently. 'For the past two weeks, he and Bill Gates have been troubling me. Bill is on the other side of the beach trying to destroy Google while buying vaccines for African children. Whenever he is free, he tries to talk to me into partnering him and buying Facebook so that he can drown Mark Zuckerberg.

He even wants me to get a really heavy stone so he can tie it to Zuckerberg's legs when he throws him into the sea.'

'It still doesn't answer why Warren Buffett tried to steal your guavas?'

'Bloody fellow! That Buffett is just jealous of me. He doesn't like it when the media calls him "*The Jhunjhunwala of the West.*"

'How's your health?' Ramesh asked totally ignoring my persecution by Warren Buffett and Bill Gates. 'Bhabhiji told me your abdomen is feeling better.'

'Saale! Tu agli baar dekh. Next time you get as much as a little sprain and I will get into your wife's ear and make such a tamasha she will send you to vacation in a *Moov Spray* factory!'

'Oh, SHUT UP! I know how much you're secretly enjoying it. I heard you even went to Vijay Mallya's villa and partied with the Kingmachli calendar girls.'

'Who told you that? Yes I did. Vijay Mallya is hiding here from Kingmachli Airline employees demanding their salaries. Apparently, the airport here is the only place Kingmachli still operates from.'

'Nice. Anyway, listen. Something has come up,' said Ramesh as his tone become heavy and focused.

Sensing the mood, I took a quick gulp of the hot, sugary coffee and said, 'Yeah, tell me. Has the world collapsed into chaos? Do they need me to fly in and save the day with my awesome superpowers?'

'Err...not quite,' replied Ramesh unwilling to make use of my superhero services. 'But you are needed nonetheless.'

'What happened?' I asked bracing myself for the challenge at hand.

Ramesh breathed heavily into the phone and asked, 'Have you heard of someone called Ramakant Shastri?'

'Hmm...the name sounds familiar.' I reminisced as the name desperately blinked from some corner of my brain. 'Is he Ravi Shastri's long lost brother? Did they get separated in the Kumbh

Mela as brothers years ago? Did one becoming an extremely annoying commentator and the other a ganglord working for Dawood? Have the two been reunited now? TELL ME NOW!'

Taken aback at the sudden flurry of questions, Ramesh screamed almost jarring my ear, 'WILL YOU BE SERIOUS PLEASE! Apparently he's the owner of a company called Notco which, get this, makes...nothing.'

'Oh! YES, YES, YES! I remember him.' I rejoiced that the name had finally been identified. Taking a breath, I continued, 'He's a lunatic. Complete gone case! After he dies, they are planning to rename the Agra mental hospital after him. He had approached me before I got sick. Hahahaha! He wanted to sell nothing.'

'Hmmm. Did you buy a stake in his company?' asked Ramesh, his tone indicating that he was simultaneously beset with thinking.

'Me? Are you crazy? Do you want the mental hospital in Agra named after you also?'

'I'm being serious boss. News on the street is that you have picked up a 15% stake in his company, Notco Industries. I saw your name on their website also right before it was banned by Kapil Sibal for...well...reasons only Kapil Sibal knows.'

'ARE YOU SERIOUS?'

'Dead serious and get this—the company got listed on the exchange four weeks ago. No one was even bothered about it then. But once news started spreading that you have picked up a stake, the share price has jumped like crazy! I mean crazy! Everyone is pouring their money into this! Everyone.'

'Dude!' I said astonished. 'This has got to be a prank or joke of some kind. I told that fellow very clearly that I had absolutely no interest in buying his company. How could you think I could possibly invest in something which makes nothing!'

'That's why I am calling you to confirm,' Ramesh declared clearing his throat. 'I'm surprised you haven't heard anything about it. All the channels have been talking about this only.'

'Kahan yaar! Biwi ne TV, newspaper, aur Internet teeno bandh karke rakha hai,' I complained. 'Phone pe bhi all numbers of the officewallahs have been blocked. Yours is the only number which can reach me. Speaking of which, why didn't you call me sooner? You said the news has been going around for four weeks.'

Surprised that I was the one with the question for a change, Ramesh paused and replied, 'I wanted to be sure it was not just a rumour. I had my guys look into the company registration and index listing papers and all. I just received confirmation a few minutes back that you have indeed purchased the stake. You are on the Board of Directors list with SEBI and as you know they won't put your name on the list unless you sign an affidavit stating the same.'

'Bloody hell! Kuch gadbad hai!' I shouted as the force of my words blew away an entire army of swimsuit models into the ocean. I wasn't worried about their safety. They were too weightless to sink.

'You're right about that,' agreed Ramesh as I began to wonder what the hell was going on. 'News is that SEBI is even investigating the rise in the stock prices.'

'Shit! I bet it's a conspiracy!' I howled, convinced someone was trying to set me up.

'I agree. It smells fishy.' Ramesh opined and asked after a minute as we both deliberated quietly. 'Anyway what will you do now?'

Realizing I needed to deal with the problem hands on, I quietly sighed and muttered as Ramesh held on, breathing through the phone, 'There's no choice. I have to get back home,' I declared.

'Hmm,' Ramesh reluctantly added. 'I'm sorry your vacation has been cut short. The point of all this was to de-stress you but now this is going to re-stress you.'

'Bah! I haven't had fun anyway. Aur gajar aur tamatar ki salad kha kha ke bore ho gaya hoon! Can't wait to get back. Let me talk to the wife.'

'Theek hai. Let me know when you arrive.'

'I will and thanks a lot Ramesh.'

'Anytime fatso!'

'EH! DON'T CALL ME FAT! I'M JUST A HIGHLY SATURATED INDIVIDUAL!' I shouted and hung up as Ramesh's voice sneered mischievously from the other end. The time to go home had arrived. I decided to explain the situation to the wife who, I knew, would be pissed off with my sudden decision to leave. I emptied the remaining coffee down my throat and left to inform her.

BACK TO BUSINESS

After having cajoled the wife who was heartbroken to part with me, I decided to take off. She was stressed that I had to leave for duty on such short notice. Since she was stressed, the best thing to do was to let her de-stress on the resort for a few more days while I set things right at home. But much to my dismay, I learnt that my private jet had developed a 'technical snag'. The pilot had gone off on an all night bender and had decorated the walls of the cockpit with vomit. YUCK!

I therefore did what any self-respecting billionaire would have done—sold the plane to a national air carrier at a profit and since those guys have a habit of throwing money away, I didn't feel one bit guilty. I was only taking advantage of a pre-existing flaw in an airline which has been a fantastic success at failing disastrously. Of course, I did send them the cleaned plane with an entire box of perfumed cockpit air freshener.

I was indeed sad as I was looking forward to watching cartoons and drinking apple juice on my jet while on the way back to Mumbai but time was of the essence and my superior wisdom and knowledge were required at Jhunjhunwala Chambers to deal with the Shastri situation.

I decided on the next available option—public transport.

So there I was at the airport counter, booking my ticket like a common passenger. Sweating and sluggish, I approached the counter, dragging my impressively rotund figure, clad in my usual full-sleeved satin white shirt and crisp anti-wrinkle charcoal black trousers. I was facing a transparent glass window at a small cubicle-ish counter; one of many in the rectangular, box–like terminal. People were buzzing about like flies on a hot afternoon.

The lady at the booking counter smiled as I crossed the yellow line in front of us. As if on cue a brash young man cut in front of me from nowhere. I screamed my head off, 'HEY! ASSHOLE! GET BACK HERE! YOU CAN'T CUT AHEAD OF ME! IT'S A CRIME AGAINST HUMANITY! THIS IS A CIVIL RIGHTS VIOLATION!'

'Chill buddy! Err…I was here already, but I had to go to the bathroom,' he said as though I was the one cutting him.

'HEY! DO NOT TELL ME TO CHILL! I WILL CHILL WHEN I WANT TO CHILL. I WILL NOT CHILL! I WILL HEAT UP!'

The boy began to tremble.

I continued enraged, 'Nobody cuts ahead of me. Don't make me buy this airport and have you ground into fish paste with a plane turbine! MORON! I will have you locked up in a solitary room with nothing but a small hole for a window and make you watch Baba Yogdev doing yoga on loop for 20 fuc*ing years non-stop. NON-STOP. YOU HEAR ME! After just a week, you'll be begging the baba to teach you something called the *atmahatyasana*. GOT IT? JACKASS!'

The fellow stepped away trembling. The people around were shaken up. The young lady behind me nervously moved around and took a step back. I snorted a 'Hmmmpf' and pushed towards the lady at the counter.

Lady: 'Hi Sir! Welcome to Kingmachli Airlines.'

Me: 'Hi. I want one ticket to Mumbai. Business class.'

Lady: 'For what time, Sir?'

Me: 'Noon.'

Lady: 'I am sorry Sir, but all seats are full on our 12 pm afternoon flight.'

Me: '1 pm?'

Lady: 'Full.'

Me: '2 pm?'

Lady: 'Full.'

Me:'2.30 pm?'

Lady: 'Full.'

Me:'3?'

Lady: 'Full.'

Me:'4?'

Lady: 'Full.'

Me:'5?'

Lady: 'Full.'

Me:'6?'

Lady: 'Full.'

I took a deep breath, grunted, and moved my head from side to side. Spotting the fellow who cut in front of me, I sneered. He shook some more.

Turning back to the lady I asked, 'Do you have a map, a compass, and directions to the nearest Nike showroom?'

Taken aback by the strange request, she asked, 'No Sir, but can I ask why?'

'I want to buy a new pair of shoes and then *WALK* to Mumbai because you people do not have a single seat for me! Normally, I would have preferred to sail, but if I dock at the Gateway of India, some people might think I am entering the city like a terrorist.'

'I am sorry, Sir, but as I told you before, there are no flights available for today,' she said apologetically.

I stood there cursing my pilot as she continued to click away on her computer for a few seconds. She then lit up and proclaimed, 'Ah! Congrats Sir. One seat has just opened up on the evening flight. Would you still be interested?'

'Maybe if I sail to Mumbai in a small boat with a tiger I might have some sort of life changing experience like that boy in *Life Of Pi.* Do you know where I can get a tiger, miss? I intend to later unleash that tiger on that fellow there who cut the line ahead of me.'

Seeming harried, the lady pressed on, 'I don't know if you heard me Sir but a seat has just become available. Would you like to book a ticket on the 6 pm evening flight to Mumbai?'

'Thank Ganesha!' I exclaimed. 'YES. Please give me a ticket to Mumbai on that flight.'

'Sure Sir', she smiled. 'Can I confirm your booking for Mumbai, Economy Class, 7 pm?'

'Didn't you just say the flight was at 6?'

'Yes Sir, but unfortunately the flight has now been delayed by an hour.'

'How the hell did this happen! You just told me it was at 6.'

'Sorry Sir, but the system was getting updated when you were asking me where you can purchase a tiger and unleash it on that man over there,' she pointed with her eyes as I slowly turned my head and looked at the line cutter again. He shivered some more.

As I thought about the delay, she tapped away on her keyboard. A neat little boarding pass popped out from a printer which she tore and handed to me along with a receipt for the ticket. I grabbed it eagerly and prepared to leave. As I was about to thank her, she asked abruptly, 'Sir, would you like to be part of the Sid Nincompoop birthday celebration festival? He's our swimsuit calendar making, non-wage paying owner's son. We offer our beloved flyers a chance to add a balloon for just 100 rupees which will be added as your gift at his birthday party.'

'No thanks,' I declined. 'Is there an option instead where I can pay to punch Sid N in the face instead really fuc*ing hard? Like so hard all his teeth fall out and he has to spend the rest of his life flapping his gums around like a fish out of water and sucking food through a straw?'

I was expecting her to say no and shoo me away but surprisingly she said, 'Yes sir! For 5000 rupees you can punch him in the face with a maximum force of 200 joules.'

'Holy shit! Are you sure? I was just kidding,' I shrieked in unexpected delight.

'No sir. We just recently introduced this offer. You see our airline is in such a bad financial situation that we are finding all sources of income, including causing grievous bodily harm to our irritating owner's irritating son. If you pay 3000 rupees, we will poke him with a stick and send you pictures and video of the same.'

Impressed, I asked, 'What can I get for 10,000 bucks?'

'We will electrocute his testicles and have a donkey urinate on him.'

'Fantastic,' I said and handed her my card again.

Handing the ticket over she smiled politely and wished me, 'Have a nice day, Sir.' I then walked off towards the boarding lounges.

It was closing in on midnight when I landed in Mumbai. Twelve hours earlier, I was part of a conversation which involved air tickets, a tiger, Sid N's family jewels, conducting wire, and 2400 volts of electric current.

That last sentence read in isolation would have led you to believe that this is some weird bestial version of *Fifty Shades of Grey*. Before further misinterpretations arise, let me continue.

As soon as I switched on my phone, my inbox erupted. Most of the texts were the usual 'I luv u' from horny women who wanted to have my baby and men who wanted to undergo sex change operations, take fertility medicine, and then have my baby. I seriously do not know where these people get my number from! There must be a secret society somewhere with its headquarters in Bombay whose sole purpose is to stalk me for voyeuristic pleasure.

Knowing that I am a married man, with a wife as protective as a tigress, these people must have realized that the only way to derive intimate pleasure off me would be by stalking me. Thus, they had congregated over the years, built temples for me, and now dance around my idol, worship my birthday as Jhunjhun Jayanti, and distribute prasad to beggars to celebrate the glorious occasion of my birth. People who start as my stalkers end up as my devotees. *It is unbelievable how I impact the lives of people.*

Buried in the millions of texts was one from Ramesh that went: 'The media is waiting for you at the front gate. Be careful'

Tch. Stupid media people! Always making me breaking news. I know I deserve to be breaking news. I know my value better than anyone else and I am willing to gladly extol how valuable I am as well to anybody who wants to or even doesn't want to know. But when they show up like paparazzi outside the airport, I have every right to protest!

My best option, I concluded, was to take the back exit.

As I exited out of the glass doors of the terminal and into the city of Mumbai, I felt the soft punch of humidity that I have been used to all my life. It's like being hit in the face with a cushion. Sort of a 'Hello! Glad to have you back' from the city.

Waiting for my Mercedes to arrive, I strolled through a few more texts when suddenly the camera lights started to flash in my face. A thunderstorm of reporters burst forth, all with their mics and camera crews hovering around me. Their lips were moving furiously like Navjot Singh Sidhu delivering idiom after idiom and their voices were louder than Navjot Singh Sidhu laughing at joke after joke on a comedy show.

The media fellows had cornered me at the back gate as well. My attempts to escape detection had failed. I was about as willing to answer questions as A. Raja at a 2G scam deposition.

I moved my hands around like a Lok Sabha speaker and shouted, 'One at a time, one at a time. Ek ek karke poochiye, I will answer all questions.'

'Sir, is it true that you are involved in insider trading of Notco shares?' one reporter asked instantly in an almost accusatory tone.

'No!' I shouted.

One by one the journos fired at me. I shall now demonstrate my responses using geometrical tabular presentation:

What I was saying	What I was actually thinking
Question: Are you saying you are involved in outsider trading then?	
No! There is no such thing as outsider trading:	You fu* kin idiot! I hope you rot in hell for asking me such a stupid question, but before that, I wish you win a free holiday to the Swiss Alps. When you take that holiday, I hope you go backpacking and see a crystal blue lake in the mountains. At this time, I wish that you take of all your clothes and swim in it like Michael Phelps. Refreshed after your trek and the coolness of the water, I hope you come out and billions of bees descend from the sky and sting your naked body in Itchguard lagane wali places. I hope they sting you so badly that you experience burning sensations every time you go to the toilet. This is the punishment you deserve for asking such a stupid question, dumbass!
Question: Since how long have you known the value of Nothing? What prompted you to buy Notco?	
I made an educated guess.	Aise prashn puchne wale ko isabgol khake chullu bhar paani mein doob marna chahiye.

<table>
<tr><td colspan="2">Question: Is it true that Ramakant Shastri is your relative?</td></tr>
<tr><td>I am not related to him.</td><td>The probability of me being related to a group of intelligence impaired buffaloes grazing around in the African savannah butt naked is higher than being related to that imbecile.</td></tr>
<tr><td colspan="2">Question: Your investment in Notco has made you the richest man in the world. Did you always know that Nothing was worth so much?</td></tr>
<tr><td>The rapid rise in Notco shares and the interest of so many people in nothing has come as a surprise to me.</td><td>Saale! I was already the richest man in the world. You think my gold Rolexes, platinum pens with diamond nibs, and the original Mona Lisa hanging in my bedroom all grow on trees or what? And if such a tree does exist, then I am the only person on this planet capable of buying it. I have enough money to hire Bill Gates and Carl Slym to clean my car!</td></tr>
<tr><td colspan="2">Question: How are you planning to deal with Notco now that Ramakant Shastri has become almost as rich as you through his company?</td></tr>
<tr><td>It's business as usual for me.</td><td>I will build a time machine and go back in time to the night he was conceived and give his parents two cinema tickets to the night show so that they would be watching a film instead of making a baby who would end up causing such idiotic problems for me after so many years.</td></tr>
<tr><td colspan="2">Question: Are you planning to buy a stake in an IPL team? Is the rumour true that you will call the team The Nothings?</td></tr>
<tr><td>No!</td><td>I want to bash your head with a cricket bat.</td></tr>
</table>

<table>
<tr><td colspan="2">Question : Did you support Ramakant Shastri when he first said that he wanted you to invest in an invisible product?</td></tr>
<tr><td>I found his presen-tation…very interesting.</td><td>Die! Die! Die! You idiots, why aren't any of you asking the right questions? Do you all really believe this 'nothing' bullshit?</td></tr>
<tr><td colspan="2">Question : Is it true that SEBI is investigating you for insider trading of Notco?</td></tr>
<tr><td>SEBI is a responsible body who are welcome at any time to investigate me.</td><td>No, they're not

Come near me and I'll kill you SEBI bastards!</td></tr>
<tr><td colspan="2">Question : The government has said it is investigating the rise of Notco shares but is also delighted that an Indian has invented Nothing. Do you think this is a bigger achievement than the invention of zero by Indians many years ago?</td></tr>
<tr><td>Let us not compare.</td><td>I am going to find out where you live, come to your house in the middle of the night, ring the bell, and run away. This will cause you to wake up. After I do this every single day over a period of a few months, I will ensure that you become a regular victim of sleep deprivation. As a result, your workplace productivity and personal life will suffer while your personality undergoes a serious shift, and then you will become a serial killer like Dexter. Then I will…huh…hold on…</td></tr>
</table>

Having had enough, I decided to push through the crowd of reporters. I was cranky and did not like the spray of camera flashes gnawing at my face. As my Mercedes pulled up, I barged through shouting, 'Leave me alone media people! Go follow someone else. Isn't there like a child trapped in a borewell somewhere who needs your relentless journalistic attention instead of me!', I dove in head first into the backseat, shut the door, and sped out of the airport.

Slowly, the car made its way through the city. The drive from the airport to my Malabar Hill residence generally makes me sleepy. I wished I had told the driver to bring my Black Corvette to the airport. Unlike my cheap Mercedes, it's bigger and the insides are totally pimped out. A year ago, I had even installed a hot tub in there. The haggard of the fly back would have been soaked away in the fizzy bubbling sparkle of a hot tub in the back of a 70 crore automobile. I noted that not asking for the Corvette to be brought as my chariot was a strategic mistake.

The car pulled up at a traffic signal. The road in front had been cordoned off. From what I gathered, a gangster shootout a few blocks away had resulted in casualties and the injured were being ferried to the hospital. Ambulance vans swiped across the eyeline, red lights blaring and all. Behind them were some media vans.

I started to think about Notco's astonishing rise in the month I had been away. Was it possible someone was insider trading? Or was this really a case of investors thinking that nothing was a solid idea? Did they think that this invisible, pseudo, emptiness they were putting their money into was actually going to grow in value and make them richer over time? Or were they all in it just for the short-term? A few months of holding the stock, ready to abandon ship the moment the thing hit a particular high price because it could, at best, be considered a fad. Something which is important because it is valuable only for a short period of time and useless most of the time thereafter, like a coalition government in Delhi?

Notco's rise needed to be investigated further. It made no sense to me especially when Ramakant was selling—nothing.

A knock on the car window made me turn. It was my favourite beggar in all of Mumbai! Chandu Thakureshwar Dinanath Mishra Upadhyay Yang Wu. (His dad is half Chinese, hence the Yang Wu. Even today Chandu can go into China and not get a Stapled Visa in return because his dad is Chinese.)

'Chandu mere bhai! Kaise ho? Bahut din ho gaye!' I roared jubilantly as I lowered the window glass in excitement.

'Kya Saab! Aap toh yahaan se aate hi nahin. Sirf madam aati hain. Aaj kal sirf helicopter se ghumte rehte hain! Kabhi kabhi aasmaan se utar ke zameen pe bhi humein darshan dijiyega!' Chandu mocked.

'Sorry yaar, bahut din ho gaye. I have been busy,' I said apologetically.

Chandu and I go way back. I started my career in the stock market and Chandu began a career in the begging industry at around the same time. Chandu was pretty much one of the best beggars in the country.

He had moved up from begging on the footpath to government offices. He then started begging outside temples and then moved to shopping areas. Nowadays he begs mostly outside fancy malls and at traffic signals like this one.

The last time I met Chandu, he gave me a case study titled 'Benefits of Investing in the Indian Begging Sector in the Modern Day Indian Economy.'

Chandu was an extremely smart dude. Many a time I had offered him a job at one of the various thousands of companies that I have a stake in, but he had refused citing a desire to expand his begging company.

I remembered his report and asked, 'So how's the company?'

'All good, Saab. My brother's company is merging with mine. Our profits as well as our manpower should double by the end of the year.'

'Very good yaar. Congrats!'

'Thank you, Sir. The begging industry, like all other industries in India, is going through times of change. We need to be able to adapt and improvise in order to keep pace with the changing extremes of business,' he said in a nonchalant manner.

Curious, I asked, 'What do you mean?'

'I mean that our country has a huge problem when it comes to distribution of wealth. Everyday thousands are losing their jobs. So many people as a result are resorting to begging. The sector has become so competitive it is unbelievable! Young students fresh out of college are walking around with two or three degrees and they want to beg. The workforce is expanding like crazy.'

'Are you worried that the Chandu begging company will not be able to match up?'

'No chance, Sirji! We will do whatever it takes. I have been in this business from the past thirty years. Experience matters on the streets of this city. I have seen the city change. Before 1992, the roads were full of cycles and Marutis, now the roads have not become any bigger but the cars have increased. This means begging potential has gone up. We have to make sure that begging capacity increases as well to meet supply.'

I looked on amused.

'Today everything is about marketing and innovation. Begging is a business. I am working on removing the stigma attached to it and apply strong corporate practices to a very competitive industry with a high entry barrier.'

Impressed with the heavy duty jargon, I opened my mouth to compliment him, but he continued, 'I have identified forty-four high beta traffic zones in Mumbai. This means I have opened forty-four branches at traffic signals in Mumbai. Each signal is headed by a family member. My wife looks after Kurla. I supervise Colaba and now after the merger with my brother, North Bombay is also covered. My children and nephews are all smart. They know how to get change from rich people...speaking of which...'

Engrossed in his business model, I had forgotten to ~~pay~~ donate in the first place. 'Oh, sorry yaar! Bhool hi gaya.' I flipped open a wallet. The street light glistened on the platinum (yes, my wallet is made of platinum) like moonlight across a dark moor. (There is no need to tell you these things, but I would be deeply depriving you of the knowledge of the luxury I roll myself around in if I didn't).

Chandu cracked a satisfied smile. The smell of cheap tobacco hit me like a bullet from his mouth. Trying to act as though I had smelt nothing, I rendered a 1000 rupee note to him.

'I'm sorry yaar! I don't have change. Do you have change for a thousand?'

'Of course, Sirji. I always have change. It's my job to have change! But if you don't have exact change, you can now pay me by card as well.'

Astonished, I asked, 'What! You now take card also?'

'Of course, Sir. We are modernizing the business. I don't understand why beggars in India don't take card payments also. Bloody idiots. Begging is a business just like any other business. If we keep concentrating on the stigma attached like I said, we will never move the enterprise aspect of it forward. We must think of the customer always. Chandu beggars now accepts card payments for begging deposits. Not just Card, we have everything—Net banking, Cash voucher, wire transfer, debit card...*basically we must make it as easy as possible for the customer to give us their money.*'

'Achha'

'We also take EMI payments. You can now pay us beggars smaller and regular begging deposits at 0% interest for the first year just like the big retail chains.'

'Dude! Beggars accepting cards and taking EMI payments. This is the shit!'

'Sirji, even Anand Mahindra said the same thing last week. I stopped outside his Scorpio at Bhayandar circle. He also didn't have change, so I swiped his card and gave him a receipt. He gave me a three and a half minute speech praising my 'entrepreneurial attitude', and the need to develop corporate social responsibility. So I have started my own trust now. Twenty percent of my income will now go towards researching environment-friendly solutions for begging. Nothing is expected to happen on that front for another twenty years, but I will get to keep the twenty percent and not pay any tax on it as I can claim my trust as an NGO. I don't know if this is what he meant when he said I should develop corporate social responsibility but I hope I have made Anand Mahindraji happy anyway.'

Not knowing if I should take offence or deliver praise, I unsurely opted for the latter. 'Kamaal ke bhikari ho yaar tum! I have never seen a more dedicated beggar than you.'

'Thank you, Sir!' he said emphatically as he swiped my card.

Signing the receipt, I put the card back in the wallet (yes, it's still made of platinum).

'Always a pleasure talking to you Chandu!' I said.

'Same here, Saab! Please keep coming this way more often. This is my head office. I have shifted my operations from outside Palladium Mall.'

'Why?'

'Ever since the traffic police increased the timer on this signal, the red signal lasts 2 minutes longer. Change collection time has therefore increased and I want to take advantage of this. Already there is a twenty percent growth in revenue at this signal because of the time increase. Can't afford to have such a high value area in the hands of a junior beggar. So I am heading the company from here itself.'

'You seriously need to come work for one of my companies. You know more about business than half the hacks I have to hire just to type a spreadsheet.'

'Thank you for the offer! You are a loyal customer always! By the way Sirji, I wanted to ask should I also invest in Notco? I heard the shares are very blue chip? I know you have a stake in the company.'

'Yaar Chandu! Please don't ask me about that company,' I said indignantly.

'Oh, why Sirji?! Any bad news? Should I short the stock tomorrow?'

'No, nothing like that. I'm just too tired to talk about shares now, especially Notco.'

'Ah! Samajh gaya Sir! You want to keep it a secret. Kahan aap aur kahan hum! When everyone else is busy buying something, you are the one man buying Nothing. This is why you are a genius aur hum jaise log beggar hi hain!'

'Nahin yaar. I am yet to decide my future with Notco. Anyway, you keep kicking ass like always.'

'Absolutely, Sirji! Thank you so much! And please keep coming by car. If you keep flying in helicopters, my collection will go down! Aapka kripa banakar rakhiye.'

'Yaar, the way you are progressing, I won't be surprised if your own helicopter pulls up next to mine somewhere in the air and your hand thrusts a bowl into my face asking for change!'

'Hehe! Let us hope so, Sirji! Sab aapka aashirwad,' laughed Chandu trying to appear humble.

'Theek hai Chandu, hum chalte hain,' I said bidding adieu and slowly withdrew my head as I was reminded of Nitin at the office.

I asked the driver to make a quick stop at a vada pav stall before heading home.

TAKING STOCK

There's a huge difference between wealth and money. I've worked a hell of a lot for both. Most people don't think it's a good thing. For some reason, the creation of wealth is considered to be the most banal of human endeavours. Being rich in India is a funny thing. Till you become rich, it's a dream. Once you become rich, it's considered a crime. If you're not, you're poor, and there is no disease people see as more harmful as being poor. The rich are criminals and the poor are sick.

The saddest thing about money is that you don't get to take it with you when you die. Nonetheless, I have never shied away from the fact that I am a creature who loves money. I love living like a deity. There is nothing wrong in that as long as the means I adopt to make cash are ethically and legally sound.

My humbleness allows me to recognize that like many people, I too am a product of India's economic boom. We, a country that 50 years ago did not even have the capabilities to manufacture as much as a safety pin, today boast some of the largest industries in the world… But the sad thing is that despite all the progress, it's never enough. It can't be when there are 1.2 billion people trying to share the economic pie. The pie is simply not big enough.

At the risk of sounding like a quasi-version of the Dalai Lama, let me move on.

The next day, I was in the office sharp at 9 am, so sharp you'd feel my sense of time sharper than the blade of a samurai sword.

My investing team gathered around the meeting table. These were the people I had handpicked to look after my investments. They weren't magicians like me. I've turned hundreds of rupees into billions of dollars so many times with magic.

The reason these guys work for me is because I can trust them. They are competent, eager to learn, and most of all, loyal. These people have weathered the storms of temptation and stood beside me at a time when employees are poached left, right, and centre from naukri.com, so much so that the government needs to promulgate a new anti-poaching law to save these innocent creatures from hunters who bait them with money and goodies only to trap them in a caged life of servitude, slowly sucking their life out and finally leading them into extinction.

We began the meeting by singing the International Jhunjhunwala anthem song. It goes something like this:

O Jhunjhunwala, you are awesome Jhunjhunwala.
You are the Pharaoh of the markets, O great investing genius,
You rock so much it's ridiculous.
The last words of the previous two lines rhyme,
And people remember you all the time!

Your intelligence is unparalleled!
Your handsomeness is unmatched!!
You are the savior of the stock markets!!!
The emperor of the commodity markets!!!!
The icon of trading!!!!!
And the knight of investing!!!!!!

Your ass—politicians kiss.
Your face—hot beauties kiss.
Your speeches—the traders never miss.
All the bears in front of you—they drown in piss.

Everyone either wants you or wants to be with you.
But there is only one you,
And that's you!

We bow down to you, O awesome one!
The market is your altar,
You are its God.
May God bless us all!

What a song! It moves me every time. It is a modest estimation of my sense of achievement encapsulated beautifully in lyrical prose accompanying harmonious instrumental music. I find it relaxing and play it in my head all the time. In my office, it is customary to sing this before every meeting. I remember a few years ago, traders all across India went on a hunger strike petitioning SEBI to make it mandatory to sing my anthem before trading sessions each day, and since that day its been sung in trading rooms and investing houses all over the world.

The team and I sat down to begin our discussion. I had convened this gathering of fine minds to discuss the Notco situation.

The creaking of chairs receded in the room. This was the meeting room located next to my personal cabin. It was fairly big, able to accommodate around 20 odd people around a rectangular meeting table. At the head of the table, I sat on a chair higher than everyone else's, placed my elbows on the table, looked at the glass jar of water upon a side table, took a deep breath, and began.

'Let's get down to business. How did this happen? I don't remember communicating with any of you that I wanted to pick up a stake in Notco.'

Rajat, my 40-something, Company Acquisition Specialist, cleared his throat and spoke apologetically, 'Sir, it's my fault. Mr Ramakant ambushed me as I came out of the bathroom. At first, I thought he was from the IT department. He stood there smiling at me eerily like a ghost from a Ram Gopal Varma film. He showed me the cheque you had signed and said it was to pick up a stake in the company.'

'This is an inexplicable breach of company protocol. THIS IS A SERIOUS INTELLIGENCE FAILURE! A rogue terrorist entrepreneur gained access to our office. He jumped the fence, escaped security, ambushed our top company acquisitions guy, and then cleverly pawned of his company on us. Unacceptable!' I blared thumping my fist on the table.

Rajat apologized, 'I am very sorry Sir! He was very convincing. He seemed to know all of our procedures very well. We had no prior intelligence that this man was going to attack us.'

Nandini, the overly obedient 25-year-old trading analyst said, 'All of us here seriously condemn the incident, Sir. We will never allow this type of thing to ever happen again.'

Iqbal, her more experienced colleague and one of my senior trading guys, emphatically reiterated, 'Yes Sir. We will increase security around the office complex and double grill the windows just in case rogue, entrepreneurial elements, non-state industrial actors sneak across our border…err…boardroom and attack innocent citizens of the Jhunjhunwala Republic.'

Heads nodded in agreement all around. Vishal, another of my senior guys in his late 30s calmly touching the bridge of his nose, interjected, 'We have already formed an investigation team to examine lapses in our office security. The HR manager has been directed to suspend the Chief Security Guard immediately.'

Rajat butted in, 'I have already withdrawn our company name from the inter-company cricket tournament Sir. We will not play cricket with Notco till this issue is resolved.'

'Very good!' I said, loudly banging my fist on the table yet again. 'That'll teach those bastards from engaging in acts of terror.'

Vishal got up and slid across from his side of the table towards the other end. He fiddled with the projector remote. For a second, I was reminded of my ward remote at JK hospital. A few seconds later, he looked up and asked, 'With your permission Sir, I would now like to present an in-depth report of Ramakant Shastri's nefarious design.'

'Proceed,' I proclaimed generously.

'Thank you. Ladies and gentlemen, this was a well-planned, well-co-ordinated, and well-executed attack on our company finances. Please look at the projector screen. Let me go over the bullet points of this attack,' Vishal said instructing Nitin who was hovering around to adjust the projector screen. I took a deep breath and opened a packet of pan masala.

As Vishal and Nitin adjusted the projector, we readied ourselves. Vishal directed Nitin to turn off the lights. In the whitish glow of the projector, we awaited the briefing as Vishal began, quoting the text on the screen.

- '2 months ago, Ramakant Shastri recced our office and memorized operational protocol when he came to meet Jhunjhunwala Sir.
- 'His singular aim was to attain the blessings of our leader, by hook or crook.
- 'Upon realizing that Jhunjhunwala Sir would never agree to buy a stake in his Nonsense, Nothing manufacturing company, he resorted to plan 'B'; the execution of which has led to the events we find ourselves facing.

'His modus operandi was simple:

'1. He was well aware of the fact that Jhunjhunwala Sir gets sleepy headed after a heavy lunch and since all of Sir's lunches are heavy, it was but expected that he would be drowsy on the afternoon Shastri approached him.

'2. Carefully timing his entry into our office at exactly 3.30 pm, the specific time when the markets close for the day and also the specific instant when Jhunjhunwala Sir's internal metabolic processes start to decompose food consumed an hour earlier.

'3. Having eaten an extra quarter kilo of matar paneer with extra paneer and extra matar, onion slices, parantha and lime, along with four large glasses of lassi to celebrate the rise in the value of *Pedo File Company*, a company whose shares we bought just a week earlier, Sir was naturally drowsy due to the extra production of amino acids released as a by-product of the metabolic digestive process.

'4. Ramakant accosted Sir in his office and triggered serial presentations on his laptop which were activated by an IED (irritating electronic device) across the table from Sir. An already sleepy Sir was attacked with slide after slide, presentation after presentation, thus leaving him incapacitated, drowsy, and numb.

'5. With amino acid levels constantly rising each second, Jhunjhunwala Sir was convinced that Shastri was a deranged entrepreneur who had been brainwashed by extremist economics and signed a cheque to rid himself of this man because his talks were not producing results.

'6. Ramakant gladly accepted the cheque and fled the scene.

'7. Jhunjhunwala Sir left for his vacation in the South China Sea to recover from severe medical complications which led his awesomix to rupture. At this time, Ramakant reactivated his sleeper cell tactics and planned a second string of attacks on us.

'8. On the morning of July 23rd, our Chief Acquisitions Officer, Rajat Mukherjee, ingested too much pineapple juice as he was a. Thirsty b. He had heard that pineapple increases sperm count. He and his wife are trying for a baby, you see.'

'Oh, congrats yaar!' I shrieked looking at Rajat, interrupting Vishal's extempore.

'Thanks Sir,' replied Rajat seemingly unhappy that his family planning plans had been rudely leaked to a room full of people. Vishal continued:

'9. This resulted in Rajat's kidneys processing the liquid content and transferring fluid residue to his bladder for urination. Unable to maintain muscle control of his bladder any longer, Rajat went to the bathroom to relieve himself.

'At this exact moment, Ramakant, who had been quietly waiting in the office lobby, slipped past the border between the lobby and the foyer and ambushed Rajat who had just emerged from the bathroom. Delirious in his own world of post urinary evacuative bliss, Rajat then proceeded to unwittingly aid Shastri in executing this attack.'

Pausing for a second, Vishal cleared his throat and sipped water from a glass. Rajat, still pissed off with Vishal, shakily sipped water too while the others all stared away at Rajat like they were a pack of wild dogs ready to devour a piece of meat. Clearly his intention to increase the headcount in the next national census had been the cause of our problems, they had summarized.

Gulping down a full glass, Vishal slowly withdrew and said, 'I shall now handover the briefing to Rajat himself.'

Taking Vishal's place towards the left of the projector, Rajat slowly limped around like a nervous contestant about to have his dish tasted by the hellish judges on Masterchef India.

'Thank you Vishal,' he said, still peeved as he took the remote from Vishal who, after passing the baton, headed over to seat himself.

'So I emerged from the bathroom and found Ramakant Shastri just standing there. At first I thought he wanted to use the bathroom but then it dawned on me that he did not work here. Before I could even open my mouth to convey that this facility was for office staff only, he fired, "Hello. You must be Rajat. I'm here to sign the Notco sale papers. Jhunjhunwala Sir had asked me to get in touch with you today to finish the deal."

'I was obviously taken by surprise. Sir had definitely not mentioned any deal regarding this matter to me. That's when he took out the cheque. I looked at it carefully and saw that it had been signed by Sir for an amount of 1 lakh.'

I was irritated at this stage and barked, 'Dude, when was the last time I picked up a company for an amount as low as a lakh? Even Sonakshi Sinha gets more for exposing her teeth in a toothpaste ad for this amount!'

Nandini complimented my sentiment almost enviously, 'I think spending more than 10 bucks on anything related to Sonakshi is a serious waste of money, but that's my opinion.'

'I agree, Sirji,' Iqbal supplemented. 'Renowned displayer cum owner of a wonderful, well-endowed jawbone AND Cricket player Ashish Nehra would have done the same ad for five rupees. His teeth are as wide as Sonakshi's forehead. I wonder if they get married and produce children, will the children have freakishly large foreheads and freakishly large teeth?'

'I was surprised Sir but then Ramakant told me that Notco was just a startup and you were on board only as a minority investor. He was very convincing, Sir. Chalu bugger.' Rajat quickly butt in sensing that the conversation was veering toward a completely different topic. Perhaps something more dental.

'Then what happened?' I asked.

'Well, I took the cheque from his hands and told him to sit down in the conference room. I called Iqbal and Nandini over and discussed the matter with them.'

Nandini muttered, 'There was no doubt in my mind that it was your signature on the cheque, Sir. I mean only you can sign your name like Ganesha writing the Mahabharata under Vyasa's tutelage. What calligraphy Sir! What an excellent, perfectly harmonious, magnificent, and splendid arrangement of letters delicately placed on paper to form your great name. It was like looking at a composition written by Beethoven, endorsed by God himself to be the background symphony of the cosmos itself. That name signed in 22 karat gold ink can only be written by you, Sir! I showed it to Iqbal as well.'

'Yes. We all saw your name on the cheque and prostrated in front of it. We were moved to tears. It was not just a signature on a piece of paper Sir, it was the word of God in gold on sacred papyrus. Any cheque signed by you, Sir, is a religious manuscript for us,' said Iqbal almost ready to prostrate at my feet again.

'And we cannot disobey the will of God, Sir. That's why I thought Ramakant was telling the truth. But as it turned out later, saala chor nikla,' Rajat affirmed.

Nandini began to tear up. 'We were missing you so badly Sir. You had gone off to the South China Sea and we were the ones drowning in a sea of despair and loneliness.'

'Oh you guys! You are bringing tears into my eyes. I am so moved!' I burst forth unable to hold myself any longer.

The entire team bellowed in chorus like a church choir, 'Sir, we love you Sir!'

Moved with their devotion, I ordered them, 'You guys! Come, let us all group hug. Come near me now. I don't want to get up from my chair. Let us hug.'

The team moved eagerly into a circle of admiration around me. Clearly their devotion had blinded them from discharging their duty. So I hugged them. My muscular arms squeezed around them till they were almost dead.

I let go sensing enough juice had been squeezed. Slowly the guys returned to their seats, puffing and panting like wild dogs. All of them were overwhelmed by the emotion of the moment.

A few minutes later, the team had recomposed. The water jar on the side table had been emptied. Rajat looked at me with a weird expression on his face. He seemed to be in pain, as though my bear hug around his chest had caused a massive shockwave to detonate all over his body, maybe even causing something to pop down there like balloons, thereby completely destroying his chances to start a family (at least naturally), but I told myself it was just my imagination. We returned to our discussion. I looked at Rajat.

'So Rajat, what happened after you showed the cheque to Nandini and Iqbal?'

'We discussed the situation. I was still unclear. I wanted to call you up but you had left specific instructions not to be bothered unless some truly ginormous emergency of cosmic proportions which could not be resolved without the grace of your esteemed presence were to occur...something like aliens landing on the planet and asking to meet the leader of all mankind. So I resisted all temptations and decided it best to not call you,' Rajat replied. His reply convinced me that he was not in pain.

'Hmmm,' I pondered aloud.

Vishal explained, 'I told Shastri to come back after you had returned so we could deal more certainly with this.'

'Why did he not leave then?' I asked.

Rajat answered, 'He produced a letter that had been signed by you saying we were to complete the acquisition of Notco by the time you return from vacation and help in enabling the company to get listed on the exchanges.'

'WHAT! NO WAY. I never signed any letter saying that! What nonsense!!'

Nandini flipped open a cardboard green file lying on the table, picked out a piece of white paper, and handed me the document. I was stunned to read it. Everything Rajat had just said was true and below it all was a signature, much like mine. It read 'Yours awesomely, Jhunjhunwala'.

'GET THE HOCKEY STICKS, FELLOWS! INDIAN OIL KA PETROL TANKER HIJACK KARO! CYLINDER LAO! DAARU KI BOTTLE LAO! WE'RE GOING TO PAY RAMAKANT SHASTRI A VISIT RIGHT NOW AND LEVEL HIS COMPANY TO THE GROUND. THE BASTARD HAS HOODWINKED US! THIS LETTER IS A FORGERY! IT'S NOT MY SIGNATURE! THIS IS A CRIME! AND I KNOW DANGEROUS CRIMINALS. THEY CUT IN FRONT OF YOU AT THE AIRPORT. BASTARDS! AAG LAGAO! BUS JALAO!' I began screaming as Vishal abruptly turned on the lights.

'What?! But how?' asked Rajat. He grabbed the paper from my hand and peered as if he was burning a hole through the thing with his eyes alone. The rest of the guys gathered over his shoulder and stared away in shock. I observed their reactions carefully.

'Unbelievable! It looks exactly like your signature, Sir! Are you sure you did not sign this letter?' a baffled Nandini asked.

'Of course! You think I would not know what I signed and what I didn't?' I sneered.

Iqbal insisted, 'No Sir. You may have forgotten...after all, you sign so many things every day. Signatures, autographs. You once signed Sachin Tendulkar's bat.'

I insisted more, 'Yes, and I remember each and everything. I still remember the share prices of Reliance from 1986 onward. This letter is a sham. It is as real as silicone tits.'

Iqbal muttered, 'But then...'

'Look closely, fellows. The signature on the letter is just as it appears on the cheque. The curves, the depth of the pen strokes, the indents—they are all in the exact same places. I think this fellow has done a good old-fashioned carbon copy trace and then filled it over with ink. No wonder its looks so genuine,' Vishal said peering at each of them like Sherlock Holmes explaining the final twist in a sensational murder case.

I screamed in horror, 'Let's inform the cops immediately. Let them arrest this dangerous criminal and imprison him!! I bet he molests children in his free time just for fun. He is a depraved and dangerous perverted lunatic who must be locked up without further delay.'

Rajat agreed, 'Yes. We need to bring the perpetrator to justice. Once the cops take over, the law will take its own course.'

I was just about to give the go ahead. The plan was to first beat him up and then break his neck to teach him such a lesson that he would never ever try to con a hardworking billionaire again.

As I pondered various types of harm upon Ramakant Shastri, a thoughtful Vishal spoke up, 'Let's think about this for a second.

We've got a company here whose boss has cheated us by forging documents. But in just two months, Notco's value on the index has zoomed. The day it opened, it was listed at 3 rupees. Today, a single share is worth 30,000 rupees! That is a phenomenal 10,000 percent rise! No one has ever seen a company share go up like this in such a short span of time! Sir owns 15% of the company. Is it really wise to send Ramakant to jail? I'm sure we can settle this some other way.'

'Oye! This is illegal. The guy fudged my signature,' I howled, appalled he was even considering this.

'Haan, agreed. But should we let go of an opportunity like this which has fallen in our lap? We've lost at most a lakh. In return, we are getting crores. So many crores! There is not enough place in the Reserve Bank of India to hold this kind of money and its only been a few weeks! Can you imagine the future, Jhunjhunwala Sir?! If we can turn this situation in our favour we would be taking advantage of the opportunity. A stock like this comes but once in many lifetimes.'

'Agreed, but I've always established my businesses on the basis of integrity. This man has tried to get me on board by lies and deceit. Why should I reward his company with the legitimacy of my patronage? It would be like Leonardo da Vinci endorsing the painting ability of an art thief.'

Sensing rationale in Vishal's diatribe, Rajat who so far supported the death penalty on Ramakant changed his position. 'But is this not an opportunity, Sir? You, more than anyone I know, highlight the role of opportunity in business.'

Even Nandini seemed to agree. 'Forget the company, Sir. We should concentrate solely on the stock. We can always sell if things get worse.'

'What worse? People on the streets are already saying I am the one responsible for this mess. That I bought into this company and the bulls are acting on my instructions to drive up the prices,'

I raved disappointed my own team were so reluctant to beat up Ramakant and burn down his office.

Vishal, spurred by the support, chimed away. 'But that's not true. Authorities are well aware that the brokerage houses are all buying into Notco. Everybody from JP Morgan, New York and Tzu, Yang and Ping, Tokyo to Kazov Sons Moscow, Vikas Traders, Andheri, Senenayake Securities, Colombo to Mate, and Mate and more Mate, Australia are purchasing the stock. There is heavy demand for this. We should somehow keep this stake. It has landed here by crook but by hook we can make it right.'

'No,' I screamed in outrage. My heart was pumping loudly. 'I will do violent things to Ramakant and then throw him in jail myself. Not just any jail, but Guantanamo Bay. I will pay the torturers to insert things into him. Actually, I will ask for those things to be set ablaze and then inserted into him. He will suffer from internal combustion. SAALA KUTRECHA! PAANI KI JAGAH ZINDAGI BHAR BURNOL PEETA RAHEGA!'

Trying to douse the fire, Rajat slowly said, 'Sir seriously. For a moment consider these 2 scenarios:

'1. We have Ramakant arrested for fraud and lose out on potentially huge gains. I mean HUGE. The value of our stake in Notco is running into lakhs of crores. It's the combined sum total of at least 20 2G scams+10 CWG scams+20 Coalgate scams. We will file a complaint in the morning. By afternoon he will be arrested. By evening he will get bail. By night he will be on TV telling people he has been wrongly accused. By midnight he will get offers to participate in reality shows. The law will take forever to punish him. The cops will take at least 3 years to build a case. The CBI Economic Offences Wing will take another 2 years to investigate the police's investigation. Meanwhile Ramakant will go to the District Court, High Court, and Supreme Court, but he will never go to jail. He will remain out on bail only. In fifteen years time, maybe the court will convict him. If it's a fast track court, it will take 5 years.

'2. Hold the stock, see how high it goes and dump it if things get screwed up. Right now we're only dealing with rumours of insider trading. They will die down soon. The media will lose interest. They will change focus to Rahul Gandhi's fantastic aphorismic speeches illustrating social problems in a manner even Einstein cannot comprehend. We are hardly losing anything. In return the gains are so much it's unreal!

'Let us at least wait and see what happens no, Sir.'

'Hmmm...'

'I agree with him, Sir,' Vishal said.

I lifted my head toward the ceiling and stared coldly at the white egg-shell coloured roof. After a few seconds, I slowly lowered my head and looking at Rajat said somberly, 'Bringing myself to agree with this point of view is something I cannot do.'

'Of course not, Sir. We all agree that what he did was illegal. That is why we are condemning this form of terrorism. All I am trying to say is that what he did intentionally has unintentionally turned out very well for us. There can be no denying that. It's just idiotic to discard the stock in my humble opinion.'

'Well, in my opinion which is even more humble, I will fire all of you guys if something like this ever happens again!' I thundered looking around and banging my fist this time so violently upon the table that Nandini's green file hopped an inch into the air like a frog.

'I promise it will never happen again, Sir. I will not even drink pineapple juice from now on,' Rajat quivered.

Vishal stoically said, 'We know how valuable it is to work for you, Sir.'

The Titan on my hand indicated 11. Adjusting my glasses, I slowly arose. The rest of the folk followed. The creaking of the chairs slowly punctuated the room.

I issued the orders. 'Let me talk to Ramakant Shastri and then decide. Meanwhile you guys devote your efforts into finding out who is buying Notco shares. The volume is incredible. I want a list of every single person who owns a Notco share. Hack into SEBI, bribe the other brokers, turn over the banks, I don't care. If they are gonna accuse me of insider trading, they've got another thing coming.'

'Yes Sir. We'll get it done ASAP,' Nandini squealed.

'Good, This meeting is adjourned.'

All of us stood up. The team pledged allegiance to the colours of Jhunjhunwala. We sang the Jhunjhunwala closing hymn which is an electrifying rock remix of the opening hymn and set out to sort the Notco jumble.

THE MAN WITH THE GOLDEN BOOTS

That afternoon I went to Ramakant's office.

I decided to go by a giant robot. You must be confused. Don't worry. You'll understand in a minute (or less or more depending on what your reading speed is).

Shastri had been holed up in a posh skyscraper 3 kilometres from Jhunjhunwala Chambers. He had renamed his own building 'Notco Towers'. The rise of Notco's shares had allowed him to lease this prime piece of real estate in the city's business district. It was a sight to behold, much like my chiseled, rock-hard yet sinewy and muscular thighs.

The dinosaurs knew that years into the future, there would come a species whose emperor would be the custodian of the most supreme set of thighs in all of eternity. Unable to cope with this knowledge, the dinos killed themselves. The extinction of the dinosaurs was therefore the largest mass suicide in history. An entire species opting to destroy itself to avoid feeling the shame of not being able to produce even a single creature whose thighs could compete with mine.

The modern theory that an asteroid caused their deaths is bullshit. The dinos didn't die of an asteroid problem. They died of a thigh-roid problem. Hahahahahahahahaha!

Coming back to more important things, the robot came to a halt outside the building. A young woman saw the giant robo head through a glass window on the 25th floor and started screaming. I waved charismatically to the rubbernecked Ramakant as he came running into the room to comfort the young lady. Jolted by the pandemonium, he looked frenzied. GOOD!

I shouted, 'RAMAKANT SHASTRI! PREPARE TO PISS THYSELF', and quickly broke through the window by poking the robot's finger through the glass and began comforting the woman who had screamed.

Poor soul, it's not every day that you see a fine creature with champion thighs peering at you from a shoulder next to a giant robot's head. Also, that's a sentence you don't read every day.

Ramakant, still taken aback at what was happening around him, mumbled to the onlookers to vacate the room. The young lady, still gasping for air, was slowly escorted out of the room. Ramakant pushed the remnants of the broken window aside and I jumped in.

'So Mr Shastri, are you impressed? Most people travel by car, bus, scooter, bike, auto, taxi, truck, tractor, cycle, etc. ME, I travel by a robot. That giant head which startled the poor woman is none other than the head of Optimus Prime. The leader of the Autobots from the *Transformers* movie. I bought this thing from the producers. Optimus is so huge, I can simply jump into people's windows. I don't have to walk through lobbies or take elevators any more. I simply find out where the concerned office is and direct Optimus to take me to the nearest window. After that, I jump in through the window and create a truly dramatic entrance. Phata poster, nikla robot aur robot se nikla hero,' I said pulling up a chair.

Shastri mumbled trying to continue the conversation, fully aware that the point of contention was about to break anytime 'Pleasure to have you here, Sir! But one question: What do you do when there's no window to enter from?'

'Then the robot shoots laser beams from his eyes into the concrete and metal and creates a window for me.'

NOTCO
RAMAKANT SHASTRI! PREPARE TO PISS THYSELF!
NOTCO
NOTCO

'Very cool!'

'I know. The producers wanted me to buy the Megatron robot but I bought Optimus Prime and whenever I need to park him he just transforms into a truck. Sometimes, I just drive the truck around for fun. It has "*HORN OK PLEASE—If you have any complaints about this truck's driving then bloody well keep it to yourself because this is not only a truck but also a giant robot and if you complain then you will be crushed by a giant multi-ton steel foot*".'

'Wow! Maybe I should buy one as well. Now that Notco is making money, I am sure I can afford it.'

'Umm, no you can't. This was the only Optimus Prime robot made, and I cut off the hands of all those who worked on making him just like Shah Jahan did after the Taj Mahal was built. Now they cannot scratch themselves in places which itch. Sorry Ramakant!'

'No problem, Jhunjhunwalaji. I'm just happy you are here,' he said sensing the purpose of my visit. At any moment Ramakant was suspecting a giant foot to hammer him down.

He wasn't far off from the truth. I had come to this office for one reason and one reason alone. I wanted to verify the nature of Shastri's cheating and then crush him under the robot's giant foot. My team had thought that it would be best to hold on to Notco shares but I was eager to literally stamp out all ties with Ramakant immediately.

'Why did you try to cheat me, Mr Shastri?' I asked looking straight into his beady little eyes.

Without hesitation he answered, 'Because I needed the backing of a big corporate or investor to sell Nothing, Sir, and you are the biggest.'

'There are other ways to get it instead of forging my signature. I gave you that cheque because I honestly felt you needed to get your head examined. You used my authentic signature on a real cheque to write a fake letter telling my essential staff to buy into an unestablished company which makes an invisible, empty non-product. Do you realize how ridiculous that's going to sound when I try to put it on a police FIR? I hope you understand that you have committed serious fraud.'

'I am sorry Sir,' Ramakant said trying hard to hide his shame. 'I tried to explain it to you but I was unsuccessful. Many people have rejected both me and my idea. The funny thing is that now that the stock is doing well, those same people are apologizing and trying to woo me back. I feel like a sauteli beti who has suddenly inherited a huge amount of wealth from a dead aunt.'

'Bhai, mujhe koi Ekta Kapoor serial ki story mat sunao. You still tried to cheat me.'

'I know and I'm tremendously sorry for that but please give me a chance. What do I do to convince you that this is a great business idea?'

'I don't trust you yaar, and I don't believe in this so called product. Moreover, why do you need me now? Your company is doing well by itself.'

'It's only been a few months, Sir. If news gets out that the world's biggest and greatest investor is offloading his stake, all hell will break loose. People will dump Notco faster than rotting onions at Nashik City market.'

I asked, 'If your product is truly great, why do you need my name to endorse your wares? The product will speak for itself.'

'I truly believe that Nothing is the future of the world. The plans I have for expanding require huge amounts of capital. No one will lend me money unless I can convince them that someone as big as yourself has already been convinced.'

'But you haven't convinced me. You've cheated me…' I said pausing to look at the sun's rays bouncing off Optimus's gleamy metallic exoskeleton.

'I apologize wholeheartedly again, Sir. If you want, I will run naked on Dalal Street as punishment. All I ask for is the chance to make this idea work. I know you don't believe in it and I respect that. I will not ask you for any more money. God promise! And I will gladly let you or anyone you appoint to oversee any aspect of my operations. They can even come and stalk me the way Ranveer Singh stalks Deepika Padukone.'

'Hmm…'

'All my life I've been doing nothing. Even when I do something people say it's worth nothing. Who better than me to sell the world Nothing? I just need your help, Sir.'

Looking at the scrawny Ramakant, it was hard to make out if this dude was stupid or crazy or both. The best entrepreneurs I had backed over the years were those who had had the craziest ideas. In that instant, I decided, contrary to my best judgment, to give this fellow a shot. My team was also in favour of me staying put, if not for the company then at least for the shares. Dumping it now would raise a lot of questions and if they were the kind I had to encounter at the airport, then I would hike all the way up Mt Everest and jump off the summit.

In monetary terms, a lakh is something I won't lose any sleep over. Just the shoelace on a single boot on my feet is worth at least a 1000 times more. The problem was trusting Ramakant…

'Here's what I'm going to do,' I said squinting my eyes and proclaiming with a sense of direction. 'You know my views. I will not back your company publicly till the time I change my mind—which may or may not happen. I will in fact treat you the way Amitabh Bachchan treats Rekha—like an unknown, unheard of entity floating around in some corner of space with no relation to him. I will not make a comment on Notco in public. I won't say anything good about you or Nothing or Notco but I will not say anything bad either. The 15 percent stake in your company which I have been conned into owning will be legalized under a new contract according to my stipulations. This is non-negotiable.'

I paused waiting for him to accept the ultimatum. He nodded in compliance.

I continued, 'My own auditor will track your accounts and report to me. At any time, either me or anyone I appoint, will oversee your developments. Lastly, if you lie to me or try to defraud me one more time, I will make sure that you suffer. The surface area of your orifices will undergo a serious change in volume if you try to con me or my staff or anyone else again.'

'What does that mean, Sir?' Ramakant asked puzzled

'It means there are various holes on your body…right?'

'Right.'

'Some holes bring things into your body while some take things away. If you lie to me again, I will remodel your interior fittings, tear apart all the holes, and rejoin them into one huge hole. You will look like a giant zero on a pair of walking sticks after I'm done with you. This will not only kill you, it will hurt you the whole time you are dying.'

Shastri gulped anxiously. 'I am once again very sorry, Sir. I will be honest with you and make sure I don't do anything which will make me look like a giant onion ring.'

Shifting my eyes from his face to the ground, breathing slowly, I caught a glimpse of Shastri's feet. The shoes on his feet gleamed under the tubelighting of the room. The cheap white light in contrast to the decadent glow of his boots formed a glittering contrast. The first time I saw Ramakant, his boots were a dull coal black leather. This time they were different, yet unmistakable. The man was wearing gold on his feet.

'Nice shoes,' I remarked.

'Thank you!' he uttered, relieved I had veered away from rearranging his inlets and oulets. 'I got them custom made. 24-karat gold foil embossed on top of 22-karat gold sheets molded onto a leather base. What do you think, Sir? Golden shoes! Don't they look awesome? '

'Gold always looks good buddy, but why are you wearing it on your feet?'

'It's something I've always wanted to wear. Gold shoes. Till a month ago, it was just a fantasy. Exactly twenty days ago, Notco shares touched 20,000 rupees and then I had these made as a sort of celebration. Every time I move my feet, I am literally walking on gold! It's the way I always dreamt it would be.'

'I hope you are happy your hard work has paid off,' I said.

Not realizing I was being sarcastic, he smiled brightly and proclaimed, 'This is just the beginning, Sir. Now that you are also on board...officially...'

'And legally,' I interjected stressing on 'legally' as I said it.

'Yes! Yes! Legally too. Notco will reach greater and greater heights. Nothing is the future!'

Nothing is the future. I pondered over it, wondering if Ramakant's enthusiasm had twirled my common sense. I called up Rajat at the office and told him to fax over the acquisition papers with a few clauses inserted. Since he had already done the drill after the forgery incident, the preparation was already on the hard drives. It was just a matter of making a few changes and faxing the papers over to Ramakant's office.

Within a few minutes, the fax machines started buzzing like rowdy MPs at Parliament's question hour. A girl brought in the papers as Ramakant fiddled away on his laptop. I was checking share prices, shooting emails to my staff for the ongoing trading session, and simultaneously viewing videos of cats practicing karate on sleeping babies on my phone. This is my idea of multitasking.

Shastri tapped his feet. The heaviness of the gold on his feet and the tension in his nerves made for a noisy beat in the 25th floor office. Cracking a wry smile, Shastri looked at his screen and said, 'Ah! Notco has gone up today again! Incredible! '

It *was* incredible. In three decades of investing, I had never—and I mean never—seen anything like this. One company rising at this pace over a period of time this short by a margin this huge was astronomical. His company was in a lot of ways already touching the sky.

Suddenly, we heard the sound of loud metal exploding. I jumped up and immediately looked at Optimus. A huge metal bar had struck him in the face and was lying on his shoulder. I ran toward the window and gazed up. A crane was moving on the terrace of Notco towers.

I screamed, 'OYE! RAMAKANT! What the hell is going on in your terrace? Why is my poor Optimus being hit with iron railings? SAALA! CHHAT PE MAYAWATI KA STATUE BAN RAHA HAI KYA?'

Shastri quickly barked out orders to his staff, 'BANDH KARNE KO BOLO! BANDH KARO!'

I looked around unable to make out what was happening. Maybe the decepticons (the antagonists in my favourite movie—*Transformers*) were attacking Optimus.

Ramakant hurried towards me and said, 'I'm sorry Sir. We are installing a blue pyramid on the roof. It's a special pyramid. You can see it glowing from a mile away. It will shoot a blue laser light beam into the sky. It will look fantastic Sir! The work people are making that noise. That's why the railing hit your robot by mistake.'

'What!' I asked, surprised at what I had just heard, 'A laser light beam? Building ke upar musical fountain laga rahe ho kya??'

'Nahin Sir. Have you seen the Luxor hotel in Las Vegas?'

'Oh yes!' I said reminiscing about the Pyramid shaped hotel on the Vegas strip. It shoots out a 50 foot neon blue light into the sky and bedazzles the atmosphere. It looks like a string of blue emeralds pulsating into the sky.

Ramakant smiled, 'The pyramid is an important shape for Notco. Do you remember, Sir, when I told you about the...pyr...'

'YES, I remember. Please don't remind me!' I said, ready to break my head on the wall. Realizing I would damage and even break off my nose, much like the Sphinx, I stopped and wondered if that's how the Sphinx actually lost its nose.

'I want to emulate that light here also. The roof of Notco Towers will be home to a 50-foot light beam, just like the Luxor hotel. It will be fantastic!' said Ramakant with enthusiasm.

I turned my head towards an abrupt knock on the door as an office girl brought the papers into the room. I signed them immediately in my eagerness to escape. Ramakant had scanned over them while I was inspecting the crane hovering over the roof and my staff had given me the 'A-OK' on the phone as well.

A few minutes later, Shastri smiled and outstretched his palm like a banana leaf for a handshake as I dotted the last of the agreement. I shook it lightly, unsure about my actions, and prepared to set foot on my robot. As I started to move towards Optimus Prime's outstretched finger pointing at the window I had arrived through, Ramakant let out a squeak and pleaded,' Sir, can I request you to not tell anyone who does not already know, especially my staff, that I tried to cheat you to get you on board. Please, dear Sir! I am sorry. I will not do it again. Please, don't let anybody know!'

'Your secret is safe with me and my staff…for now,' I said, unsure what else to say.

'Thank you Sir! And welcome aboard Notco…legally,' he sighed with a sense of relief.

I waved a goodbye at the man with the golden boots, hopped aboard my robot and went back to my office, with the robot stamping down the roads and scaring half of Mumbai along the way. TOTALLY WORTH IT!

MARKETING MEETING 1

A day after legalizing the documents, Shastri invited me over to Notco Towers. I decided to oblige as I was curious to see how Shastri intended to make something out of nothing (pun intended).

It was 5 pm when I arrived at the towers. The beam was being built at full swing. Earlier in the day, I could see the crystalline, pyramid-shaped structure being assembled like a jigsaw puzzle on the roof of the Notco building from the top floor of my office building.

Making a rather quiet entrance this time, I walked into the same conference room I had spoken to Shastri earlier and seated myself at the table. Shastri and three other people were already seated around it with their laptops facing them.

'Jhunjhunwalaji. I'm happy you are here. This is the marketing team we have hired. Meet Bipasha, Sachin, and my sales head Nitin,' Ramakant said as I squeezed into the swiveling grey rotating chair at the head of the table.

Taking a look around the table, I observed that all of them looked to be a few years younger than Ramakant, in their late 20s or early 30s. Their eyes signaled the onslaught of a reaction all too common the very first time someone encounters me—*heart attack from adulation.* I looked at each of them, weighing them with my eyes, and smiled that luminous crunk smile.

'Hello Ramakant's associates. You now have my permission to worship me,' I declared.

Their faces exploded immediately into spontaneous euphoria. The guys began to cry. The girl was hyperventilating.

It's a process in which light reflects off my body, enters their eyes, crawls up their optic nerves right into their brain's visual cortex, spreads all over like a rash and completely floors every memory, action, and collective experience they've ever had. All that remains at the very end is the stupendous realization that the one standing before them is ME. The result is a cataclysmic collapse of their emotional system. A raucous degeneration of their very consciousness. Hearts race, hormones overflow, they bite their lips, cry their tears out, quake with anticipation, orgasm into bliss, drown in ecstasy, and finally collapse before me.

It's called awesomeness.

'So you are the people who will be marketing Nothing, huh?' I enquired stroking my chin as the group slowly coalesced back into their senses.

The scrawny, clean-shaven, late-20 something boy spoke first, still breathing heavily after witnessing my divine presence with his own eyes. He gently adjusted the screen of his laptop and squealed loudly as he looked into my eyes.

'Yes Sir! We are delighted to be working with Notco. Our company *Force Marketing* has come up with excellent ideas to market and advertise Nothing.'

Still rubbing my chin and a tad bit distracted, I uttered, 'What is your name again? I'm sorry I didn't catch it when Ramakant told me. I was thinking of the time a bird tried to recently defecate on my robot's head the last time I was here.'

Still trying to make sense of what I had just said, the boy answered with a jolt, 'Oh! It's Sachin, Sir.'

'Tendulkar… Ah! SachinTendulkar, Very nice name.'

'No Sir…Joshi. Sachin Joshi,' he stressed making it a point to highlight 'Joshi'.

'Don't worry Tendulkar. You have a nice name,' I complimented and comforted at the same time.

'Thanks Sir… but my name is not Sachin Tendulkar. It's Sachin Joshi.'

'But why? You should change your name to Sachin Tendulkar. You can market yourself more effectively that way…you know?'

Looking confounded, he blinked for a moment and then proceeded to slowly say 'Well, you can call me just Sachin.'

'Ok *Just Sachin*… I will call you *Just Sachin* from now on.'

'Just…Sachin, Sir,' he stressed, again taking care to highlight 'Sachin'.

I looked around the table at the others who were unsure if I was joking or purposely trying to aggravate poor Tendulkar. Grinning mischievously, I said, 'I'm also saying that…*Just Sachin.*'

'No Sir, not *Just Sachin*…just…only Sachin…not…just Sachin…Only Sachin,' he reiterated by slowly measuring out each word, trying his best to make sure that I got his name right.

I shrilled loudly, taking special care to make it sound as though my deliberate taunts were actually a burst of anger. I was intent on making Tendulkar believe that this was all his fault and his nomenclature had been specially designed just to confuse the fu*k out of me. 'Arre yaar! Now you are saying your name is *Only Sachin* and not *Just Sachin.* Why are you confusing me? That's why I said you should change your name to Sachin Tendulkar. Then this *Just Sachin, Only Sachin, Not Sachin* confusion business will stop!'

Shastri leaned forward in his chair and trying to pacify the situation said, 'Jhunjhunwalaji, his name is Sachin. You can call him that and by that I mean Sachin and not actually "that".'

'And this is Bipasha,' Sachin immediately interjected trying desperately to divert my attention to anyone but him. He pointed to a thin, skinny, pony-tailed girl who seemed to be around the same age as him.

My investigation into poor Tendulkar's name had escalated the atmosphere. Ramakant's pencil thin moustache was flaking in the gentle breeze from the window. A quiet fan rotated above. I could see that the air conditioner was also switched on. *Just* and *Only Sachin* who was not Tendulkar was waiting for me to say something. The other fellow was looking at the girl who was in turn looking at Ramakant who was in turn staring at me like a gap-toothed idiot.

Deciding to break the silence, I swiveled the chair a little and asked as I shifted my gaze from the girl (whose name I had once again failed to catch) to the other guy. 'So I know this is Sachin. What about you two?'

'I'm Bipasha, Sir,' the girl answered stoically.

Turning towards her again I exclaimed, 'Bipasha…ah…Bipasha Basu. Very nice name!'

Bipasha Basu then looked at Sachin Tendulkar who seemed to be getting irritated for some reason.

'And my name is Nitin, Sir,' the other fellow said courteously. He looked older than the other two. This one was in his late 30s. His moustache was much thicker than Shastri's who was sitting next to him. They looked like brothers.

'Nitin Gadkari? Achha…okay,' I acknowledged. 'You all have nice names. Sachin Tendulkar, Bipasha Basu, and Nitin Gadkari. Solid marketing team banayi hai aapne, Ramakant!' I complimented Shastri who smiled eagerly, glad that I was having a bit of fun this time instead of disfiguring him into a giant onion- ring shaped mass of meat.

Nitin then proceeded to cut right to the chase and turning his laptop screen towards me, announced, 'We'd like to present our marketing, publicity, and advertising plan for the revolutionary Nothing product Sir. We were discussing that only with Ramakant Sir before you came in.'

'Hmmm, okay. Let's see what you've got,' I obliged.

Nitin handed me a brochure from his bag on the ground next

to his chair and moused over his laptop. Looking as though he was about to deliver an election speech, he spoke with an air of confidence.

'Jhunjhunwala Sir, we at Force Marketing believe that what Mr Ramakant has created through his hard work and genius is extraordinary. We are proud to be involved in marketing Nothing. Basically, we want to adopt a 3-point strategy to market Nothing. Firstly, a publicity campaign to build brand awareness. To tell the customer that such a product from such a company exists.'

'Hold on,' I interrupted. 'But I thought the product doesn't exist.'

'You are right. What I meant was that we will start by publicizing that the product does not exist but it is being sold by Notco headed by visionary entrepreneur Ramakant Sir!'

Ramakant beamed.

Nitin continued.

'It is a positive development for us because Nothing has already garnered publicity via headlines because of its rise on the stock exchanges. Now we want to increase this coverage by launching a full-fledged marketing campaign.'

'We're talking billboards! Print media! TV ads! Radio and Internet! Celebrity endorsements! Already Alia Bhatt has told me this product is very close to her heart. We only have to pay 50 lakhs for her to endorse Nothing. Such a nice girl! She even gave me a Coke to make me feel loved,' Bipasha added wiping a tear from the overwhelming act of generosity she had been reminded of.

'We'll do that Facebook and social media thing. We can start a Facebook page and have a contest. The people can "like" Nothing on Facebook and if they win a lucky draw, they will win free Nothing!!' Sachin said eager to give his inputs as he frantically tapped away on his keyboard.

Nitin then added, 'We'll do the same thing on Twitter. Our agency will try to trend the hashtag #nothing and make it a trending topic.'

Stroking my chin again and feeling that the crux of the issue was being lost, I said dismissively, 'All that is fine but what is the core reason people are going to be driven to buy this product?'

The team members exchanged glances guessing who would answer the question. It was then that Shastri who had been silent all this while said in a heavy tone, 'The core reason is simple—its boredom.'

'Boredom?!' I yelped.

'Yes. We highlight the boredom in people's lives. Boredom which has set in like tooth decay—monotonous, unavoidable, stinky, infected, pus-ridden. Boredom, with everything else money can buy, has led the average consumer to be sad.'

'If the consumer were a smiley, he would be a sad smiley like this :-(,' Nitin said and drew the smiley on a piece of notepad paper which he then held up for me to see.

'Everyday he works hard always looking for newer ways to spend money, but there's nothing new or exciting that can earn his attention,' Bipasha added and then turned to Shastri for approval.

Ramakant nodded at Bipasha and then looked at me and explained, 'This is where we introduce our product. Nothing removes the sadness, the gloom, and boredom of everyday products and fills the customer with a sense of happiness and excitement. It gives him that feeling of money *well spent*. That's what Nothing is—a creator of satisfactory feelings.'

Unconvinced, I halted the explanation as Shastri was about to continue. Looking around I asked, 'Simple question guys. What is the *need* for the customer to buy the product you guys are so eagerly marketing?'

'That's the second point.' Nitin swooped in. 'Highlighting the need to use Nothing. *The need is to remove boredom. They will buy this simply because they are bored.* They already have everything in the world but that does not make them happy, so they will now buy Nothing instead which will actually make them happy.'

'And you think people are stupid enough to buy this?' I asked beginning to scratch my head.

Shastri replied, 'Crores of rupees are spent on market research that indicate how stupid people are our #1 customers. We are finding out where huge pockets of stupid people are found to live—not only in India but also the world. The plan is to market our product extensively in these areas to build an initial customer base.'

'That's crazy!'

'No Sir. It's market research. We should never underestimate the buying power of stupid people.'

Sachin added, 'After that we will start a marketing campaign to target intelligent people also.'

'In time, both stupid and intelligent people will start using Nothing.' Shastri declared as though he were reading the last line of a fairy tale. The others nodded in agreement, exchanging satisfied smiles with each other.

'Fantastic,' I said in contrast, sarcasm, and bewilderment dripping like saliva from a buffalo's mouth.

Sensing my apprehension, Shastri explained further, 'What we will do is that we will come up with a punchline to highlight the most important aspect of Nothing.'

'What is that?'

'The fact that Nothing is invisible.'

'Eh?'

'The tagline we are going with in this initial phase of marketing is 'INVISIBILITY ROCKS!'

'This summarizes Nothing in two words and it captures the minds of our main customer segment,' Sachin said, looking at Shastri and then at me.

'Who? The youth?' I asked.

'No. People who have eyes. More specifically those who can see,' he replied.

I squinted my eyebrows and stared transfixed at Sachin Tendulkar. I had been fed more bullshit in this one meeting than a dude who has watched every single episode of 'MTV Roadies' every single day for years on end till his brain decides to start banging itself against the inside of his skull and terminates itself.

Realizing that the explanation was confusing me further instead of making things clearer, just like Rahul Gandhi's speeches. Shastri adjusted his chair and resting his elbows on the table, said, as he flapped his palms about, 'I think what Sachin is trying to convey is that we have no use for blind people. They cannot see invisibility so there is no point in selling our products to them.'

'Because they cannot see something that is not visible!' I asked in exasperation as I squinted my eyebrows even more.

'Exactly,' he declared taking his hands of the table with an expression of 'finally! You get it.'

I hadn't however, got it.

Leaning back on the chair and then catapulting back into an upright position, I asked loud and forthright, 'Look, just forget the tagline for now and for heaven's sake explain to me why a person will spend his money to buy something which is

'Shapeless

'Formless

'Invisible

'Expensive

'Cannot be touched, cannot be held and most of all

'Is of no use.'

'Jhunjhunwala Sir. I agree Nothing is shapeless, formless, and invisi-bles, but tell me this—have all the things in the world made of all possible shapes, present in all possible sizes, seen in all possible colours, bought in all possible quantities and available in all possible prices ever made man happy? Has he ever felt happy with everything around him ever? He's only happy for a while with that new thing he just bought. Then it gets old, he gets bored with it, and throws it away, waiting for something newer to come along. If he's already spent too much money on it then he just keeps it and uses it because he has no other choice. All the while he wishes he had that new thing out there so he tries harder to make money with which he will buy it only to get bored again and the whole process repeats again and again and again. It's like a vicious cycle,' Ramakant explained shaking his head about like an epileptic rabbit on crack.

Pausing for a few seconds, he stared intently at me and asked slowly 'Now my question is why?'

'Because it's his nature?' I answered.

'Exactly!' he declared even more vociferously than the last time and continued, 'Man will always get bored of what he has even if he has something which already fulfils all his needs, he'll still want something else. That's the problem with products which have shapes and forms. They bore him.'

'And speaking from a marketing and sales point of view, boredom is an extremely lucrative market. We should take advantage of his boredom with visible, shaped, and formed products and give him invisible, shapeless and formless products instead,' Nitin insisted as he adjusted his screen and wiped it lazily with his finger.

'What Nothing will do is remove his boredom by giving him a feeling of happiness. So even though Nothing has no shape, no form and is invisible, it can be felt.' Bipasha added waving her right hand in the air.

'The customer *feels* that he has bought a product which is no longer boring. It gives him a feeling of satisfaction which is what any product tries to do,' Sachin added.

Shastri kicked the floor and moved the chair a few inches back. The clank of his golden boots tapped the floor and my ears. Adjusting his chair some more he surmised as he looked at me. 'Every product tries to make man feel happy. Companies try really hard to give us things which are supposed to fulfil our needs and make us feel good but they fail because what man wants is not for his needs to be fulfilled but to feel fulfilled itself.'

I adjusted my spectacles and sighed willingly. What they had said was making sense. I still felt that their reasons were all wrong but it was impossible to argue with the fundamental basis of the premise. Man as a creature wants to feel good and content. He buys, eats, drinks, smokes, drives, watches films... basically everything he does, everything we do, we do to feel. Shastri was right about that.

I sipped from a glass of water as Ramakant continued.

'Nothing simply makes the customer feel good. We don't need a shape or colour or form or substance for that. We've just skipped all that and gone straight to the crux of making him feel good.'

'And since we take money for that, it's obviously a business, not a charity,' Nitin added.

Though not fully convinced, I conceded unwillingly and placing the empty glass on the table said, 'Okay fine. But how do we go about this? How do you convince an entire population that they can feel good with Nothing? How do you convince them to pay for colourless emptiness?'

'Through marketing and positive perception creation. Leave that to us Mr Jhunjhunwala' Nitin said emphatically as the other two marketing people smiled away like mad scientists about to open a Pandora's Box of Frankenstein monsters.

Apparently relieved that I had conceded for the moment, Shastri recapitulated, 'So to sum up, we are going to aggressively expand Nothing in high-profit sectors. We'll first target stupid people who are bored and then sell Nothing to them. They'll buy Nothing because our marketing campaign will harp on the fact that they will feel good after buying Nothing. And after they buy Nothing they will tell other stupid people to also buy Nothing and once all the stupid people have bought Nothing, we'll market Nothing to intelligent people but since they are so few it won't matter. Basically we are creating a positive association in marketing terms with our invisible non-existent product and this positive association factor paradigm will be our third point in our marketing strategy.'

Nitin declared immediately, 'We'll be creating positive association by sponsoring and powering a few TV programmes. That's how we'll begin.'

'What do you mean "powering"?' I asked.

Nitin smiled at Bipasha who, taking the smile as a cue to answer instead of him, obliged her senior colleague and looking at me and asked, 'You ever see the title card of a show like "The X Factor"? The full title will be something like *"Hindustan Lever presents X Factor in association with Nokia Lumia Smartphones POWERED by All Out Mosquito Repellant"*. Have you ever observed that?'

'Yeah.'

'So we'll be the *"POWERED BY"* guys.'

Squinting my brows yet again, boldly risking another long winding explanation, I asked, 'Why *Powered*?'

Nitin and Bipasha exchanged glances. The question had caught them on the backfoot. Ramakant opened his mouth and made a mumbling sound. Before he could make a coherent sentence, Sachin jumped up in his chair and yelled, 'BECAUSE IT IS GETTING POWER BECAUSE OF US!'

'HUH!' I responded taken aback with the sudden burst and the absurdity of the answer which didn't make sense to the others as well. Bipasha stared a hole into Sachin who quietly slunk into his chair.

Trying to do some damage control, Nitin insisted, 'Arre don't worry Sir. It's just brand association. *Power, Sponsor,* whatever, our name is publicized for money that's all. Speaking of Nokia Lumia phones Bipasha just mentioned, Notco will also be making smartphones enhanced with Nothing.'

Immediately turning my head towards Shastri I howled, 'Whaat! Why are you making smartphones now? I thought you made Nothing.'

'I'm glad you asked us that,' he replied calmly and stood up. 'Notco, like I said, will focus on bringing Nothing into all high-profit sectors. We will use Nothing in smartphones and then diversify into other things as well which I will also make clear soon. This way we combine the usefulness of Nothing with something already useful in the market, which people use. Nothing+something =High quarter growth projection!'

'For the moment, check this out Jhunjhunwala Sir,' said Sachin who had almost disappeared after the fiery warning gaze and tried to restart operations. Fishing out a white phone from his trouser pocket, he held it up and announced, 'It's called the Notco Smartphone. It's from the 9987 series. It has the latest Android Jellybean, 22 megapixel camera, HDMI recording, latest apps, and the coolest shiz in it that will blow your mind!'

Immediately, Bipasha, seemingly forgetting her anger towards Sachin, pulled out a pink phone from her small handbag slung over the chair, and holding it up like Sachin, declared, 'And this is the Notco 9900 smartphone in multi-coloured back panels, Android custard apple, 26 megapixels, video recording, and check out the colour—it's pink which means it's women friendly and gay friendly.'

Nitin thumped his palm on the table. Distracted by the sound, I turned from Bipasha and Sachin seated next to each other holding their phones up to Nitin who proclaimed immediately 'Jhunjhunwala Sir, forget about these. Look at my phone—it's the Notco 9999 smartphone with 36 megapixels, HD recording, Android Chocolate Shake 4.4 operating system, and everything the other two phones have. It also has an app you can download to launch intercontinental ballistic missiles across the border, very popular in North Korea and Iran.'

It was like a pissing contest. I turned forward to see Ramakant already holding up a black phone. Like Nitin, he proclaimed loudly, 'You wait Sirji and see my phone. It's the best, Notco 99999999 series with Android diabetes 5.6…'

'Yaar, aap log number bana rahe ho ki phone bana rahe ho? Yeh kya business chala rahein hai aap?!' I hollered out of confusion and irritation.

'Sirji, hum tarah tarah ke phone number bana rahein hai…' Sachin said keeping his phone on the table and abruptly stopped as Bipasha once again stared at him angrily.

Ramakant stood next to Nitin and, holding his phone a tad bit higher than Nitin, said, 'I think you are confused because each phone looks the same but trust me Sir, this is not the case. My phone is 38 megapixel while Nitin's is only 36 megapixels. My phone is better.'

'Why? Because you're phone has two more megapixels than his?' I asked.

'Yes!' he squealed in delight.

'So how does that help you?' I countered and pointed at his phone with my finger. 'What are you getting with the two extra megapixels?'

Looking seemingly unhappy that perhaps I had not acknowledged the greatness of his integrated-circuit based, Internet enabled, Made in China, Telecommunication device, he replied nonchalantly, 'I don't know what the consumer is getting but I know I am getting 2000 rupees more.'

'Huh?'

'My phone with 38 megapixels is 38,990. Nitin's with 36 megapixels is 36,990. Sab kuch same hai bas mera phone mein do pixel zyaada hai aur jab consumer mera model kharidta hai instead of Nitin's for those 2 extra pixels then I am getting 2000 rupees more'

Ramakant added putting the phone into his shirt pocket, 'Sirji, why do you break your head over this? My phone costs more because it has more megapixels and consumer wants to pay more so he can also have more megapixels, so I am making a phone with more megapixels. Zyaada megapixels se woh kya kare mujhe kya? Mujhe toh sirf MRP dekhna hai bas!'

Seeing that I was getting irritated, Bipasha coughed and, nodding at everyone, declared, 'So to sum up…again, we market by publicity, emphasizing the need for Nothing and by creating a positive association with the product.'

Moving the chair back, I looked at all the faces at the table and replied in an uninterested tone, 'Fine go ahead. Do what you want. I'm late.'

It was almost 6. The grey of dusk was cascading in as I got up, frustrated that what was stupid some time back didn't seem so stupid now. I knew it was a farce, yet Shastri and his team had analyzed consumer psychology pretty well. Sooner or later this was going to turn into a clusterfu*k for me and I knew it.

GEOFFREY'S

Geoffrey's is the world's coolest bar. It's so cool that a fully-clad Eskimo, sitting inside the stomach of a polar bear moving around in Geoffrey's, would catch a cold. For the record, the previous line is only to demonstrate the coolness of Geoffrey's. No real polar bears or eskimos confined to the stomachs of polar bears were harmed during the writing of this paragraph.

I make it a point to visit Geoffrey's at least three of four times a week. After a hectic day of ruling the markets and managing the different contours of money in equities, commodities, properties, bullion, and foreign exchange, there's nothing better than settling at the Geoffrey's bar side and guzzling Black Label whiskey while munching on masala cashewnuts and poppadums.

It's my way of rewarding myself for making such a ridiculously obnoxious amount of money during the daytime.

Drinking at Geoffrey's is special. Imagine Sachin Tendulkar batting at the Wankhede versus batting anywhere else in the world. He's told me many times—especially while he's busy thanking me for teaching him how to paddle sweep—that batting at the Wankhede is the greatest experience ever. My greatness experiences similar sentiments while at Geoffrey's. Being a champion at drinking just as Sachin is a champion at batting, I consider Geoffrey's to be the best watering hole in the world.

I've achieved many milestones here such as gulping down two hundred shots of Cocoroco, Bolivian badass liquor—97% alcohol, 3% water, and 10,000% awesomeness. This is a drink so dangerous it is banned in 129 countries across the world.

The double hundred is the hardest achievement in the drinker's playbook. Till I achieved the feat, many were convinced it couldn't be done. There's an entire platoon of doctors standing by to give you a liver transplant when you pass out after attempting a double.

In my case, I needed neither a liver nor a medical team after scoring the double hundred. I scored another double hundred immediately after and then hopped on the next flight to London and took part in the Olympics where I won 10 gold medals in Javelin, Archery, Wrestling, Sculls, Swimming, Badminton, Table Tennis, Rifle Shooting, Boxing, and Judo… all on the same day.

I know. I will give you a moment to applaud.

So there I was, looking at my glass and admiring the viscosity of the brown liquid within, dazzling in the light like a shiny disco ball. The shade of brown reminded me of my remarkable foresight to have invested in Asian Paints a long time ago. Within two years of me laying my magic fingers on them, the stock price had exploded(in flying colours), and I was able to buy my first nitroglycerin-powered autorickshaw.

Laugh all you want but a nitroglycerin-powered autorickshaw is a class ten vehicle. There's enough firepower in this to destroy ten full-sized, army battalions. It's sanctioned only to people with extreme knowledge of handling explosive material and since the regional transport officials are well aware of my wife's anger, they readily decided to approve my rickshaw buy order.

Now since it's so rare, my rickshaw obviously costs a lot but man can it travel! With the nitro-thrusters on, it rips on the road faster than a Ferrari. The producers of the *Fast and Furious* franchise are genuflecting before me, hoping I'll lend my autorickshaw to them for their next.

Speaking of *Fast and Furious*, there is one person who gives my blood pressure a fast and furious shakedown. All I need is to see this guy and every single atom in my body starts to zing around like coffee in a percolator on a high flame.

Earlier in the day, after having met Ramakant, reluctantly agreeing to stamp my name on Notco and then explaining the situation to my staff and a swarm of media guys who were constantly buzzing around the office ever since they had ambushed me at the airport, I decided to rest my hot brain in some cool alcohol at Geoffrey's.

Geoffrey's relaxes me.

Geoffrey's has a nice dartboard neatly pasted to one side of the wall adjacent to the bar counter with the mahagony table. The proprietor/bartender manages the show for us humble bevda log from behind the counter. It is a pub with a very British feel. Even the menu boasts of fish and chips. Modern times have however forced the management to dole out nachos, French fries, and sandwiches. For us desi folk there's always a bowl of freshly fried moong dal, salted almonds, cashewnuts, and lime-coated paneer tikka.

Popping a cashew into my mouth, I waited for the masala to explode upon my tongue. A couple of youngsters were throwing darts in one corner. Geoffrey's veterans sat upon the bar stools next to me, drinking quietly. I was getting set for a quiet evening.

Thats when I knew HE was in the vicinity.

I could smell his 50-year-old, shifty, moustached, greasy haired, stench-bearing, filthy carcass of a human body from yards away. Slowly, his footsteps grew louder, the thud of his boots inching closer to me...

They stopped. I heard him breathing behind me. It was time to put my glass down, turn around and face him. Business was about to pick up. A quiet evening it was definitely not going to be... It was time to confront the biggest bear on Dalal Street, Enemy # 1...the man called STINKER.

'Well, well, well! Look who we have here! Still stuffing your face with food and drink as always, fatso?' Stinker said condescendingly, smiling away like the Joker from underneath his walrus moustache.

I retorted honestly, 'Eh! Don't call me fat you bloody asshole! I'm not fat. I just happen to wear a protective armour under my skin instead of over it and it just happens to be made of adipose tissue. It's a shock absorber for my six-pack abs!'

'Yeah right! You are fat. You're so fat that if you had travelled on the Titanic, the ship would have sunk just from your weight. You weigh more than the iceberg which sunk it.'

'OH YEAH? Well you're so thin that I could lift you up and use you like a toothpick to clean my teeth!'

Stinker sneered mockingly 'HA! You're so fat and you eat so much that even if you use me as a toothpick, I'd only find enough food material stuck between your teeth to feed an entire country full of hungry people for the next 5 years!'

I could hear my heart pounding. I shot back 'WELL YEAH? You're so thin that you teach anorexic runway models how to look stick thin by puking! And don't talk about my teeth. I'll have you know that I use Vicco Vajradanti with *Sodium Dotjartiminin and Bhramarishi jadibooti* with microgranular technology approved by 9 out of 10 dentists registered with the Indian Dental Association.'

Completely disregarding the statistic evidence I had just given him and thereby drowning out any opportunity to discuss dental hygiene, he yelled, 'YOU'RE SO FAT THAT YOU ONCE SAT ON AN iPAD AND SQUASHED IT INTO AN iPHONE! BLOODY FATTY!'

Aroused by the commotion, people began to gather around us.

I was thinking of an appropriate comeback when he blasted, 'You're so fat that if you take all the flubber from your body, it would be enough to fry an entire family of blue whales so fine they'd be crisper than a Mamata Banerjee tongue-lashing!'

Fuming away impulsively, I yelled back to defend my honour, 'YOU...YOU...YOU...WELL YOU'RE SO THIN THAT I'M RICHER THAN YOU!'

Got him! STINKER (spelled in CAPS because I cannot emphasize how much he STINKS) hates the undisputed fact that I am richer than him. In the last thirty years, he and I have gone toe-to-toe on some of the biggest block deals on the market. We've been engaged in a battle of mind-tennis and I have trounced him all the time!

Unfortunately, the guy's got the resilience of a zombie. No matter how many times I kill him, he keeps coming back—more dead, more bloody, and more stinky than ever.

The very first time I met him more than 15 years ago, it was hate at first sight. The moment I saw him, *I knew* he was the worst person in my entire world.

During our first encounter, he had uttered a name his parents had given him—'Shukla', 'Sharma', 'Deepak', 'Paapi Aulad'... something like that. Pretty soon it became clear that we were as different as night and day. If I'm Batman, he's the Joker. If I'm Udit Narayan, he's Kumar Sanu. If I'm Kumar Sanu, he's a piece of chewing gum stuck to Kumar Sanu's boot. If he says I am Pepsodent, then I say he is Colgate. If I'm MDH Garam Masala, he's Everest Garam Masala. If I'm a glass of chilled Haywards 5000, then he's a mug of hot donkey piss. If I'm as glorious as the game of cricket, he's the BCCI.

I have always hated bears and Stinker is the biggest bear on Dalal Street. For the uninitiated, a stock market is a place where two fundamental approaches prevail. Depending on which approach you follow you are either termed a bull (YAY!) or a bear (Boo!). Without getting too technical, a bull, which is what I am, (and everyone else should be) is someone who buys a company stock first and sells it second. I wait for prices to go up. I am an optimist.

A bear, which is what stinky STINKER is, sells a stock first and buys it back second. He waits for prices to go down and is a pessimist.

Our very DNA is different. I am built like a God and he is built like a rat. I wait for companies and people's lives to increase in value and profit off it. Stinker and his kind profit off a company's declining fortunes. He likes to call himself a realist. I like to call him an asshole.

In our very first conversation he had called me 'FATSO'. In response, I had responded with 'STINKER'. The names have carried on ever since.

Stinker, despite his best and most sinister Machiavellian schemes, has been unable to rule Dalal Street. In our many battles, he's always given me a good fight but when I fire, they all burn. Stinker hates it when I replay this fact over and over like a catchy ringtone. Rupee for rupee, dollar for dollar, gold bar for gold bar and Nestle Bar-one for Bar-one that my net worth is fantastically, stupendously, gigantically more than his.

Add to this, the fact that I'm hotter, stronger, smarter, more talented, more fantastic, and more excellent than him in every way possible and the writing is on the wall. I am awesome. Stinker is not. Even my wife is hotter than his wife. Even my wife with a moustache is hotter than his wife.

For guys like us in the markets, the methods we adopt—bull vs bear—is more than that; it's our philosophy, our way of life, and when the both of us follow completely different ways of life which contradict and clash at every single turn, enmity becomes inevitable.

Stinker had started to simmer. Perspiration was brewing on his forehead. The tirade had just begun…

'What happened, butthead? For 30 years you've been fighting me and you still haven't, for a single day, managed to overtake my net worth. The only thing you've done in these three decades is grow a moustache and let me tell you—that thing on your face looks like a monkey shat on your lips and let it dry.'

He fumed furiously, his eyes turning red as the moustache I had attacked growled ferociously.

'Can't digest the fact that I'm richer than you? Tanki bhar bhar ke gelusil aur kayam churna peena shuru karo. Digestion problem ke liye achha hai.' In no mood to stop, I mocked as the folks around us tried to digest my vicious and deliberate barb.

'SHUT THE FU*K UP FATSO!' Stinker yelled, outraged at my comments. 'Don't mock the fact that you have better accountants than me. That is the only reason you're richer than me!'

'Hahaha! You're just too dumb. Your methods suck! You suck! I'm richer than you.'

Stinker fumed some more. The rest of the crowd at Geoffrey's had gathered around us. Stockbrokers, fund managers, finance dudes and dudettes, traders, market analysts, and the rest of the general population had divided itself into two opposing factions, each cheering their preferred bar warrior in the mix.

I popped another cashew in my mouth and gulped a cool swallow of whiskey. STINKER had wiped the sweat off his brow. Removing his jacket, he looked me in the eyes and sat down on an opposing stool.

The crowd moved in. A big-fight feel was forming at Geoffrey's. It was on…

'You want to fight! Let's go fatso!' he yelled.

'Hell yeah, stinky face!' I blasted back, totally up for the challenge.

'I'm so rich I'm that I'm on the cover of *I'm Rich* magazine!' Stinker yelled as the crowd raucously chanted, 'FIGHT! FIGHT! FIGHT!'

'I'm so rich that I'm on the cover of *I'm Filthy Rich* magazine!' I said aloud, brushing him off easily.

'Oh yeah! I'm so rich that I drink mineral water specially flown in from Belgium. My kidneys aren't used to anything but the purest spring water from the Alpine forests.' STINKER furiously salvaged.

'Screw you! I'm so rich that the mineral in my mineral water is gold. I piss gold…BITCH!' I yelled back immediately.

The crowd went crazy. The chicks started salivating. The waiters were rushing around refilling everyone's drink. The cash register was ringing at Geoffrey's. Even the sole guy in the corner throwing darts had abandoned the dartboard and was cheering me on.

'You're a joke fatso! You're so god damn pathetic that every time I look at you, I feel mercy killing should be made legal!'

'FU*K YOU, you stupid doorknob. Before you call me "Fat" look at your pathetic face. Look at your moustache! Saala! Mooh pe M-seal chipkake baitha hai! Your own dad is rolling around in his grave thinking of how pathetic you are and he isn't even dead yet!'

'KUTTE! MOTE BHAINS! Baap pe mat jaa! Don't talk about my dad, okay! He's extremely proud of me because I'm so rich that all my VISA platinum cards are made out of actual platinum.'

'So? I'm so rich I threw out my platinum cards years ago and got uranium cards. I once tried to pay with my visa uranium credit card when I was bitten by a spider. The radiation from my uranium card infected the spider and when it bit me, I became Spiderman!'

Looking at me as if I were dressed like Spiderman, Stinker, quickly realizing his stock was taking a beating, shot back, 'I'm so rich I bought Antarctica just because the ice tray in my freezer was empty!'

'I never remember selling Antarctica to you,' I answered, cool as ice.

'Thats because I'm so rich that when I cash a cheque, the bank bounces!'

'Boo! Like I haven't heard that before asshole.I eat gold biscuits. When I take tea and Parle-G biscuits, the "G" in Parle-G actually stands for gold! I'm so rich that I'm under treatment for gold addiction from Dr Bappi Lahiri.'

'Grr...Grr...I'm gonna kill you, Jhunjhunwala! If it's the last thing I do. Just you wait...one of these days ...I'm gonna get back at you...' STINKER muttered hopping mad. Waiters were running around taking orders furiously. Everyone loves a good fight as long as you aren't in it. Stinker and I had become the evening's entertainment.

'Fu*k you bear!'

'Double fu*k you you fuc*in fuc*er !'

'Infinity times fu*k you!'

Because this book is rated U/A I shall censor the next few gaalis with ****'s

'**** your **** with ***** and **** till your Gall bladder blasts out of your **** while the **** makes your head look like wet cement!' he exploded like a hand grenade.

I grinned nastily. The masala and the whiskey had done their job. Grenade ka jawab missile se dena tha. I launched off' **** your toad face with Chilli powder so bad that your **** hand is pulled up your **** virus infected **** hanging in that ***** rubbed with rat flesh so hard you need an welder's blowtorch to surgically separate your **** leaking **** in your rotted up backside and your **** up your **** goes for a toss!'

Stinker shook his head in confusion, trying to make some sense out of what I had just said. Quite abruptly and sheepishly, he asked, 'I hate to ask but what is a **** up your *****?'

There is no point in giving a gaali if the opposing party does not understand it. I therefore obliged out of a sense of duty and explained my most recent barrage. 'You know when your **** is set fire to with the blowtorch and then rubbed with dead rat flesh?'

'Yeah.'

'The **** up **** is what happens when you take those burnt remains and sink them in buckets of Hydrochloric acid before sticking them up your *****'

'Oh! You mean before the blowtorch? Right after the road roller goes over my **** which was stapled with dehydrated fungus ridden wooden board wrapped up in plastic and exploded in my *****?'

'Exactly!' I shrieked, glad he had finally understood it.

'Thanks,' he said coldly.

'You're welcome,' I said and relaunched the attack. 'Now go ***** your ***** in gutter liquid!'

Suddenly, the cheering audience went more silent than a minister facing corruption charges. The bartender intervened at this point. Wiping a beer mug he looked at us, stone-faced, like a librarian chiding a bunch of kids making noise, 'What are you doing, Sirs?'

'Nothing yaar, just chanting random alphabets,' I replied, trying to desperately avoid eye contact as a part of the audience booed.

'Yeah absolutely,' STINKER reluctantly agreed. 'It's been a long time since we left kindergarten so we were just testing our memory to see if we can still remember A,B,C,D.'

The bartender placed the mug on the table, outstretched his arms and smiling maniacally raised his voice. 'Gentlemen, as the supreme authority of this fine establishment AND as the Chief of the Bar Federation Of Asia, let me tell you, that if I hear such disgusting language in my bar ever again, then I will personally KICK BOTH OF YOU AND BAN YOU FOR LIFE! YOU GOT THAT?'

Stinker and I looked at each other. The bartender's diatribe forced us to call upon a ceasefire. Both of us nodded slowly. The crowd slowly began to dissipate as the bartender went back to wiping his mug and continued to patrol us with his eyes.

After a minute of silence, STINKER turned towards me. 'Don't try anything funny with Notco, fatso. I'm watching. I don't know what your game plan is yet, but let me tell you right now that if you sell the stock I'm gonna short the hell out of it so fast the value of your holding will be worth less than a peanut.'

'Boy, you are so stupid that you went to the circus, kidnapped a dwarf, dressed him up in chaddis, stood outside the Bombay Stock Exchange and started taking bids for him because that's what you understood by the term SHORT SELLING'!' I yelled.

The bartender looked at me from under the TV.

'Cheers!' I said eager to not have my drinking license suspended. 'Another double,' pointing the glass towards him.

STINKER continued, 'I'm serious, fatso. Every bear on the exchange is ready to go to war. All they need is a word from me. I'm sure you're upto something with Notco. that's why the price is zooming. You had better not be rigging the price, fat ass.'

'SHUT UP STINKFACE!' I yelled. 'I love the markets too much to disrespect it by rigging or pulling some stunt like that.'

'Whatever. Just know that my friends have also bought shares of Notco. Moreover, if you try to sell the stock then by God you will have a bloodbath on your hands. Those analyst idiots on TV can run around like headless chickens all day screaming. I don't care. For every one share you buy I'm gonna sell two. Watch out!'

'Are you trying to scare me? Go read a history book pigface! You can't beat me. You can keep trying and keep failing. I've already kicked your ass so many times that there's a permanent imprint of my size 11 footprint all over your buttocks. Every time you experience a bowel movement, it's like a roller-coaster ride with the tracks laid out in the shape of my foot rambling all around in your derriere!'

'You are the most idiotic son of a bitch I've ever seen!' STINKER whined frustratingly.

'I'm a freakin genius! You're just too stupid to realize it.'

'You're gonna pay, fatso!'

'Fu*k you stinker! You're more irritating than listening to a credit card telemarketer playing a broken violin on the phone while downloading a pirated movie at less than half the speed of a three-legged tortoise!'

'I'm warning you, Jhunjhunwala! Don't pull any stunts with Notco. You haven't seen the worst of me,' he yelled. Clearly this man had no intention of maintaining the ceasefire.

'You think you're so smart don't you just because you have a comeback for every single thing I say? You've made more comebacks than Uday Chopra and Aftab Shivdasani combined, but let me tell you this! This isn't a war of words. It's a game of numbers and a game of thrones and if you even try to... '

'Yeah! Yeah! Yeah!' I cut him off rudely and gulped down some more whiskey. 'You've already threatened me about Notco about ten times today. Personally, I think your threats sound like a little kid mumbling nursery rhymes. I get your point. Now fu*k off! Just in case you've forgotten, this is my bar. Go back to your watering hole on the other side of the street or go find a lactating hippopotamus, attach yourself to its teat and drink milk!'

Stinker arose almost toppling over the bar stool and angrily stomped out. 'Fine! I'm going, but just remember if you rig Notco...'

'DIDN'T I TELL YOU ALREADY, YOU BLOODY STINKER! NOW GET OUT OF HERE BEFORE I CLOBBER YOU! I'LL SMASH YOU SO MANY TIMES THAT WHEN THEY TAKE YOUR X-RAY THEY'LL FIND YOUR BONES TURNED INTO CALCIUM TABLETS,' I shouted, unable to tolerate his presence any longer and willing to finish off the war once and for all.

Perhaps experiencing a similar sentiment he shouted, 'Fu*k you fatso!'

'Fu*k you Stinker!'

Before we could go another round, the good bartender, chiding the both of us with his eyes quietly, escorted stinker out and refilled my glass. I did go another round after all! YAY!

THE FIRST LAWSUIT

It was 8.30 am when I woke up the next morning. Realizing I had to rush before the markets opened in 30 minutes, I zipped through my ablutions faster than the Ghatkopar-Dadar express.

Hot water still steaming off me like butter on a pav-bhaji tava, I threw on my usual white satin shirt and black trousers and jumped into my Black Hawk helicopter screaming to the pilot, Captain Topinath (his name was something else but ever since he joined the AAP party, he wears a white topi and has legally changed his name to 'Topinath'). 'Onward my good man, there is money to be made, fly me to headquarters, and for heaven's sake do not vomit in my plane. I don't want to fly Kingmachli again!'

'Yes sir!' he saluted enthusiastically and the world's awesomest billionaire was off on his way to the lab ready to create another monstrous fortune.

A bull's eye view from the sky (see, I used 'bull's eye view' instead of 'bird's eye view'. You may consider this a demonstration of my high IQ. Only Einstein can match it, but he's dead. That makes me the most intelligent person on the planet…no in the universe…no, in the multiverse. I am willing to prove this by beating Vishwanathan Anand in chess while simultaneously solving 56 rubik's cubes with my wiggly toes, thereby demonstrating phenomenal brain computational skills and freakish toe elasticity) revealed the plight of the working, common man. Stuck in his car, pushing his bike, jammed in a train, ploughing in a rickshaw, hopping along on a cycle in a modern metropolis' rush hour.

Oh the perils! The roads were blocked. The city's infrastructure had been based on one fact and one fact only—pack as many vehicles as you can on the road. Every year the city added thousands of vehicles but it never added enough roads, like Chandu said.

I had foreseen this problem years ago, so taking Ravi Shastri's advice, I decided to take the aerial route. I bought a car company, then I bought a bike company. After their prices catapulted, I sold the car company and the bike company, and bought a helicopter company. It's the same company which ferries around our MPs when they go on their foreign study tours.

From my Black Hawk, I could see the streets stirring with traffic. Vehicles everywhere, lining the roads up like cholesterol on blood arteries. No amount of Saffola oil with extra protein heart power could help reduce this cholesterol. Somewhere below, Chandu was running around entrepreneurizing the begging industry.

The temple called the Bombay Stock Exchange came into view. I folded my hands to the great citadel. In a matter of seconds, my office too was in sight. In another few seconds, Captain Topinath had landed the hawk on Helipad #2 on the roof of Jhunjhunwala Chambers. I strode out like the terminator, ready to kick ass.

I rushed into office, just three minutes to market opening. The staff waved their good mornings as I walked into my office hurriedly. I gave them all high fives as this is good for employee motivation according to employee motivation expert Dr Shiv Khera.

Nitin was summoned as I barged into my cabin and sat on the throne, all seven trading screens on my station switched on. Ready to roll.

'Fatafat ek cutting chai aur misal pav,' I ordered Nitin.

'Ji saab!' he said and scampered away. In the rush to get here, I had abandoned breakfast at home. A text message blinked on the mobile. It was from the Mrs, 'Don't forget your diabetes, appendicitis, liver, kidney, pancreas, BP, and arthritis tablets.' 'P.S—you have more medicines in you than a bloody pharmacy. Take care of your health. XOXO.' I texted, 'I heart you XOXO' in return.

Nitin scampered in, placed the chai and misal pav on my table and disappeared as I watched the screens intently. Notco had opened to yet another high. It was up a further ten percent.

Nitin, who had so generously fetched breakfast, knocked again on the door and impishly proclaimed 'Saab, koi lawyer aaya hai aapse milne'.

'Theek hai. Bhejo andar,' I commanded and returned my gaze to the screens. The screens were blinking furiously in red and green. The markets were livewire.

Nandini had walked in meanwhile through the open door. I transfixed one eye on the screens and another on her as she shadowed the area. Sensing she did not want to disturb me but needed to say something, I looked at her.

'Good morning Sir,' Nandini said flowering into a smile, relieved that she had caught my attention.

'Good morning,' I said as I continued shifting my gaze between her and the screens.

'Sir, there's a lawyer with a summons here to see you,' she said.

'Nitin just told me. But what sort of a summons does he have? Who dares summon me?' I immediately said aloud, surprised the word 'summon' and 'me' had even been used in the same sentence!

'The Honorable High Court summons you, Mr Jhunjhunwala,' a voice crackled in the near distance.

Immediately, I shifted my gaze from Nandini to a figure at the door.

'Who are you boss?'

'Hello. My name is Pankaj Mishra. I'm the lawyer representing Notcorp and we are suing you for infringing on our patent.'

'You're the Notco lawyer?'

'No. I'm the Notcorp lawyer. NOTCORP, CORP. With an RP at the end,' said the man stressing on 'RP' as he walked closer.

'What's a Notcorp? Corp with an RP?' I asked, amused and curious at the same time.

'I'm surprised you haven't heard of us. We make Nothing. Notcorp is the company Notco stole the idea of Nothing from. We invented Nothing. We made it first!' he answered, displeased with my lack of awareness of the subject.

Aghast and jolted, I exclaimed loudly, 'Hold on! You're saying your company invented Nothing and not Ramakant Shastri?!!'

'Exactly. *We* invented Nothing. The only invention Mr Shastri can take credit for is stealing our idea and since you are on the Board of Notco Directors, you are culpable in abetting him. Therefore you are being summoned and you face a real chance of being indicted for this crime.'

I took a sip of tea and looked at the lawyer. Seemed to be in his 40s. Streaks of white adorned his temples. He was dressed in a crisp white shirt, a pair of black pants, and a black blazer that finished off his stereotypical lawyer presentation. Holding nothing more than a roll of papers, he approached closer.

'Please sit down Mr Mishra,' I said pointing to the chair on the other side of my table.

As he took the seat, I instructed Nitin to fetch the lawyer a glass of water. I quickly shot off a text to Nandini as well. 'Call Ratmalani. Tell him to get his ass here immediately. Brief him.'

Nandini who till now was standing by my table, hurried out of the room to fetch Ratmalani. Ratmalani, so named as he possesses the tenacity of a rat, is the baddest, most cut-throat, sinister, weasely, scheming, wicked, opportune, dirty, corrupt, horrendous, lying, foul-mouthed skunk-faced sack of maggot meat I've ever laid my eyes on and those are just his good qualities.

He's so rotten he once competed in a 'Who's More Rotten?' contest with a barrel of rotten apples, a jar of cockroaches, a bowl of tuberculosis bacteria, dead vultures with cholera, and a diseased horde of sewer rats, and he still won emphatically. I'm proud to have him as my lawyer.

'Would you like some tea, Mr Mishra?' I asked looking at him seated on the chair.

'Thanks, not really.'

'Okay. So you're saying your company...uhhh...Not...corp invented Nothing?' I asked, still trying to come to terms with what I had just heard.

'Yes,' he replied emphatically. 'Our founder Ajay Agarwal filed this patent with the Office of the Controller General of Patents, Designs & Trade Marks or CGPDTM, commonly known as the Indian Patent Office way back in 1997 under the name of his own company Notcorp before Ramakant Shastri even registered Notco in 2012. It was his idea to suck Nothing from nowhere.'

Reaching over from the chair and unrolling the papers, he ironed them with his palm and handed over the stapled sheets. I looked at them, leafing over each sheet carefully. They were xeroxes of the original patent application.

'So what do you want now?' I asked. My amusement had now turned into mild irritation that I was talking to this fellow instead of trading my beloved stocks in this first hour of a new market session.

'Only what is fair. Ramakant has made a lot of money after having stolen our idea. He is liable to pay Notcorp every single paisa he has made and since you Mr Jhunjhunwala are on the board of...'

'Directors as a major shareholder. Yeah, yeah I know,' I said cutting him off. 'Let me call up Ramakant. Hold on.'

'That won't be necessary Mr Jhunjhunwala.'

'Why? Let me find out if there is truth in what you are saying.' I quickly texted Ramakant as Mishra tried to dissuade me from talking to Shastri.

'My client is willing to let this matter go if the Board of Notco financially compensates him. Give us 5000 crores right now and we will drop the case.'

'How about you go fu*k your own face instead?' a voice boomed on the computer monitor.

It was Ramakant. I had texted him to Skype with me. The lawyer had been unaware that Ramakant had appeared online in the last few seconds and had tuned in. Slowly I turned the monitor facing me towards Pankaj Mishra sitting on the other side of the table. Ramakant's dhamakedaar entry had jolted him.

'No need for abuses, Mr Shastri,' Mishra warned at the sudden outburst. 'You very well know that you copied Mr Agarwal's idea. You have copied everything. Even the sucking technology your company uses is based on our patented technology. You suck just like we suck. Even the name of your company is copied from the name of Notcorp. RP hata diya, Notco bana diya.'

'Bullshit! I invented Nothing. I was sucking way before your boss could even process the market's sucking potential.'

'You may have started sucking first but we invented sucking!'

'No! My sucking is not based on your sucking and you know it!'

'We suck!'

'I suck!'

The conversation was turning into a paradise of double entendres. I quickly interjected, 'Hold on boys. Don't get mad. You both suck OKAY. Let's sort this out.'

Mishra stepped back. His spectacles fogging. The day had begun abruptly. Quickly I disposed off breakfast. While the two were talking about sucking, I had managed to score necessary quick bites. Folding the paper with traces of Misal Pav, I chucked it into the trash, had the emptying sip of chai, and got ready to examine the lawyer and the accused.

'Ramakant, did you file a patent?' I asked staring at the screen.

'No Sir. That was my mistake. I should have.'

Mishra was about to open his mouth. I flashed a stop sign at him. Reclining back on his chair, he nodded unwillingly.

Ramakant continued angrily, 'This patent proves nothing, Sir. It only proves that a patent was filed. Do you know how many patents have been filed for the telephone after Graham Bell's death? Yet, only he is the undisputed inventor of the telephone. What these people are doing is extortion! They discovered that I had forgotten to file a patent which I had forgotten in the first place only because I was too busy changing the world with my remarkable invention! It's a patent lawsuit. Oldest trick in the book. I'll see them in court! I invented Nothing, not them!'

'Mr Shastri, is it not true that you and Notcorp founder Mr Ajay Agarwal worked on the design for the first, Nothing-sucking motor. Wasn't using a funnel his idea?' asked an indignant Mishra.

Immediately I butted in, surprised as hell, 'Hold on. You know this Ajay guy?'

The lawyer answered on his behalf, 'They were classmates in college. They've known each other for more than twenty years. Ajay Agarwal and Ramakant Shastri started an agarbatti manufacturing company years ago. It shut down within months but this is where Ajay came up with the concept of Nothing and invented the technology to extract it. Since Shastri was his confidant, he told him all about it.'

'Bullshit! *I* told *him* about it. He wanted to continue selling agarbattis. Bloody fool! Copied my idea first, then tells people I copied it from him. I feel like A.R. Rahman arguing with Music Director Pritam over the validity of my own compositions. Tell that besura client of yours to stop ripping off my ideas and then telling people that I ripped off his!' burst Ramakant, eager to rip apart Mishra with his words alone.

'Mr Mishra LLB, does your client really believe that this idea is worth 5000 crores?' I asked trying not to get swayed by Ramakant's emotions.

'How does it matter, Mr Jhunjhunwala? You are a stock market man. You know its worth. If people are paying for this, it's only natural we get paid our share. After all, we invented the idea.'

Ramakant erupted. His voice boomed on the computer speakers. 'NO! JUST BECAUSE YOU KEEP SAYING YOU IN-

VENTED THE IDEA DOES NOT MAKE IT TRUE. JUST BECAUSE I EAT PIZZA ALL THE TIME DOESN'T MAKE ME ITALIAN.'

Amused and simultaneously outraged, I looked at Ramakant's pixelized face on the Skype window, then turned to the lawyer across from me and asked, 'This is Nothing, you realize that no? It's absolutely Nothing. If this is worth 5000 crores to you then imagine how much real shit is going to be worth. My stool sample alone is going to have to be worth at least a million dollars, especially because I'm so awesome.'

'Don't insult us, Mr Jhunjhunwala. Just because you are rich doesn't mean you have to rub it in our faeces…err…faces. If it's so worthless, then why are you a holding shares in Notco? Answer me!' the offended lawyer demanded.

'Don't answer him, Sir!' Ramakant shouted. 'This is our internal matter. Neither of us need to justify why we are partnering with each other.'

The lawyer reasoned aloud as though I was a judge in a courtroom. 'Because it's making a lot of money and I mean LOTS! The *Economist* magazine is doing a cover story on Ramakant Shastri in their next issue. We know all about it. They're calling him a genius and a gamechanger, a visionary, man of the century, Czar of Nothing, and what not? Ridiculous. It should be Ajay Agarwal on that cover instead.'

'You go tell Ajay I will see him in court,' Ramakant said grinding his teeth.

The lawyer, losing his cool more than before, muttered, 'Fine! And let me tell you this Mr Jhunjhunwala, you are the king of the stock market but you are not king of the courtroom. We will take every paisa from you. Every single one! And Ramakant, after my team is done with you, you're gonna be in jail rotting away like stale bread for the rest of your life!'

Ramakant was upset. I could see it in his face. The lawyer had turned aggressive. All the while Mishra and Shastri were trading barbs, I was googling 'Pankaj Mishra lawyer' on my phone. This fellow had won some pretty important cases and was fast establishing himself as a very astute intellectual property rights lawyer. His most recent victory was against a British Pharma company. The court had ruled that the damn Brits had stolen an Indian entrepreneur's patent (just as they claimed Chicken Tikka was their invention). The result—the Indian was now richer than the Queen of England. Mishra was making a statement. He had walked into my office and tried to punk me out with a court ordered summons. No more Mr Nice guy!

I grinned mischievously, eager to stomp him into the ground. 'You know I get the fact that you're suing me, that you are suing Ramakant and everyone on Notco's BoD, that Ajay Agarbatti… errr…Agarwal…might have a really good shot at all of us. However, for you to come in here, to my office, the inner sanctum of my chambers, and say that you are going to take my money! You've got balls lawyer, but here's the thing—my balls are bigger than your balls.'

'No need to be rude Mr Jhunjhunwala,' he said twitching a little.

'I'm not being rude. I'm being awesome. Even my enemies quiver in their undees after they threaten me. They call up their henchmen and scream in panic—OYE! GET 50,000 GUYS AND COME HERE IMMEDIATELY, JHUNJHUNWALA IS COMING… ALONE.'

The lawyer squirmed uncomfortably and tentatively sounded off. 'Well, that maybe so but this is a court case. It will be fought in the courts.'

Do you know who my lawyer is?' I asked.

'I've heard you have an entire team of lawyers, so I'm not sure.'

'Ratmalani.'

Mishra gulped. On the screen, Shastri cracked a smile.

Looking into the lawyer's eyes, I said pouting my lips, 'Ratmalani once went to court and created so much confusion that the judge sentenced himself to jail.'

'I am familiar with the International Geography Society vs BMC case of 1999. Mr Ratmalani became a legend after that case,' the lawyer said trying to appear unruffled.

'No,' I said sensing Ratmalani's name had sparked a mini-panic in the lawyer. 'He was already a legend before that. He actually became a legend when he proved that a chicken shot an innocent waitress in a crowded Delhi bar and not the actual criminal—a politician's son.'

'Err...'

'Ratmalani once proved in court that fire doesn't burn and water isn't wet.'

'I am aware...'

'Do you even know how screwed up Ratmalani is? He once got bitten by a venomous cobra and immediately the cobra vomited three times and died from severe neurotoxic posioning!'

The tables had turned. Mishra looked unsettled and squirmed vigorously in his chair.

'Once I tell him to get on the case, he will turn this thing into the biggest clusterfu*k circus you, my friend, have ever seen. He will throw so many laws, in-laws, by-laws, bye-bye laws, so many amendments, adjournments, indictments, attestants, informants. So many witnesses, illnesses, and highnesses...just so many... problems at you that at the end of it, all you'll want is to just hang yourself from the nearest ceiling fan,' I raved.

The lawyer, knowing his own defence was weakening, truthfully said, 'All I am saying is that you should examine the truth in this matter.'

'I thought this wasn't about the truth but about money. 5000 crores worth of it especially over something as ridiculous as Nothing,' I reminded Mishra as he tried to look away.

'But you endorse Nothing,' he pointed out. 'Why else do you hold a stake in Shastri's company?'

'Why should it matter to you why I buy what I buy and what I endorse and what I don't endorse,' I asked daringly. 'I dont come to your house and tell you what to eat, where to go and how to dress, what cases to take and which ones to drop. Since when have my trades become your concern?'

'They're my concern because you are trading in a company whose entire existence and success...'

'Aha! So it is about my success, isn't it?' barked Ramakant pouncing upon the lawyer even before he completed the sentence. 'I bet if I were still running around from bank to bank applying for a loan with my mom and wife's jewels you'd have absolutely no interest in what Notco makes. If I was still selling agarbattis with Ajay, going temple to temple and telling each pujari that our agarbatti contains jasmine and lavender, and its God's #1 preferred aroma, then he'd be as delighted as a cow defecating at a bio-gas plant.'

The lawyer sickened with the analogy shouted back, 'You could be selling Jeera powder for all I care. What we are saying is that Notco copied Notcorp's idea. We came up with the idea of selling Nothing first and we will prove it in court!'

'That's nonsense! Everybody knows that manufacturing Nothing was my idea! You bastards are lying!'

'Mind your language Mr Shastri!'

'Nahin karoonga mind. Kya ukhad loge bey?'

'Why don't you come to court? I will show you what I will ukhado.'

And back to square one. Before any more talk about *ukhadoing* got underway, I clutched the court order and arose. Sensing rightly that I wanted him to leave, the lawyer got up, abandoning his argument with Shastri for the moment and walked towards the door as I escorted him out of the office. 'I'll see you in court my friend,' I said.

FUNNELHEAD

Two hours later, the plasma TV in the conference room began to flash:

'BREAKING NEWS: Company sues Notco over patent violation.'

'Notco CEO under investigation by CBI over alleged patent violation.'

The same news anchor who had delivered the news of the babies dying in the incubators reappeared. He was more animated this time and bobbed his head around like a rabbit on viagra. 'Ladies and gentlemen, in a truly shocking development, Notco Industries Chairman Mr Ramakant Shastri and the Notco Board of Directors, including famed investing God Jhunjhunwala, have been summoned by the Bombay High Court in connection to a case filed by lawyer Pankaj Mishra on behalf of little known company Notcorp. That's NotcoRP with an RP.' I gritted my teeth in annoyance.

He continued, 'Notcorp has alleged that its founder Ajay Agarwal is the brain behind the Nothing revolution sweeping the world. Notcorp is alleging that it is Agarwal and not Shastri who invented Nothing and is demanding sweeping damages of 10,000 crores from Notco. If Notcorp wins, it will be the single largest settlement in the history of settlements.'

'Didn't the lawyer say 5000 crores just two hours back?!' a perplexed Nandini asked. The team had gathered around the conference table to watch the unfolding circus.

Ratmalani had arrived an hour back and had joined us in the conference room. Ramakant was on his way.

I was shifting priorities between the TV screen and the trading screen. Notco had erased its morning gain. It was now in the red, down 5% solely on the news of the lawsuit.

The anchor continued, 'Sources now say that Mr Agarwal and Mr Shastri were at one point closer than brothers. In fact, they were known as the *agarbatti brothers*. The following photo available exclusively with our channel proves how close they were. Here they are seen being close by closely holding an agarbatti close to each other. As the court date gets closer and closer, one can only wonder what is going through the minds of these once-close partners. India is closely watching.'

The stress of the entire situation was getting to me. Rich people like me aren't supposed to be worried by petty problems like these, I theorized. Confident in the skills of Ratmalani and believing that Ramakant was telling the truth about inventing Nothing, I breathed heavily, relieving clouds of tension from my nostrils. Ratmalani was busy scratching his bald head and pensively looking at the TV, concocting some sort of jhamela in his bhayankar lawyer mind.

The video cut from the anchor to a live report. A bunch of reporters surrounded Mishra. For the first time I saw the Ajay Agarwal chap standing next to him. They were outside the court. The reporters were hounding him, sticking the microphone so far up Mishra's nose that I could hear the phlegm moving inside. Reporters of each channel smudging into each other to get that exclusive sound byte. It looked like BEST bus passengers circling the conductor to buy tickets.

Mishra snorted, swatting a mic away, 'My dear media friends, we are confident of winning this case. We will produce all the necessary proofs and witnesses. Justice will be done.'

The video cut abruptly back onto the anchor.

'Breaking news: Notco Chairman, CEO, and *alleged* Nothing founder Ramakant Shastri arrives at Jhunjhunwala's office. We now cut live to outside Mr Jhunjhunwala's office.'

'HUH!' I exclaimed, bamboozled that the media were at my doorstep. Ramakant got out of his car looking…HOLY SHIT!

'What the hell is he dressed like?!!! And why does he have a goddamn funnel on the top of his head?!!' I hollered, absolutely stunned at the visual staring me in the face.

Vishal with a similar expression squeezed out a sentence, 'Sir! Is that Ramakant for sure?'

Ratmalani began to laugh. The 60-year-old, cherubic, manipulative lawyer gleamed with delight and confusion. A very unhealthy combination. 'HAHAHAHA! This is the guy I have to defend in court? He looks like an upturned samosa! HAHAHAHA!!!!'

It was a sight to behold. Ramakant Shastri had just stepped out of a black Mercedes. The city lights had descended on Shastri. Here he was in all his resplendent glory, golden boots, a bejeweled funnel on his head, diamond studded black square sunglasses shielding his eyes and a fur coat so thick you'd think he had a white grizzly bear fused to his skin. The result of the consummation of a bear-human love story which had resulted in an offspring that looked both human and bearish.

A stunned Iqbal shrieked, 'I think there's a peacock feather on top of his head. Why does he have a feather on his head?'

All of us peered closely at the screen, pondering the absurdity of the question itself. Iqbal was right. There indeed was a feather sticking out from the funnel spout on the top of his head. What the hell was going on? This guy was off his rocker! I couldn't believe it. But before we had even begun to process our outrage, the…creature…on the screen…started speaking.

'Mr Shastri, why are you dressed like this? Is this a statement you are making to Notcorp?' fired a reporter.

'Ramakant Shastri doesn't need to make a statement. Ramakant is dressed in his natural avatar and as far as Notcorp goes, let me emphatically tell you that my company and I alone are the inventors of Nothing. We invented Nothing through our hard work. Ajay Agarwal is trying to extract undue benefit by dragging my name into a dirty controversy. Ramakant and all the shareholders in Notco have full faith in the Indian judiciary. Justice will be done and truth will prevail,' Ramakant unequivocally answered.

Another reporter shouted, 'Is it true that you and Mr Agarwal were once business partners and friends?'

Without hesitation, Shastri spoke as the feather is his funnel swayed to a breeze, 'That was a long time ago and let me make it very clear, *WE WERE NEVER FRIENDS*. At least before this lawsuit I had some respect for Ajay, but now even that is gone.'

It was at this junction that a young, meek-looking reporter seized the silence of a few milliseconds after Ramakant's answer and asked the most important question of the decade, 'Sir, why is there a funnel on the top of your head?'

A murmur broke out. The unruly reporters were cursing themselves for not asking the question themselves.

Ramakant answered squarely, 'It's not just a funnel. It's also a crown. It's a funnel-shaped crown.'

'Are you saying you are a king and that's why you are wearing a crown?' the girl asked again.

'I am not saying that. I am only *dressing* like that. It's a matter of personal choice. Also, aren't you guys calling me the Czar/ The King/ The Emperor of Nothing? This is my personal style statement! Most of all, funnels are very important to Notco's Nothing extraction process. It is simply an extension of my company's technology that I have integrated with my personal sense of style!'

The astonished reporters began to murmur to each other as another reporter fired, 'Don't you think that by dressing like this you are hurting your chances in court?'

Sir, why is there a funnel on the top of your head?

'Why? Justice is blind. Why would a judge care how I dress? Moreover, any court values honesty. By dressing like this, I am only being honest about myself to the whole world. Just because I am a businessman doesn't mean I can't have a sense of style or dress the way I want. We are a democracy afterall! I'm only expressing myself with my clothes. It's called self-expression. *So what if there's a funnel on my head?*' countered a fighting Ramakant with a question the poor journalist had absolutely no way of answering. There really is no comeback to *'So what if there's a funnel on my head'*.

'Somebody ask him if he's escaped from a mental hospital!' an irate, perplexed, frenzied Rajat yelled! I was guessing pretty much everyone, not just in this room but everyone watching this anywhere on the planet, was thinking the same thing.

An ice-cream cone wrapped in colour paper with a bunch of earrings on. That's what Ramakant looked like. If this media question was in a multiple choice format, then Ramakant would be forced to pick one of the following options:

Are you:

a. A deranged lunatic.
b. An attention-seeking pinhead with the self-esteem of a professional rodent fungus remover who needs to validate his existence by dressing like a transvestite hippy clown suffering a serious case of wardrobe malfunction.
c. A multi-coloured flower vase wrapped in plastic sheet and spray-painted in gold glitter to give everyone the impression that you are a senile jewellery box which has forgotten its true purpose.
d. All of the above.

The questions continued while Ramakant dragged himself through the bevy of onlookers. The media were hammering him with one question after the other, most of them repetitive, to get that first exclusive 'reaction' to be plugged incessantly on their respective employer's newspaper, TV channel, website, or any other form of information exchange mechanism.

Shooting through that volley, one reporter shrieked, 'Do you think that Notco industries is facing such allegations because of its tremendous success in such a short time? What do you have to say to all those people who are still doubting the potential of Nothing? I mean those calling it a passing fad?'

The noise dimmed like a light bulb. The other journos wanted him to answer. Ramakant obliged steadfast and unmoved, 'Let me tell those people right now that a so-called *fad* cannot become a *Fortune* 500 company within months of starting. Our revenue from sales alone has catapulted Notco into the big league! Obviously there are some jealous people who cannot stand the fact that a middle-class boy with humble roots has managed to build such a ginormously successful company in such a short amount of time! Nothing is the future! The future is Nothing! The future is Nothing!'

For a second, the hush prevailed. Immediately after, it was back to the chatter. Shastri's two big bodyguards clad in black held the glass doors of my office building ajar as the camera showed him walking in. Ramakant's little excursion outside the office would be action replayed meticulously till the channels had run out of satellite space. It was therefore time to discuss things with Ramakant off-camera. I muted the TV.

Pretty soon, Shastri emerged from the lift with two bodyguards in tow. The little receptionist was startled. Iqbal moved out into the lobby and fetched Ramakant. My team along with Ratmalani waited confused and alarmed as Ramakant walked in, leaving his guards outside the conference room.

Iqbal shut the door as he walked in behind Ramakant.

Before Shastri could sit down, I uttered, 'DUDE! What the hell happened? Why are you dressed like that? You look like a goddamn farm animal!! This is bizarre! Have you gone insane?!!!'

Ratmalani chuckled. The fur on Ramakant looked astonishingly heavy, even thicker than the image I had seen on live TV just a minute or so ago. Along with the funnel-shaped head dress, he was wearing a ring on each finger, including the thumbs. Rubies and emeralds set in 22-karat gold. Each ring larger than a five-rupee coin. A couple of thick golden chains were also hanging around his neck. Ramakant smiled back and sat down.

'Ramakant likes to lead a good life. Ramakant is dressed like this because it brings out his true personality,' he muttered.

'Yeah and what personality is that? A clown?' Rajat commented.

'Please respect Ramakant. Ramakant makes more in one day than you do in a year.'

All of us were taken aback. Before Rajat could say something, I stepped in.

'You must respect my staff, dude. Most of us here are taken aback with the lawsuit and now with you like this...'

'Ramakant apologizes for his rudeness but please don't make fun of Ramakant's clothes. Ramakant doesn't tell others how to dress...right?' he said pointing his eyebrows from under his glasses.

'Right,' replied Rajat with an air of disgust. We looked at each other. I nodded my head up and down slowly. Rajat, realizing more important issues were at hand, sat back in his chair.

Ramakant had grown a stubble. The pencil-thin oily moustache had coalesced into the blackness on his jaw. Slightly adjusting the crown/funnel, he removed his glasses, opened his eyes wide, looked at me and started to speak.

'Please don't worry. Ramakant assures you that everything will be fine. Ajay will not win the case. Ramakant has spoken to the other directors and has their hundred percent support.'

'Dude! Why are you referring to yourself in third person? From the time you've walked in, you've stated your name like a hundred times. Even while talking to the media. What's going on?'

'Ramakant is trying a new thing where Ramakant refers to himself in third person from now on.'

'Why?'

'Because Ramakant has decided he will call himself Ramakant instead of I. Ramakant's name is Ramakant. Ramakant's name is not *"I"*.'

'Ok, but *why*?'

'Because Ramakant feels that is the correct way to talk about Ramakant.'

'Dude! Seriously. What's going on with you? When we Skyped this morning, you were fine. Did you have a brain transplant in the last two hours or something? Full personality change!'

'Chill, Mr Jhunjhunwala. It must be hard to accept Ramakant like this at first, but trust Ramakant, you'll all get used to it. Ramakant is now a rich and prestigious businessman. Why should Ramakant hide all the prestige he has attained?'

I had had enough and was ready to pulverize him right there. 'YOU WANT PRESTIGE! GO BUY A BLOODY COOKER THEN! DO NOT EVER COME INTO MY OFFICE AND DISRESPECT MY STAFF AGAIN… ESPECIALLY DRESSED LIKE THAT. YOU LOOK LIKE A BLOODY CARTOON!'

My staff approved, shaken though at the fury of my temper. Some of them, especially little Nandini, vibrated like the feather in Shastri's funnel.

Ramakant, trying to look unfettered, leaned forward and said, 'People say that only because they are not used to a businessman dressing like this. I…err…Ramakant will change that perception. Many business guys, politicians, and actors are congratulating Ramakant for proudly flaunting this flamboyance. In time, everyone will accept and applaud Ramakant's originality, just like they have accepted Nothing.'

'Fine! To hell with this,' I shouted. 'Dress however you want. Want to wear a funnel over your head? Go ahead. Want to stick a peacock feather, no, an entire peacock in your head, go ahead! Let me just say you're wearing multicored pants dude! It looks like as though an entire nursery of babies ate hundreds of packets of Cadbury's gems and vomited all over your your freakin trousers!'

'Ramakant understands your frustration but is confident you will see things his way soon.'

My appendix was hurting. A light sweat was breaking out on my temples as my cheeks flushed with hot blood. Yet again, Ramakant had managed to raise my blood pressure. I screamed, unable to withstand the tomfoolery anymore. 'YOU REFER TO YOURSELF ONE MORE TIME IN THE THIRD PERSON AND I WILL BITCHSLAP THE FU*K OUT OF YOU, GOT IT!'

Ramakant jolted up as echoes of my voice reverberated across the room. A sudden hush broke upon the room. My team preferred to keep quiet, hoping not to irritate me further.

Drinking a glass of water and adjusting my glasses, I addressed Ratmalani, hoping to move on from funnels, fur coats, shiny fabrics, and peacock feathers. 'So, what's our strategy for the case?'

'I am currently preparing...'

Shastri butted in, not allowing Ratmalani to complete. 'I thought since I am also being accused, we could fight the case together...'

'NO!' I thundered. 'I am not going into court with you looking like that. Get your own lawyer.'

Shastri squirmed uncomfortably almost sliding out of his bear skin.

'When is the hearing date?' Iqbal asked.

'A month from today,' Ratmalani answered and then looked at me. 'You won't even be required. It's just a preliminary hearing.'

'Then why so much tension?' Nandini asked quite innocently.

'Because we cannot let the media believe that Notco stole this idea. Public perception is very important in these cases,' Ramakant answered. The staff shook their heads in agreement and disbelief. Agreement over the sense his answer made. Disbelief that it had emanated from someone who looked like a pimp in a rap video.

'So what do we do?' Iqbal asked after a minute as we deliberated upon our next move.

'I've been in touch with an international American PR firm—*Stew, Pid, and Jack.S*—to tackle any PR issues on a massive scale,' said Ratmalani.

'Aren't they the same guys who used to do PR for Gaddafi, the genocidal Libyan dictator?' I asked, relieved Ramakant had finally dropped the third person lingo.

Ratmalani perked up and said, 'Yes! They're very good. Gaddafi was once nominated for the Nobel Peace Prize because of them. I have friends there. Very good company.'

'Hmmmm. Why am I not surprised you have friends there?' I asked looking at Ratmalani.

'Hehe. Our work is similar, you see.'

'Ramakant is confident that we will win this case. It is just a short-term hiccup in Notco's long and prosperous future. More and more people are starting to realize the benefits of using Nothing. We are expanding. Even export revenue is growing. Like Ramakant said earlier to the media, Nothing is the future,' Shastri said looking at me with a look of *'I will continue talking about myself in third person even if you shout at me loud enough to break the sound barrier.'*

Unwilling to school him and tired from the pain in my abdomen, I resigned myself to his fancy dress.I said slowly to Ratmalani, 'Do you know what must be done in case the PR propaganda does not work?'

'But Sir, isn't using propaganda tactics wrong?' Nandini asked.

Ramakant cackled away as though encouraged by my passive surrender to his sense of dressing. 'Hahahaha! Do you think the guys from Notcorp aren't already engaging in propaganda?'

Nandini simply said, 'I guess they are.'

'This is a battle. My company has been attacked for 10,000 crore rupees. With so much money at stake, they will spare no expense to hurt us both in the eyes of the public and the court. We too must be prepared and respond appropriately. We must act like the Indian Army, proactive and ready. Not like the Indian government, bumbling and useless.'

A sense of patriotism and focus emanated from the room after this statement. For the first time, the clown had managed to instill some confidence. Despite the outward appearance, he seemed convinced on the inside that Notco was in the right.

It was almost 2 pm. The post-lunch market session had begun. The ticker running at the bottom of the channel showed Notco down a further 3% from before. News of the lawsuit would keep playing around for a few more weeks.

'Okay. It's lunchtime. I'll talk to you later Ramakant,' I said arising from the chair, hungry, in pain, and eager to rid myself of the lunatic in the room.

'Ramakant is happy to talk. By the way, do you think you could do an interview for *ET Now* tomorrow? They called asking for Ramakant but Ramakant is going to South America tonight to negotiate setting up our factory there. They also have lots of Nowhere. Will be back next week. Ramakant thinks it is necessary someone from our side addresses questions regarding the lawsuit. It would be a confidence building measure among our shareholders,' the lunatic proclaimed as he arose as well.

'I agree,' Vishal said. 'Maybe you should think about it, Jhunjhunwala Sir.'

Realizing that my involvement was required, I reluctantly accepted. 'What is there to think? I am required to make supreme sacrifices for the sake of my investments. You may tell them I will give them the interview. Tell them to give my secretary the details.'

'Yes Sir!' Shastri said and got up and departed with his bodyguards as I secretly wished the lunatic had gone to the doctor with the cheque I gave him. I also pondered if I was the lunatic here because I had partnered with this individual.

NEEDS AND WANTS

Dalal Street. Mumbai 400001. Midnight. Under the cover of darkness, the superhero in me was on the prowl. Unfortunately, improper insulin production in my body has rendered me slightly 'fat' and diabetic. As a result, I despise jumping from rooftop to rooftop like the Spiderman (aka Makdi Babua in Bhojpuri) or the Batman (known as Chamgadad purush in Hindi). I already fly, thanks to machines running on aviation turbine fuel, so the necessity to do a Superman thing in the sky is unnecessary, but I can really, actually, *fly*. No really! Air traffic control actually calls me to carry passenger jets facing engine failure in mid-air to safety and I do this by flying at super hypersonic speed, lifting the plane out of the sky with my bare hands, placing it on my back, and flying to the nearest airport after blowing a flying kiss to any cute air-hostesses on board.

My ultimate superpower is my phenomenal ability to make money. Two places form the source of my powers. One is the muscle between my ears—an extraordinarily special contraption called my brain—fired up with billions upon billions of neurons each flickering synapses permuting trillions upon trillions of money-making fundas one after the other.

The second is the heart of the modern day market economy—the stock exchange—not just a concrete structure but a living, breathing entity whose very pulse beats within me. The *Phiroze Jeejeebhoy Towers* standing 29 floors tall, 18.9 degree north latitude, 72.8 degree east longitude. People are a bit more familiar with it as the Bombay Stock Exchange building. I call it HEADQUARTERS.

When I walk into it, brokers pour rose petals over me. They chant my name and call my praises. They tear their shirts and ask me to sign their man-boobs. They orgasm at the very sight of me, fawning, roaring, and moaning till ecstasy reaches its zenith in the cry of my name and my name alone. Indeed the market is my altar. I am its God.

I have deliberately not used exclamation marks in the previous paragraph because this is a common, everyday occurrence.

Right in front of the BSE is a bronze statue of a two-horned bull standing pristine on a small green lawn. It was here that I sat, waiting for Ramesh after having the daylights shocked out of me, first with the patent lawsuit and then with Ramakant exploding onto the middle of the affair with a batshit lunatic costume—funnel embellishment and all. I cannot stress the latter enough.

It was past midnight. An abandoned Dalal Street glittering in the orange street lights lay in front of me. A solitary food cart loomed in the corner selling bhel-puri and chai. The vendor, a man named Mani from Mylapore, Tamil Nadu, had set up his cart here fifteen years ago. Many a time I had stood by his cart and gobbled up bhel while working late nights in the early days, much before trading stocks was done electronically.

In those days you had to fill up forms by hand. One form for each share and I'd buy hundreds of shares daily. I filled in more forms than an RTO Inspector sorting driver-license applications, not like you people sitting in bed these days, laptop in front, eating pizza with one hand, buying stocks in one browser window while ordering this book from Flipkart on another. Useless fellows! (Tell your friends to buy this book as well. I promise to donate 50% of the proceeds to some charity run by well-known farmer Robert Vadra).

In the distance, the Colaba night traffic could be heard. I had decided to take a drive down to clear my head.

For me, in Mumbai, the night is the best time to chill out without being mobbed. While driving here today, I had met Sachin Tendulkar driving his Ferrari. As a sign of respect, we got out of our cars and exchanged gifts. He gave me a signed bat and I gave him a signed Demat account form. Sachin and I often run into each other during our night drives. We exchange trivia. He tells me how great I am and I tell him how great I am.

As I stood by the bull, another car blurred into the horizon. It was Ramesh.

Ramesh's maroon-coloured Volkswagen sedan pulled up. He flashed a smile as he got out shutting the door and clicking the key to lock the car. The beep of the central lock set off a nearby brown coloured stray dog on a barking spree. 'Oops! Sorry my friend,' Ramesh said adjusting the zebra inspired striped shirt on his back as he raised both hands up at the dog in an 'I surrender' pose. Gently he walked over after patting the dog for a few seconds who had seemingly accepted the apology and sat down next to me on the lawn.

'What's up, fatty?' he said taunting me mischievously. 'Saw your boy on TV today. Did the media kidnap him from a fancy dress competition or something?'

'Eh! First of all, DON'T CALL ME FAT! It's just liquid weight. You know I drink like a fish. All this chubbiness is just *liquor liquefaction*.'

'Huh?' he said quizzically as he adjusted himself next to me on the long white stairs at the entrance of the exchange.

'Liquor liquefaction buddy! It's when the cells in your body develop the ability to accumulate booze and hold it for long periods of time for future use. I am a walking storehouse of liquor and DON'T CALL THAT JACKASS SHASTRI MY BOY! Dimaag kharab ho gaya hai. I've decided to exit the Notco stock.'

'You told me yesterday you were thinking about holding on

and that you had worked things out with him?' Ramesh asked as I fumed in anger.

'That was yesterday before he started to dress like a...'

Before I could complete the sentence, Ramesh cut me off. 'So you're going to dump the guy based solely on how he dresses? WOW! You're no different than my ex-girlfriends.'

'No...'

'Then?'

'He can dress any way he wants man. Bottom line is he a. Tried to cheat me b. I am not confident in his ability to run a successful business. c. I cannot reconcile doing business with someone who wears a funnel on his damn head!'

'What are you talking about? Who cares what he's wearing on his head? I know he tried to cheat you but his business is minting money, man. I mean...it's off the chain. Everywhere I go, it's only Nothing...Nothing...Notco this...Notco that... I just returned from Finland. *Fortune* magazine is running Ramakant on the cover in Finland. All I kept hearing in the country was how awesome Nothing is and how great Notco is and what a genius Ramakant is.'

'What are these people seeing in this?' I asked, perplexed that his legend had reached Finland also, which is at best a contender for an 'emerging nations' spot in the ICC T20 Tournament.

'I don't think they are seeing anything...literally,' Ramesh replied.

'You know what I meant. Why are they finding absolute emptiness so...so...why are they buying this stuff in... I can't even say tons or kilogrammes because it doesn't weigh anything. It's not even real!'

'Jhun. How does it matter if Nothing weighs or not? Whether it can be seen or not. Whether it even exists or not?'

'What are you saying?'

'You asked me why Nothing is selling so much, right?'

'Yeah'

'Nothing is selling *because* people are buying...'

I looked at Ramesh wondering if my dear best friend had just left his brain behind in Finland. 'What does that mean? That's obvious.'

'No, I don't think you understand, fatty. *Nothing is selling because people are buying Nothing.* It's really *that* simple.'

'I don't understand...'

'Its basic supply and demand. People want Nothing. People like Ramakant are giving them Nothing. These people are then buying Nothing. This is why Nothing is selling.'

Convinced that he had indeed left his brain behind in Finland and convinced I must approach the Indian Ambassador to Finland and ask for Ramesh's brain to be exported back to India, I yelled, now more perplexed than ever, 'But what is the reason they are buying!'

'They are buying it for the same reason anyone buys anything.'

'I know why anyone buys anything, dammit! Tell me why is everyone buying Nothing.'

'Imagine I am Alexander Graham Bell. The inventor of the telephone.'

Not sure why Graham Bell had been dragged into a conversation, I said, 'Okay. You are Graham Bell. Who am I?'

'You are nobody.'

'Screw you! I am awesome. I am me!'

'No baba. In this example you are nobody and I am Graham Bell for explanation sake.

'Okay, and?'

'Now imagine I have walked into the 21st century. I invented the telephone to solve people's need to talk to each other even over long distances.'

'So?'

'Why are people then using a mobile phone when a telephone is readily available and has been available from two hundred years?'

'Because its smaller, faster, and does more stuff than a regular telephone. Heck, you can play Angry Birds on a mobile. You can't do that with your telephone Mr Graham Bell! You suck!' I fumed in outrage and stated loudly, 'If you weren't my best friend I would totally bitchslap you! I hate you Alexander Graham Bell!'

'Be serious, Jhun! People are using mobiles because they aren't happy with the old telephones. They've grown old and outdated. Only useful in India's Telecommunications Ministry or in a BSNL office.'

'Right,' I agreed, assured Graham Bell knew full well that only BSNL was still using the original model of his telephone.

'But why do they need to use a mobile?' he asked.

'To play Angry Birds?'

'No.'

'To play Temple Run?'

'No.'

'To play *Krrish 3, Krrish 4,* and *Ra.One* videogame?'

An irritated Ramesh stressed, 'No! Because they *NEED* to use a mobile...'

'Matlab.'

'Matlab and read my lips—they *NEED* to use it.'

'Well obviously they need to use it Einstein...I mean Graham Bell...that's why they are using it. If they didn't *NEED* it, they wouldn't use it. What sort of an insight is that? I tell you Mr Graham Bell, you aren't impressing me very much. I bet you didn't invent the telephone at all. You just copied BSNL's original idea of the "ANTARASHTRIYA DURSANCHAR UPKARAN" and claimed it as your own.'

Totally ignoring that I had accused him of plagiarism, Alexander Graham Bell Ramesh continued, 'If they didn't *need* it—key word is NEED—they wouldn't use it.'

'Yes, I get that bit. But why do they need Nothing is my question. It serves them no purpose. Adds no real utility or value to their life. How does it fulfill any need?'

Ramesh paused for a second, convinced his telephone idea was not working out. A second later he said, 'Imagine three kids.'

'What happened to imagining Graham Bell?'

'He's there.'

'Where?'

'Here only.'

'Then why are the kids here. Are they his kids? How did they get here? You mean to say in the time we were talking, Graham Bell found a woman, married her, and gave birth to three kids.'

'Yaar be serious,' Ramesh argued, unwilling to accept that Graham Bell was multiplying his genetic material faster than an amoeba reproducing itself. 'Imagine three kids. They're all playing with building blocks. Suddenly one child finds a ball nearby and starts playing with it.'

'This child has attention deficit disorder. If the kids are all playing building blocks then why is this bastard child of Satan spoiling everybody's plan and playing with a ball? I TELL YOU THIS KID SHOULD BE ARRESTED IMMEDIATELY. EDUCATION SYSTEM IS GOING TO DOGS BECAUSE OF KIDS LIKE THESE WHO SHOULD BE BUILDING BLOCKS INSTEAD OF PLAYING BALL. I HATE YOU, BASTARD KID! I HATE YOU!'

'Jhun! Shut up and listen! If you don't take this seriously, I will leave!'

The brown stray had found another canine buddy. Together they were inspecting the street tottering up and down like beat constables. Mani's cart had disappeared. I looked up to see a white moon in the sky. Made for quite a scene. Two grown men talking about imaginary children by the side of a bronze bull under a tall white building canopied by a grey sky overlooking a golden-lit Dalal Street at midnight.

'Okay, Okay, ' I calmed down. 'Tell me about the three kids who are building blocks, but now one of them has found a ball.'

'Yes, this kid finds a ball. Starts to play with it. The other two kids see the ball. Now even they want to play with the ball so they stop playing with the blocks and start trying to play with the ball.'

'Okay.'

'But the kid who found the ball doesn't want to share the ball with the other two kids. He wants to keep playing with it himself.'

This convinced me that this kid was indeed a problem child of the highest order. Someone who created more problems for his parents than Lindsay Lohan. I yelled, 'I hate this kid! He has caused nothing but problems all day long. This is why parents should teach their kids to stop watching Nickelodeon and Cartoon Network and start watching Sanskar channel. At least then kids will learn to share.'

'Concentrate yaar!' Ramesh pleaded, trying to be the one guy who still believed in the kid. 'As I was saying, the kid wants the ball all to himself and keeps it to himself, so the other two kids start to cry because they want it too but can't have it. Meanwhile, the building blocks, being played with a few minutes ago, are lying discarded on the ground...what was wanted a minute ago is no longer needed. These kids who till a moment ago were blissfully playing blocks because they wanted it and not even aware of the ball, are now desperately hankering after it...they want something else now...and they want it because someone else also wants it even though both of them don't need it!'

'Then what happens?'

'The kids are still crying.'

'Poor kids!'

'Anyway, so the mothers now arrive at the scene, thanks to all the crying. They learn that their kids want the ball but the other kid won't share, so they immediately go to the store outside and buy two balls. One for each kid.'

'Yay! How awesome was it that the store selling balls was just near their house! Thank God the kid found a ball and not an assault rifle. The store outside wouldn't have probably had it. They'd have to order the gun online. That would have taken at least two days for delivery. I wonder what would happen to the kids then. I'm happy the kid found a ball in the first place and NOT an assault rifle. Considering his inane criminal temperament, I have no doubt this child would have grown up and become a Somali pirate!'

For some reason, Ramesh seemed to be getting pissed. I think even he didn't like the stupid ball stealing kid and the problems caused because of his selfishness.

'Okay then?' I said, pressing Ramesh on to finish the saga of the selfish kid.

'So, now all the kids have balls to play with and they all start to play with it but after sometime the kid who wouldn't share realizes his ball is old and the other two have newer, shinier balls, so he tries to take it from them. However, neither of them allow it and so now he starts to cry.'

'Serves him right! Selfish bastard.'

'So his mom now gets him a new ball.'

'Bloody hell! So now he has two balls? This is bad parenting. Why are these stupid people, who don't know how to raise children, being allowed to make babies?'

Ramesh paused and finally got around to wrapping this up. 'What I'm trying to tell you is that we buy what we buy based on two demands a. Our needs b. Our wants.'

'It's consumer psychology…'

'Right. Now if I'm thirsty and I'm given an option to choose between water, juice, and milkshake, I'll choose water because I need it but if I'm not thirsty, I'll probably choose the juice or milkshake because I want it even though I don't need it. I guess what I'm trying to tell you is that Nothing is like the ball which the kid found. The building blocks were more useful, maybe even more important, but the kids *wanted* to play with the ball. There was a *demand* for it. That's why their mothers bought three brand new balls. At this moment all that matters is that people are buying it because they want it. That's why it's selling.'

I asked perplexed, 'So you're saying people are buying Nothing because other people are buying it?'

'Yes. That's exactly what I'm saying. Ramakant has managed to create a demand for a product he controls the supply of. He has convinced people they *need* it. It serves no need but it appeals to people's wants. The only *need* it fulfils is the *need to want it*.'

'YAAR! THIS IS TOO COMPLICATED. NEEDS. WANTS. GRAHAM BELL. BALLS. SELFISH KIDS. ALL THIS TALK ABOUT NEEDING AND WANTING! I need to watch Salman Khan's *Wanted* now to uncoil my brain from all the knots your lecture has twisted it into,' I said in frustration.

'So you're leaving?'

'Yes! I'll call you tomorrow. We'll meet sometime in the evening. I have that stupid TV Interview at 9. Bye! I need to want to need to… Screw it! Bye! AND BY THE WAY, I HOPE YOUR STUPID BALL KID DIES IN A HORRIBLE CAR ACCIDENT OR SOMETHING! BASTARD! DIMAAG KHARAB KARKE RAKH DIYA SAALA!' I fumed as I got into the car and left.

'So you're saying people are buying Nothing because other people are buying it?

'Yes. That's exactly what I'm saying.'

A BAD ENVIRONMENT

I was at this point a fit candidate for bheja fry.

Bheja fry is caused when your brain's ability to process bullshit is greatly reduced—*The overwhelming power of bullshit far exceeds an individual's ability to overcome it.*

Aspiring MBA students imprisoned in B-schools are being taught about the harmful effects and types of bullshit in an effort to enable them to sell such bullshit on behalf of the companies they work for, to customers, who, like Ramesh said, are convinced they need it, no matter what the cost. The dispensers of this knowledge, the righteous professors of said students who Google complex questions and paste them in entrance examination question papers, have even created an objective index called the Bullshit *Quotient or BQ.* The BQ is a score of BS taught in B-Schools. It is a quantifiable measure of an individual's tendency to tolerate bullshit floating around in the environment.

The BQ is based on the following well-known assumption: '*Given a working bank balance, a person whose BQ has been breached will inevitably end up buying a product he does not need, to impress people he does not like, with money he does not have, but has to work labouriously to earn from a job he does not like while working for people who do not want to pay him.*'

BQ is found out using this formula:

BQ = (average no. of idiots met on a daily basis x no. of idiotic ideas generated by each idiot)/(no. of times your blood pressure rises every single time you hear each idea x no. of times you wish you were dead)^ **level** of most gruesome death imagined *

*[for example, throwing yourself from the top floor of the office building because you can't listen to any more bullshit, is a level 5]

Having hungry sharks rip your arms while all your exes punch you in the face with boxing gloves as your boss and mother-in-law thrust barbed wire coated screw drivers at you and simultaneously make you watch Karan Johar's *Kabhi Khushi Kabhi Gham* extended Director's Cut with scene by scene special commentary is a level 500. (Imagining you survived all of this is level martyrdom—it is when you become one with the bullshit around you. You have attained nirvana).

I had gotten up the next morning with a very high BQ. My subconscious had dreamt up a situation where my bullshit quotient was compounding itself at the speed of light. It had reached infinity. The subconscious had also dreamt up a sequel (I am the only guy in the world who dreams in sequels. I once dreamt about my awesomeness in a trilogy—*Lord of Awesome: the Fellow of the Awesome, Lord of Awesome: Too Awesome,* and *Lord of Awesome: the Return of Awesomeness*) where the amount of ***NOTHING*** on the planet had become so great that it had absorbed everything in its wake like a blackhole, devouring space and time itself. It was astronomically, humongously, indescribably big. At one point, it gained self-awareness and started to eradicate mankind. Soon all the human beings had been eliminated. All intelligence had been stamped out. Human beings had been encompassed by ***Nothing.*** Only *Nothing* remained, unconquered, to rule the world.

Then, I was jolted out of my sleep—startled like a batsman wrapped on the pads, convinced that there was no way the umpire would out him only to see the dreaded finger of doom. Betrayed.

The day began with the ending of a nightmare. Reality is

something I usually enjoy. It seemed these days reality was getting very confusing. Maybe my subconscious was telling me something. If I went to Sigmund Freud now, he'd probably tell me that I had a Nothing complex and that I really wanted to just have sex with Nothing.

In the past week I had come to know that I had been cheated into signing a treaty with a company headed by a funnel-head which sold Nothing, sued by another company which had claimed selling Nothing was its idea, advised by my best friend and threatened by my worst enemy into not selling my stake to exit the company, only to watch the whole thing blow up in my face because everyone on the market and in the streets were buying Nothing. *Worst of all, I had still not understood why they were buying it in the first place AND very few seemed to even care.*

My dilemma was about to get worse.

After waking up in a rather unexpected fashion, screaming 'HELP! Nothing is destroying humanity', and clutching pillows like Dushasana clutching Draupadi before dragging her into the wager hall against the Pandavas, I decided to skip work that day.

Eating breakfast, I called up Vishal and left instructions for everyone. I didn't expect the market to do much today because, well, the only one who can make it do something is me.

I needed to do something that would take my mind off things from work. The idiot Ramakant was not in town as well to bother me. I had a media interview at 9 in the evening. I decided that I would drink virgin pomegranate and play golf till then.

Golf relaxes me. After Cricket, WWE wrestling, Table Tennis (I'm a big fan of Tei Sing Ping from Chinese Taipei—she's hot), weight lifting (huge fan of Olympic gold medalist, World Champion 200 kg weight lifter Gultark Jotguthnkisiv from Serbia), it's the only other sport I enjoy.

I decided to take my dog Princy along with me to the golf course. So, I tucked the little black and tan dachshund under my left shoulder, holding her like a handbag with her elongated tubular body resting on my forearm as her tail wagged happily behind my elbow. I said tata to the wife, swallowed my various pills, got into the helicopter, and flew away.

Five minutes later, I was at the Mumbai golf course. Petting Princy, I stepped onto 8 acres of golfing greens. I ran into Anil Ambani as I walked in.

'Oho! Jhunjhun bhai? How are you boss?' he greeted me warmly, smiling away to glory.

'I'm fine man. How's the empire?' I said as I handed over Princy to a steward who walked off to find her a treat or a bone.

'Bah! Don't ask,' he whined. 'Say, are you going to be attending the *annual super rich people talking about problems rich people face conference?*'

'Haven't made up my mind. The World Economic Forum in Davos is a big drag every year.'

'You should come, Jhunjhun bhai! This year the theme is *"How to avoid paying Value Added Tax in 15 easy steps".*'

'Well, I guess it's better than last year's topic—*"Practical Ways to import Ferraris without paying customs duty".*'

'I also heard that Narayan Murthy is not coming this year. Poor Murthy is sick. He was walking in the night when he saw someone shivering in the cold...so he removed all the clothes on his back and gave it to that person. Then he walked back home in the chilly night air and now he has pneumonia. Murthy is so humble...just like you Jhunjhun bhai!'

'Hmmm. Let's see, Maybe I'll come, but the problem, you know Anil, are the beggars. They stand outside the conference rooms every time and hanker you till you give them cash and then they don't even use that cash constructively.'

'Yeah. I know what you mean. Those World Bank and IMF gandus are always a problem. Last time something called the *Unn* took cash from me and sent me a thank you note saying they're using my money to feed an entire African village or something like that.'

I looked at Anil wondering what an 'Unn' was. Soon it hit me, 'Uh. It's not the Unn dude. That was the U.N. YOUUU... ENNN...You gave them a donation?' I asked.

'Oh! So that's what it was,' he squealed in delight as though he had just discovered a brand new gas reserve in the Krishna–Godavari basin before his brother. 'No wonder they've been pestering me to get on the advisory council of the UNNISAFE.'

'You mean UNICEF.'

'Yeah. But Jhun bhai, I don't have the time these days. I am already the Chairman of 60 companies with various interests in different verticals. Can't handle even more unnecessary responsibilities,' he complained.

'Dude! All those 60 companies are your own under the Reliance banner.'

'Yes exactly. That is why I have to take care of them. I can't advise other people about educating children. Even my own wife won't take my advice on educating our own children.'

'Why? What's the problem?'

'I want to send our youngest son to Harvard but she wants him to go to Oxford. It's so distressing, I tell you! Sometimes I feel being this rich is a curse.'

'Poor you!'

'By the way Jhunjhun bhai. Did you get my proposal?'

'Kaunsa proposal bhai? Shaadi ho chukki hai meri. Bees saal ho gaye.'

'Arre! I sent one last week. Reliance ADAG wants to partner with your new friend Ramakant Shastri to manufacture and market Nothing in other countries.'

'No man, I haven't got any proposal.'

'Bloody hell! I am sure I told my assistant to send it. Somebody must have done something at the courier. I bet it's one of Mukesh's men. My office is crawling around with his spies!'

'Well, I haven't got anything,' I reiterated.

'Sigh! I'll resend it today itself. Get Ramakant to partner us no, Jhunjhun bhai. As it is, you are on the Board. With Notco, I can finally cross my brother's net worth.'

I was briefly reminded about mentioning to Ramakant about how pissed Anil is that his brother's market value is slightly higher when I was goading Ramakant to see a shrink.

Anil quickly ranted, jolting me back into the conversation. 'I mean now even Ramakant is part of the billionaire club. Fastest one to get there! For People like us, our fathers had to work their entire lives so that we could inherit their money and become billionaires ourselves, but this Ramakant, he has just shot into the billionaire club out of nowhere in such an incredibly short time. This Nothing is genius!'

'You really think so?'

'Absolutely!'

'Hmmm. Okay, let me ask him.'

'What ask him, Jhunjhun bhai! You are richer than me and Mukesh combined and multiplied 100 times. You just tell Ramakant. Do some setting for us with him no Jhun bhaiyya! Please!' Anil pleaded fervently.

'I'll see what I can do,' I said, eager to dispose off with this conversation immediately. Afterall, I was at the golf course for pleasure, not business.

'Thank you, Jhun bhaiyya! I hope you come to Davos. We'll talk in detail. I'll send the proposal by tonight,' Anil smiled, happy I had acceded.

'Okay. Take care Anil,' I said as I walked to the canopy on the golf course from the office area.

'Bye Jhunjhun bhai! I have to go to the office and fight with Airtel's Sunil Mittal. Bloody fellow is hogging all the broadband Connections in India with Airtel Internet. How will Reliance Communications increase Internet browsing speed from 3 mbps to 100 mbps at this rate?'

Once he left, I made my way onto the canopy overlooking the

sprawling greens. It seemed like I was walking into bits and pieces of an assorted jungle. The office area where I had just met Anil was an airy lounge, floor lined with wooden boards and walls decorated with golfing memorabilia. The main wall had a giant metallic coat of arms of the golf club embossed into the cement. A tiny gift shop selling golf merchandize ranging from mugs and t-shirts to clubs stood in a corner.

On the other corner was the entrance to the greens. I pushed the twin doors aside and peered into the beautiful horizon as I set foot onto the canopy. My helicopter was parked in the distance. From this angle, it looked like a miniature white coloured Black Hawk.

I instructed an attendant to fetch Princy. It was time to play some golf. Appropriately, I pulled up a chair and sat down in the shade of the canopy.

You're probably confused. Let me explain. I play golf sitting down. I'm very rich. This is an established fact. I don't need to actually, physically, painfully walk around hauling a metallic iron club over acre after acre under God's hot sun, sweating like a hound dog just to put a ball more dimpled than Priety Zinta's cheeks and smaller than Stinker's brain into hole after hole!

I'm so rich, I hire Tiger Woods to play golf for me. I play golf by watching him play golf. He's my golf proxy. I follow him around in the golf cart eating seedless mangrapes (a fruit I invented by combining mangoes and grapes to create a super succulent deliciously sweet hybrid called the *mangrape*. I won my third Nobel prize for genetics last year for inventing it) and he walks around being athletically inclined to putt every single ball straight into all 18 holes on the golf course.

At this point, I am obligated to tell you that I am also the greatest golfer in the world. I've won every golf tournament there is without even being on the golf course. I go into the golf Hall of Fame next year.I'm the only guy to have also won the Football World Cup and Wimbledon...simultaneously...because both, the

Spanish football team and Andy Murray, play football and tennis respectively for me.

My shady grove offered a decent view of the proceedings. So far I had completed four holes in four minutes on a par-4 course. Tiger Woods was stroking the ball like a genius.

'Good shot, Tiger!' I yelled as he prowled the greens wearing a red striped T-shirt, a pair of black trousers, white golf shoes, and a black sports cap.' Thank you, Sir! 'You're really playing well today, Sir,' yelled Tiger, really happy with my performance.

The steward carried Princy over to me. I don't like it when she is made to walk. That's why I've purchased for her, her very own Black coloured Porsche with her own chauffeur.

I eagerly took her from the steward, thanked him, and set her down beside me after petting her a little. She got down to chewing on a bone by my side.

I was starting to feel better in the shade, playing golf while drinking ice-cold orange juice and club soda under a hot sun in the midst of a grassy golfing meadow. Slowly my breath was becoming rhythmic, harmonious, quiet …relaxed. Baba Yogdev would be proud. Apart from the sound of Princy's happy nibbling, the occasional chatter of the staff in the concrete office behind and Tiger Woods' club stroking the ball, there was nothing else to disturb the peace. With the birds chirping away, I descended into a mid-morning siesta right there…without a care in the world.

BANG!

'I demand to see Mr Jhunjhunwala!' a shrill voice thundered in the background. Jolted out of my slumber, it took a second to realize that the voice was real and had uttered my great name. Princy was barking. 'I demand to see Mr Jhunjhunwala! I demand to see him!' The same voice howled almost militant-like.

I glanced at my watch. I had dozed off for about an hour. Before I could get out of my chair to see who it was desiring my esteemed presence so badly, a horde of kurta-pyjama clad individuals broke through the doors like an angry mob. They had seen me through the glass and were walking towards me with the ferocity of a herd of women ready to plunder a just-opened, limited-time only, saree sale at the local Nalli emporium.

'Whoa! Whoa! Whoa! People. Just relax. I'll sign your merchandise. Bring out your Jhunjhunwala T-shirts and posters! One by one, one by one,' I screamed as I got out of my chair in a huff.

The horde moving like a swift cloud stopped in front of me. Princy was about to explode; she did not appreciate her bone break interrupted. Before she could do that, I picked her up and held her close. Princy, like me, was also under stress. Off late a bunch of grasshoppers in her doghouse mansion had been bugging her. Her therapist in Luxembourg (whom she flies to once a week to meet with) had warned me to keep her on a tight leash.

I stood back alarmed, wondering who these folks were when a crispy, sharp female voice spoke aloud, 'Hello Mr Jhunjhunwala. Tell me Mr Jhunjhunwala, do you like shampooing your hair with the germ-ridden placentas of infected, pregnant women?'

'Eh!' I exclaimed, stumped at the sheer magnitude of the question.

The mob raucously nodded in agreement as the same voice fired away angrily, 'Does a great multi-billionaire like you enjoy feasting on the rotten entrails spilling out of the maggot-ridden cadavers of aborted foetuses? Do you take special pride in sitting around a table with your billionaire buddies drinking the blood of the innocents you have slaughtered as their own families dance around your table eating pieces of discarded food you've thrown while you point and laugh at their pathetic, poverty-ridden lives? Do you hire cancer to affect the poor? Do you age cancer tumours like mushrooms and inhale the spores on them because that is your twisted sadistic idea of oppressing the impoverished because you are a capitalist Nazi!'

'Oye! What the hell are you talking about?' I shouted and looked at the mop-haired woman clad in a maroon salwar whose voice had awakened me from my siesta. 'And I don't eat foetuses.

Yuck! And what nonsense is this about placenta in my shampoo? Are you people crazy?'

Soon it became clear that the woman was the leader of the mob. She stepped forward and ranted away with her mates loudly encouraging her as a few stewards tried to eject them from the course. I motioned to the stewards to let these people finish their talking. 'Men like you disgust me! You suck on the teat of mother earth only to cannibalize her other children like a piranha in a goldfish pond. You suck her blood like a leech and leave her dryer than a factory chimney. I bet you build great fires into which you throw in the bones of everyone you've screwed. You wear their skulls around your neck like a garland and dance around with their women as you employ their children as slave labourers to toil away for you in sweatshops smaller than a village post-office!'

Struck by the scathing attack, I retaliated, 'Whoa! Hold on! Before you accuse me of any more blood-spilling, child slavery, ritualistic savage bonfire dancing, debauchery, vampirism, and whatever else you seem to be suggesting, can you please tell me who in the hell you are and what in the hell do you want?'

'We are from an NGO called Sapna,' the woman proclaimed proudly. 'We work with the Ministry of Environment, Health, and Public Safety…'

Before she could continue with her description, I rudely and gladly interrupted, 'Well congrats! You've just created a bad environment for everyone. You've also totally increased my dog's stress levels. Her health and my health are under threat! I have awesomitis. Our lives are being threatened. There is no safety here at all! You people are terrorists! One of you even scared away Tiger Woods. Look! he's hiding in that tree over there but none of you ladies should go near him. He's more dangerous than Shakti Kapoor!'

'Look at you with your little dog playing your rich man's game while millions in this country starve without food! You feast while the poor scrap. You are a vulture, picking the meat off the rotting corpses of the indigent destitute laborers who struggle to build your pyramid while you sit atop your pharaoh-throne seeking salvation.'

'Hey! I am not a vulture, okay? And what is it with you and corpses, lady? Did you grow up in a Ramsay Brothers film? I'm a vegetarian, and moreover, I'm an investor, not some sort of megalomaniacal fascist overlord. You people clearly have me confused with Mukesh Ambani or Rahul Bajaj.'

'No one is confused. We are all here to tell you that we are suing you for endangering and exploiting the lives of hundreds of thousands of people. Furthermore, we are also suing you for destruction of property, illegal trespassing, and causing irreversible damage to the environment. You have caused tree genocide.'

'What the hell are you talking about?!'

'Your factory in Rikhitpur.'

'What factory?'

'The Notco factory in Rikhitpur is giving people cancer.'

I erupted, 'Crap! Bas main hi mila hoon kya case karne ke liye? I'm already fighting because of Notco!'

The mob cheered her on. Determined to inflict as much pain on me as possible, the woman continued yelling, 'We know and now you will fight another one. This one is far more serious than that one. Your factory in Rikhitpur began operations two months ago. Since then, 200 people have been diagnosed with stage 3 irreversible, fatal butt cancer.'

'Butt cancer!'

'Yes butt cancer. It's a cancer of the ass. Logon ke pichwade pe nariyal jaise bade-bade gole khade ho gaye hain. It's so dangerous even pregnant women in the area have had to abort their foetuses because of medical complications. I guess rich people like you are just not interested in the consequences of your actions. All of you want to only make money off the earth and money off the people even if it's at the cost of…cost of…'

'Shut up! Not all of us do that. I for one don't do that, OKAY! And I swear I had no idea about any of this. I didn't even know Notco had a factory in Rikhitpur,' I interrupted.

'That factory was built on land acquired illegally. There is already a case pending in court. Farmers had sold their land to a real estate developer who had promised them high returns and flats in the residential complex he would build there, but after the farmers sold their land to him, he went ahead and leased the land to Notco and didn't even give them compensation. Your factory then gave them cancer!'

'Hey! It's not my factory, okay. I don't make these decisions. I'm only on the board of Notco.'

'That's not our problem Mr Jhunjhunwala. We believe that as the world's greatest investor, you surely had a hand in the decision-making process. We are sure you helped set up the factory and we are also sure that all the Nothing that is being sucked from the nowhere around Rikhitpur is dangerous and is causing cancer to the people and the workers of the factory and the surrounding area.'

'Hold on! You're saying Nothing is causing cancer?'

'*Absolutely*. We have experts and doctors who have studied the area and they are convinced beyond a shadow of doubt that the Nothing here is extremely dangerous and since the company sucking it has not only not taken proper precautions to contain such a dangerous substance but also exposed it to the people in that area, it is therefore directly responsible for this.'

'Have you gone mad!' I shouted in disbelief. 'Since when did Nothing start causing cancer?! It doesn't even exist! How can something that does not exist cause cancer?'

'Mr Jhunjhunwala, you've been making tons of money selling this product. If it can make money, it can definitely cause cancer also.'

'Why only cancer then? Sue me saying Nothing causes AIDS also no?'

'We don't have any evidence that Nothing causes AIDS. We still believe AIDS comes from watching English movies, holding hands in public, and kissing on the lips before a rose gets in the way. We suggest the use of condoms to prevent AIDS,' the lady laughed as if she were trying to lighten the mood with a joke.The rest of the mob burst into peals of laughter delighted at their charismatic leader's attempt at comedy.

'At least that makes sense,' I said.

'Yes, if you put a condom on the rose then you can prevent AIDS,' she said as the mob laughed even louder.

I snarled. It wasn't funny that I had been interrupted and clearly my BQ score was increasing at this point. I looked at the woman and asked plainly, 'Is this a joke?'

'No, Sir,' she responded without hesitation. 'We are from an NGO also supported by the government. Two ministries are behind this. All 678 parties which are part of the coalition are supporting us on the issue. It's not a joke. The government doesn't have a sense of humour.'

'I don't believe it. I don't know what you're trying to pull here okay, but to suggest that Nothing is dangerous and causes cancer is ludicrous!'

'It doesn't matter what you believe. All that matters is what the court believes and let me tell you for a fact the court has believed stranger things. Last year a Court sentenced a monkey to 7 years rigorous imprisonment for stealing a banana.'

I waited for the mob to laugh thinking the woman had tried another joke. The mob didn't even let out a whimper of a laugh. I surmised that it wasn't a joke. The monkey was really in jail.

She paused to adjust her kurta and continued, 'Two months ago, the women were all healthy. The people were also healthy. The government hospital conducted a check-up on all of them. Then the factory came up. Bulldozers uprooted trees, pulled out crops, levelled the place totally. The site which was as hairy as Anil Kapoor's chest was now balder than Anupam Kher's skull.

'Within days of the factory coming up, people started to sneeze and cough.'

'That only proves there might have been a flu in the area,' I said.

'Yes but after that something more serious happened.'

'What?'

'They started to die.'

'Oh!'

'Yes. They sneezed, then they died. God bless them.'

'When production capacity was increased with the installation of more funnels in the area, people stopped dying.'

'Oh good!' I said, relieved that the deaths were over.

'Yes, but they got cancer instead and that's why we are suing everyone on the Notco Board,' said the woman turning my short-lived relief back into frustration.

Just 24 hours ago, I was getting sued for being on the Board. Now this. I didn't want to think about 24 hours from now. Is this what it feels like to be Jack Bauer or Anil Kapoor in *24*'s Hindi remake?

The woman was determined to frustrate me further and continued, 'Our doctors and scientists tested samples from the area. They have concluded that Nothing is leaking from the factory and into the surroundings and that's why the people are getting butt cancer.'

'Wow! Tell me how does one test a Nothing sample?'

'The test finds out a reading. The lower the reading, the more carcinogenic, or in simpler words 'cancer-causing' the sample. Nothing is highly carcinogenic. It causes cancer very rapidly. All the Nothing samples registered a 0 reading and since 0 is lower than all other numbers it is obvious Nothing is the most fatal cancer-causing substance known to man.'

'Oh boy! Ratmalani is going to make a fortune this time,' I said sarcastically.

'What now?' the lady asked perking her ears.

'Nothing...I mean...screw it. I'll handle this later. Send the summons to my lawyer's office. How did you guys know I was playing golf here?'

'Someone at your office told us when we called for you. We shall take your leave now. We have to sue the MD of Tide washing powder. The company did not specify on their packet that the contents are a detergent powder and not bathing soap. Ten people mistakenly bathed with it and now they all look whiter than vanilla ice-cream.'

I lamented, 'Such bright futures...'

'Whitewashed just like that because rich companies and rich people like you think they can get away with anything.'

'Hey lady! I've had enough of you and your lot. Please go from here. You are discriminating against rich people! This is income racism!'

The woman fumed as the mob egged her on, 'You can eject me from here Mr Jhunjhunwala but our struggle against the corrupt, corpse feeding, imperialist capitalist, cancer- causing, butt-ruining, selfish, greedy, face bleaching autocrats of Tide and Notco is far from over. We will see you in court!'

'Whatever,' I muttered as they departed. I decided to stop playing golf and head to the office. I waved goodbye to Tiger, clasped Princy tightly, and left. The nightmare was coming true.

FROM THE STUDIO FRYER TO THE RESTAURANT FIRE

'Studio leke jaana,' I said to my deputy chauffeur (he's my driver's driver's driver), crackling open a new packet of gutkha as I stepped out of the office. Ravindra smiled graciously and started the white Chrysler stretch limousine (it comes with its own anti-gravity floatation chamber). An escort of six Harley Davidson Electra Glide motorcycles in front and four in the back revved up. I got in, closed the door and vroom, vroom, we were off. I was headed to the *Times Now* studio in Parel about 10 kilometres from my office.

For all the money that the Bennett Coleman Group makes, you'd think they'd install a helipad on their office but no! Misers. They'd kill me and then send me the bill for my own funeral, even if I was in hell.

I had been asked to provide my presence on TV to explain the Notco situation by Ramakant who had run off to Argentina on business. I was sick of having TV crews set up station at my office in a bid to extract my precious wisdom (I'm interviewed at least 50 times a week by TV people across the globe including *Sonetsu Channel*—Kenya's Number One Business Network and *La Business Sola,* Uruguay's premier television conglomerate) so I decided to show my sociable nature by going to the TV studio for a change and interacting with India's finest journalistic minds.

The entourage ploughed through the streets. It was shortly after 8.30 pm. My private security force of elite US Secret Service, British SAS Guards, and Dara Singh's Pehalwan Emporium rode out with me. I spent time sipping champagne and playing Super Mario on the Xbox One hooked up to the 50 inch LED TV in the car. Fun!

An epic battle was underway. Mario the plumber, having eaten his 27th Mushroom, was on the way to encounter the evil Bowser's evil Son in level 4-4. Princess Peach, the victim of a brazen kidnapping operation was suffering all alone in a lonely, fire-engulfed castle under the watch of an evil tyrant. Suffering silently, she waited for me as Mario to arrive, to slay her abductors, vanquish her kidnappers, and finally carry her out with my big burly arms into the comforting hands of safety.

People around me often remark how a 50+ multi-billionaire tycoon shouldn't be playing something as inane as videogames. These people I sincerely consider my enemies. I chop their heads off and parade them on a spike. As the popular saying goes, 'Videogames are awesome! Reality is for losers who do not play videogames.'

'Screech', the tyres ground to a halt. Mario was just about to enter a pipe into a different world filled with weird characters when Ravindra said, 'Sirji, studio aa gaya'. Rolling down the window and keeping the joystick aside, I raised my head and looked up to see the big, white banner on the greyish, cylindrical building: '*Times Now, India's No. 1 most watched news channel*' in huge letters and below, *'65% of India watches us'. The other 35% must be the sane ones,* I thought as I exited after thanking Ravindra.

The entourage stayed behind. Four guards accompanied me inside. The rest would guard me from outside. I paused to take a look at the blue pillar lighting up Mumbai's skyline in the distance. Ramakant's pyramid beacon was now functional.

I strode into the building, remarking to the guards that Shastri's building consumed 80% of Maharashtra's electricity grid. They nodded nonchalantly, only eager to take a bullet for me but not interested in anything else. The prime-time studio was on the fifth floor. A lift transported me there and lo! I had arrived like Mario into a strange world.

It was a newsroom alright—loud, rambunctious, and zippy. People were moving around like electrons in a heated steel spoon. Things were definitely on the boil. 'Live' screamed one. 'Cut' screamed a reporter to her cameraman. 'Ready' screamed another. 'I'm going to kill myself' screamed another. 'I'll help you' screamed one to the one who wanted to kill herself. Young India's finest journalistic minds were all engaged in spreading the gospel of *Breaking News* to 65% of India.

Many were tapping away on their keyboards. Women dressed in anything from salwars to jeans to sarees. The guys sweating away under their shirts despite the air conditioning on at full blast. A young intern greeted and escorted me to the news floor.' 15 minutes, we go live Sir,' he said seating me down at a huge desk in a blue and white studio. 'Sir will talk to you shortly,' he said.

'Sir' was the boss. The big bad dude of Indian news. Confrontational, probing…annoying. He wasn't just a journo, he was also a showman. Many nights I had seen him badger people into submission at primetime. He bellowed fire and preached integrity, used words like 'the nation', 'mother India', 'corruption', and 'we the people'.

They called him the bespectacled assassin. His staff and devotees called him '*the saviour of journalism*', his critics called him a '*joke*'. I simply decided to use his name and call him *Arnab*.

The intern remarked proudly, 'It's very nice of you to come to our studio, Sir. I mean you could have gone to any studio to get interrupted by any other anchor but the fact that you chose to get interrupted by Arnab Sir on our channel… When he talks it's like making sex to your ears!'

'I didn't come here to get interrupted!' I said dismissing his comment wondering if it was a barb.

It seemed like it wasn't. The intern immediately boasted, 'But Arnab Sir is No. 1 in interruption. Last year he became the first anchor to score 200 interruptions in 1 minute. It was a world record.'

'Was?'

'Yes Sir, he broke that record just last week by scoring 300 interruptions in one minute. WHAT A MAN! He broke his own record.'

Surprised with the level of admiration the intern had for Arnab, I vocalized my intentions a bit amused, 'You seem to like him a lot little boy!'

'Of course, Sir! Arnab Sir is a legend!' He asserted joyously 'What I like about his journalism is that he doesn't let facts and opinions get in the way of his interruptions.'

About 12 minutes remained for the clock to strike 9. Arnab dispersed into view. The entire floor was just one big rectangular space partitioned into smaller spaces by plastic and plywood. In the centre of it all was one big table with computers lying back to back in the middle. People sat on either side. It was a huge station with at least 40 people sitting at it. This was the news desk with a big banner hanging above: *'Journalism is about the nation wanting to know'.*

8.50 pm. Arnab was busy hovering around the characters at the news desk. Moving his head up, he waved to me. I acknowledged with a gentle Mario-like bob of the head.

The set-up was in front of the cameras. I was sitting just in front of the news desk. One girl was waving her arm in front of a green screen. A TV nearby showed her indicating a weather pattern over the Andamans.

Seated next to me were a few other characters. One was an ad guru, another a writer, another a filmmaker. Arnab slowly approached me. 'Good evening Mr Jhunjhunwala. Thank you for agreeing to talk to me,' he said smiling unevenly through his teeth.

'You're welcome,' I said without intent, just eager to get this done with as soon as possible.

'We'll get started in a few minutes. The other guests are already here. We'll also be cutting across to some guests via satellite,' he said as I observed that he was wearing a white full-sleeved shirt tucked into a pair of jeans and a blue jacket.

'What other guests?' I asked, peeved. 'I thought this was an interview.'

'It is an interview. I am interviewing 10 people at the same time.'

'That's not an interview. It's a panel discussion.'

'What to do, Sir? No time to interview each one separately. A discussion is just as good. More points of view.'

'Hmm,' I muttered, pissed off that the very tamasha I was trying to avoid had been sneakily unleashed on me by Ramakant while he was conveniently gallivanting in South America.

'Please be seated. Ashok, put a mic on Sir,' instructed Arnab. 'I'll be back soon. See you in 5.'

The young intern patched up a mic on me as Arnab strode away. I sat at a table with three other people. They were elated to see me. This was where the ~~interview~~ panel discussion would take place. A raw feed on an opposite monitor showed my face in a little square on the left corner. Reduced to a square! Pathetic!

With two minutes to go, Arnab strode in, having changed into a freshly ironed light grey suit and tie. Arnab sat down and started barking orders. He was a lot more energetic and simply…Loud.

He looked at us rotating his head from side to side and, viciously stabbing the air with a pen stuck between his fingers, barked out loud, 'Okay. This is the rundown folks. Let me just see who will say what on today's debate. We will start at 9.05. Till then the cameras will not focus on you.' Two big cameras stared at me. I could see silhouettes of the cameramen behind both.

Arnab rambunctiously hollered, 'Starting from my left, you

Mrs Choudhry, you are from the government and will defend everything the government does.'

Turning to me he said, 'Mr Jhunjunwala. You be yourself.'

'Oye! I am always myself,' I said, outraged Arnab could even imagine me being anyone apart from me.

'Mr Ravi Markand Joshi—you are from the opposition, so you oppose everything,' Arnab furiously spoke into the other camera as a pony-tailed, skinny woman danced behind the camera flexing her index and middle finger indicating that the show would start in exactly 2 minutes.

Looking into the cameras to talk to some guests and to the in-house panelists around him seated to his left, Arnab nodded at the girl, adjusted his glasses, and rattled off like a machine gun. 'Rahul Pandit—you oppose both the government and the opposition.

'Lata Kulkarni—you will support both the government and the opposition. You will blame China, Pakistan, and the US for everything.

'Ramchandra Guha—you will be the intellectual. You will state mundane facts which have no impact on the debate but people will think you are really intelligent.

'Prahlad Kakkar—say anything you want but be sure to indicate that you are wearing a hat.

'Mallika—you are a celebrity…err…we will figure out what to do with you later. I'll ask you a question when everyone else is tired talking.

'Professor James Roberts from Cambridge University—Can you hear me Professor? You will be the foreign expert. You will say the same things the Indians say but people will pay more attention to what you say because you are a foreigner and you have a classy British accent.'

The already confused Professor looked more confused. *This isn't the BBC. Welcome to Times Now,* bitch! I thought to myself in glee, realizing Arnab would have driven the British away years ago had he been born in that era.

'And finally, joining us by satellite via Jaipur Zoo will be a chattering monkey to bring a unique animal perspective to the debate,' he concluded. I scratched my head as the others looked around confused wondering if they had heard 'monkey' right.

'Follow my lead. Okay, let's go. We roll in 1 minute. Begin countdown. Hit the music. Line up graphics! Move! Move! Move!' Arnab shouted as he stabbed the air with even more fury and adjusted an ear-piece into his right ear.

The theme music echoed and before you knew, the show was on! A resolute male baritone echoed throughout the studio. 'LIVE FROM THE TIMES NOW STUDIO: This is the Newshour with Arnab Goswami.'

Arnab ranted off as we went live. 'Good Evening. Our country is a strong nation of 1.2 billion people. When our forefathers fought to gain freedom from the British, they did it to provide us a democratic home free from an autocratic imperialist rule and frankly, what have the British ever done for India or the world? The only good thing that came out of Britain was James Bond and let me tell you folks that ACP Pradyuman from CID can solve crimes much faster than James Bond and if he were younger, more women would sleep with him than James Bond. My point is that India is the best.

'Now, this broadcast is not about the British, James Bond, or ACP Pradyuman. It is about India.

'One of the foundations of our democracy is the right to do business. But business as such cannot be business if it stands for cheap profit at the cost of human life and the methods employed to make profits are disgraceful, dirty, and illegal.

'Our issue tonight—Is the government responsible for the Notco mess or is Notco responsible for the Notco mess? Is this even a mess or am I just saying this is a mess because my own head is messed up? Is India's fastest rising company a copycat and a cheat? Have they profited off the hard work of other entrepreneurs like Ajay Agarwal? AND MOST IMPORTANTLY, do the millions of people exposed to Nothing now have a very real chance of dying from butt cancer as an NGO, implicitly backed by the Ministry Of Health, Environment and Safety, drags Notco to court? Joining us tonight will be a host of experts, including the Director of Notco, famed legendary investor Jhunjhunwala. *Tonight's Newshour debate is about Corporate India's business practices—ethical or corrupt?*

'But first a quick look at the headlines!'

The music restarted. Arnab ran through the headlines. Under the impression I would only talk about the patent issue, I had agreed to the interview. I was now gonna be talking about patents and patients. Dammit!

I sat there quietly, moving only to adjust my glasses as the anchor yakked away.

It was only a matter of seconds before the feed changed from the anchor doing the news to the anchor panelising all of us.

'*And now Live from Mumbai the newshour debate*', the deep baritone echoed as the headlines were exhausted.

The cameras focused on Arnab and us. The scene played out fast, furious, and continuously.

Arnab: 'Our 5 minutes of news are up. We now begin 55 minutes of analysis. Tonight's Newshour debate is about Corporate India's business practices—ethical or corrupt?

'A few months ago, a virtually unknown company called Notco got listed on the Bombay Stock Exchange. The Nothing company as it's now known in a matter of months has become a Fortune 500 company. Notco is the world's leading manufacturer of Nothing and a highly successful corporation but earlier this week it was sued for allegedly violating another company's patent. Did Notco steal the Nothing idea?

'More importantly, just today an NGO moved the court holding Notco responsible for mass deforestation in the Rikhitpur valley. Is Notco also the reason more than 200 people have got cancer of the ass in Rikhitpur? Did the government err in not establishing proper

safeguards for companies processing a potentially dangerous substance like Nothing? Is the cancer-devastation-deforestation scandal a slap in the face of honest corporations? Isn't corruption a bigger cancer than cancer itself! Who is responsible for Notco gate?

'Joining me on the Newshour tonight. Famed legendary investor and Notco board member—Jhunjhunwala!

'From the government, the woman whose department is pursuing the case against Notco, Environment Ministry Spokeswoman Mrs Renu Choudhry!

'From the opposition party, BJP Environmental Cell Member and renowned government blamer, Mr Markand Joshi!

'We all know him from his book "The Self Help Idiots Motivational Guide To Losing Weight By Drinking Chicken Soup for the Soul In 5 Easy Ways and Getting Rich by Being Happy", well-known writer, social commentator, critic, and fashion designer—Rahul Pandit.'

Rahul Pandit: 'I'm also a theatre artist, bungee jumper, and malnutrition expert. Did you know that only 1 out of every 5 kids are able to get food. What is the government doing? Do you know?!

*Arnab: 'The nation also wants to know. Back to our panel. Lata Kulkarni—I don't know who she is or why she's here BUT THATS OKAY BECAUSE I AM SAYING HER NAME IN A REALLY FUC*IN LOUD VOICE!*

'Specialist TV panel discussion contributor and Guinness World Record holder for maximum opinions given on maximum number of TV shows—Prahlad Kakkar.

'Rounding off our panel are Professor James Roberts from Cambridge and well-known knowledge enthusiast—Ramchandra Guha.

'Mallika—young bollywood actress whose uncle was killed by the notorious ass cancer of Rikhitpur. She will be portraying herself in a film based on her life.

'And finally, for the first time on TV, an animal panelist—a chattering monkey named Sonu from Jaipur Zoo. Welcome Sonu!'

The screen focused on a caged monkey jumping up and down. BLOODY HELL!

Arnab: 'Mr Jhunjhunwala, my first question to you—Notco has been accused of not only stealing someone else's patent but also being unable to process the Nothing in Rikhitpur. The Nothing fields of Rikhitpur have become the killing fields of Rikhitpur. Sources are saying that the Nothing here is in its most dangerous form and because Notco has not taken the necessary precautions to handle its toxic state, it is leaking into surrounding areas and causing butt cancer. People are not being able to go to the toilet because they cannot even squat properly because of this medical condition. How do you respond?'

Me: 'I don't want to comment on the patent issue because the matter is in court. All I can say is Shastri has said the patent was his…'

Arnab: 'But, papers filed by Ajay Agarwal's counsel in court clearly indicate that his patent application predates Shastri's.'

Me: 'Like I said, I can't comment on that, but as far as Notco's factory in Rikhitpur goes, it is inconceivable that Nothing causes cancer. It must be something else.'

Lata Kulkarni: 'How can you say that? Come on, tell me! Are you a doctor? We have a government report here saying 200 people have got cancer because of Nothing. Not something. Nothing!'

Renu: 'You see Arnab, this is the problem. Rich people in this country think they know everything about everything and Nothing.'

Me: 'Oye! I don't know everything about everything. Who do you think I am? Suhel Seth?'

Renu: 'Let me complete…'

Arnab: 'Mrs Choudhry, Mr Jhunjhunwala has just taken Mr Suhel Seth's name who by the way is at another channel's panel discussion. He will join our debate soon and after that he is going to another channel to take part in another debate. That guy doesn't have a home. Every TV studio has a room reserved for him every night which he occupies if Prahlad Kakkar isn't using it himself.'

Kakkar: 'Arnab, haha! Suhel is a good friend but the crux of the issue is…'

Renu: 'Arnab, let me complete…'

Arnab: 'Mrs Renu, how can you say with 100% accuracy that Notco's improper sucking practices have led to leakages which have caused cancer.'

Renu: 'Because Arnab, we sent a team of over 10,000 doctors and researchers to Rikhitpur over a month ago at a cost of 1000 crores. They conducted comprehensive tests on the water, the air, the soil, the plants, the people, the animals, the birds, everything and everyone to discover which pathogen was causing the cancer. They found Nothing. And since they found Nothing, the conclusion was therefore that Nothing was causing cancer and since Notco is the only factory there, it is obvious the Nothing THEY make in their factory is the one causing the cancer!'

Me: 'That doesn't even make sense! It only proves they haven't found the real reason…'

Renu: 'Arnab, please tell Mr Jhunjhunwala to not interrupt me. I didn't interrupt him when he was talking.'

Joshi: 'You see Arnab—this is typical of the government. Ever since they came into power, they have been misleading the people like this. I want to know why they gave permission to Notco to set up their factory in Rikhitpur in the first place, especially when they knew Nothing causes cancer?'

Renu: 'We didn't know Nothing caused cancer. We came to know only a few days back.'

Arnab: 'So why didn't the government know sooner? WHY? Isn't it the job of the government to know? The nation wants to know!'

Renu: 'Let me complete. We took immediate action by taking them to court. On the other hand, when there was a chicken pox outbreak in Gujarat, a state with the opposition state government took more than a month to act during which hundreds of innocent children died.'

Joshi: 'Arnab, Arnab, Arnab. In Andhra…err, the state formerly known as Andhra Pradesh but now called Telangana and Seemandhra, which has a government headed by their party, thousands have died because their government failed to act against AIDS.'

Renu: 'Ask them whose party was in power when lakhs died because of cockroach plague in Haryana?'

Joshi: 'Tell them to first answer how many crores have died because of malnutrition in states with their government!'

Renu: 'Before that, let them inform us how many tens of crores have died…'

Arnab: 'Folks! Folks! Let's focus on the topic. Is corporate India guided only by profits? Why is Notco not being held accountable for this mess?'

Renu : 'Arnab…Arnab…Arnab …let me complete…'

Arnab : 'Mrs Choudhry…Please don't talk when I am interrupting you…it's very rude!'

Me: 'It is being held accountable, that's why the matter is in court.'

Arnab: 'Then the nation wants to know why it isn't being held more accountable! Why is Ramakant Shastri not in jail? Why is Notco still making Nothing? Shouldn't its offices be raided and other factories be sealed shut? Why isn't the government acting? Why is the opposition not taking the government to task over this? Why isn't the Ministry of Corporate Affairs taking heed and scrapping Notco's business license? Why am I not in a mental hospital instead of TV? Why? Why? Why? Why? Why? Why! The nation wants to know!'

Rahul Pandit: 'You see Arnab, corporate India and the rest of India have two separate sets of rules. Corporate India thinks it can buy its way out of anything just because it has the money. It is the corrupt unethical rot that is being allowed to propagate by graft and corruption which is truly hurting the Indian democracy. If this was China Ramakant Shastri would have been hanged!'

Kakkar: 'Arnab, this makes me very sad…'

Arnab: 'Thank you Mr Kakkar. Ramchandra Guha, how did you feel when you were told about India's butt cancer epidemic?'

Prof .Roberts: 'Before that I'd like to say two things Arnab.'

Arnab: 'No, you say only one thing. We have to take a break.'

Guha: 'Arnab, let me also say one thing...'

Joshi: 'Arnab, you didn't allow me to say my one thing so how can you allow Guha to say one thing?'

Renu: 'That's funny how the opposition has time to say one thing and do another thing.'

Arnab: 'Folks, folks, folks! Please...let Mr Roberts finish. You will all have time to say your things. Professor, please continue.'

Prof. Roberts: 'You see, there is a wonderful dichotomy here. On the one hand we have a fabulous story. I mean even a year ago if someone had said they could sell Nothing, we would have laughed at them. But Ramakant Shastri has proved everyone wrong. Right from America to Antarctica, people are frantically seeking Notco products. Like Shakespeare once said "All the world's a stage and we are just actors who are trying to act in the heralding glow of...uh..." Well I don't want to go into what Shakespeare said exactly but just remember if he were to say it now then this would be a perfect situation to say it. Notco's is a fantastic tale...but now you hear that it's been achieved by copying someone else's ideas and by putting people's lives at perils. It begs the question: is this the only way to do business? Maybe we should all be realistic about things. Maybe people have to get cancer if India has to succeed.'

Joshi: 'OYE! We have to get cancer? Yeh firangi phek raha hai. Simon go back! Tu chamaila. Tere Shakespeare ki... SAALA KUTRECHA! TERE MAA KI...*'*

Prof. Roberts: 'What is he saying!'

Lata Kulkarni: 'He is saying your mother...'

Renu: 'Ha! These are the opposition leaders we have. Let the country know how they talk to foreigners.'

Joshi: 'It's much better compared to all those foreign women who are getting raped in your state ruled by your party!'

Arnab: 'Gentlemen, let's all be civilized here.'

Guha: 'Arnab, Arnab, Arnab, I have a totally different take on this issue. Why can't we build a factory on the moon? It's the perfect solution. It's just hanging in space. I mean surely there's a lot of Nothing there. I can't imagine why a country of 1.2 billion people cannot even build a rocket and send our people so that companies like Notco can extract Nothing from the vast space lands on the moon without causing any danger to the people here on earth.'

Arnab: 'That's an excellent suggestion, Mrs Choudhry! Why can't our government direct ISRO to build a factory on the moon? Is it because the government has no money for a space program of this nature? Where have all the funds gone?'

Joshi: 'You see Arnab…this corrupt government has failed on all fronts. The PM should resign immediately! They have also failed to bring back the black money from the Swiss bank accounts which could have been used to launch a space program to build Nothing factories on the moon and in space.'

Renu: 'This is not true Arnab. We are already taking the necessary steps to bring black money back. When Joshi's party was in power, I don't remember his party doing anything to bring black money back…'

Joshi: 'That was because we never allowed black money to get out of the country.'

Renu: 'Or is it because under your rule GDP was so low that no one had any money to eat, let alone put it in a bank account in Switzerland. Our government has at least delivered an 8% growth rate.'

Joshi: 'Your government has also delivered an 80% rate of corruption. Why is the government keeping silent on who issued Notco the sucking license. Agreed Notco has a sucking patent but a public sector company could have done the same sucking in a much safer way without endangering the lives of the people of Rikhitpur.'

Guha: 'All of this would not be happening if we had built a factory on the moon.'

Prof. Roberts: 'Hold on, I'm confused…'

Arnab: 'Let's go now to our chattering monkey. MONKEY! What do you think?'

Monkey: 'kikikikikikikijkiikikikikik.'

Arnab: 'Oh great! The monkey is showing his teeth and is now urinating in his cage.'

Joshi: 'Prime Minister should resign…'

Choudhry: 'The monkey is still more well behaved than the opposition in Parliament…'

Arnab: 'Let me now bring in Mallika into the debate. She's been waiting for over twenty minutes to say something irrelevant and totally pointless. Mallika, what do you think? Who is right and who's wrong in this situation?'

Mallika: 'I think ours is a great country…'

Arnab: 'INDEED! India is great. Finally there's something we can agree on. India is a great country. The greatest country on the planet and butt cancer or no butt cancer, no one can stop us.'

Mallika: 'Let me complete…'

Arnab: 'We'll be back after a quick break folks with our next debate—Is the National hair council of India's move to rename beards and moustaches as "facial accessories" seen as a case of caste-based, gender discriminatory, communal politics and if not, then why not? We'll be right back!'

The theme music cut in for 5 seconds and moved to the ad break. Arnab approached me as I stepped down from the stage, ready to leave.

'I'm sorry you couldn't say more. We have to limit our time. Hope you were happy we at least covered the main issues.'

THE TIMES NOW DEBATE
INDIAN BUSINESS PRACTICES – FAIR OR CORRUPT
YOU DECIDE
WHO IS RESPONSIBLE FOR NOTCO SITUATION
PARTICIPATE! We really care about your opinion.
Tweet with #NOTCOGATE—YOUR OPINION MATTERS!

'Definitely dude. Building a factory on the moon will solve all our problems. Though, you did forget to cover the most important issue.'

'What's that?'

'You forgot to debate the point of having eleven people yack away on complicated issues for just a few minutes, night after night. Do you realistically expect a reality show...err...a news debate to be a meaningful solution to our country's problems?'

Arnab's beady eyes flickered. 'But all the channels are doing it.'

'Maybe that's the problem.'

Before he could process the full impact of my barb, I reminded him, 'You better get back to the desk dude. The break is about to end.'

'Oops, thanks for reminding me Sir. I'll talk to you later if you don't mind. Also let's have a TV debate about what you just said about the media debating issues. We'll do a serious debate with only 8 panelists instead of 11,' and saying so he rushed back and I rushed out with my bodyguards in tow. The young intern escorted me to the lift. I thanked the boy, gave him my autograph, and left.

Few minutes later, I decided to meet Ramesh at the *Blue Jasmine*—a 7-star luxury hotel. I was famished and a good meal at their restaurant was just what I needed after the mindfu*k at the studio.

We arrived a few minutes later. Ramesh was already inside. I pulled up the chair across from him, sat down, and called the waiter.

'Roti, paneer makhani, and sweet lassi please.'

'I'll have a cutlet,' said Ramesh. The waiter sped off.

'Nice debate!' Ramesh lit up mischievously as I painfully looked at him in the soft orange glow of the overhanging table lamp.

'Shut up.'

'It wasn't that bad yaar. You did okay.'

'I always do okay. I am the best. I am going to start my own TV show in which I will interview myself. This is the only way I can speak all I want without having to say "Let me complete".'

'Dude! You already have four shows on your own channel—Jhun TV. "Jhunjhunwala knows best", "Jhunjhunwala is awesome", "Jhunjhunwala hunts and violently kills annoying MTV Roadie contestants", and "Jhunjhunwala's highway on Jhunjhunwala's plate". Now you wanna start a news show as well?'

'I don't know why I don't have a news show!' I complained. 'I mean it makes so much sense to have a news bulletin informing my devotees about my life. Even Baba Yogdev has Aastha TV to cater to his followers. Manmohan Singh has DD News.'

'Shut up!' Ramesh sneered. 'So when is the Notco exit?'

'Still working on it. Have directed the staff to sell Notco in small bunches. I don't want Stinker to know I am exiting Notco.'

SEBI notifies the public the moment anyone sells or buys more than 1% in a company. It's the law. I held a 15% stake in Notco and I wanted to exit it, which means I needed to sell it all off, though Ramesh and the rest of the world thought I should hold on because the business of Nothing was lucrative, as evidenced by the lakhs of empty boxes Ramakant was selling to idiot buyers.

Usually, when I plan to exit a company, I do so over a period of weeks or months. I reduce my stake till it eventually reaches zero. The problem with reducing Notco was that there was no way I could dump the company without word getting around that I was dumping it. I am way, way too important for my actions to go unnoticed. If a single hair were to fall from my scalp right now, it would become breaking news for the rest of the month.

If word got around that I was selling Notco over a period of days, Stinker and the bear cartel—who are basically a bunch of bear traders who work together to drive the price of a stock down—would get wind of it and attack. Let me explain.

Long after the Harshad Mehta scam was another scam headed by a bull named Ketan Parekh in 2001. Stinker was ruthless with

Parekh. KP, as he was called, had a huge bank backing his every move. When a bank backs you, you have enough money to buy whatever stock you want and in huge quantities. That's exactly what he did. It's like shopping with a credit card which has no spending limit or as Paris Hilton calls it, *'Asking Daddy for money'*.

KP started buying stocks in bulk. He bought so many of them in such huge numbers that their supply started to dwindle. That's when the rest of the market started noticing. The very act of his buying was driving the price up because the shares were becoming rarer by the day. Demand and supply.

Once the prices shot up because KP was buying them, people started to think it would rise higher. The paid experts on TV would all attest to this 'high growth' story like chattering monkeys creating enough public opinion for an average common man to also put his money into this stock. That's when KP sold off his stake at two or three times the price of his buying. A bloody scam. He was the reason prices were rising and he had engineered it to exit the moment they rose higher because people thought they'd rise even higher!

Over a course of few days, he would exit the company. The rally would run out of steam and people would see the value of their investments plummet. They were left high and dry while KP was roaming high and mighty.

Stinker got wind of KP's scheme. He mobilized every bear on the market to attack KP. The next time KP zeroed in on a stock, Stinker was waiting. KP bought shares of a company but for every one share KP bought, Stinker and his cronies sold 2 or 3. As a result the price of the share never rose. In fact, because supply was increasing, the price started to fall. KP had no idea he was in a bear trap, so he borrowed more money from his bank which sought more customer deposits to provide him the cash.

Finally, the bank ran out of money and KP ran out of the cash he needed to create a rally, all because Stinker was selling more shares than KP was buying. Selling, unlike buying, does not require you to put money down beforehand. It was the scam in reverse, a scam within a scam like that *Inception* movie no one understands.

This is what Stinker would do if he found out I was dumping Notco shares. He was under the impression that I was driving up the price of Notco by buying shares. He had accused my integrity by insinuating I was scamming. Unfortunately, he wasn't the only one. SEBI had formed a committee to look into the rise of Notco shares. If there was even a hint of my name, the media would be all over it like hungry hyenas on a lamb.

I could picture the headlines—'Investor Scams Market', 'God Turns Devil', 'Big Bull Bullies Market'. Oh the sheer wordplay of the headlines would kill me. Worse, I'd have to give a million interviews to clear my name. I'd have to even return to Arnab's show…what! NOOOOOOOOOO!

Most importantly, I wasn't going to lose to Stinker. It would mean the end of the bull reign. The other bulls would be leaderless. Common people on the street would live in a market era of gloom and shadow. A world where their investments would never give them bountiful returns!

'How's the food?' asked Ramesh as I popped back into reality.

'It's good. Let's leave in five minutes. Can you please tell him to get the bill please?' I said as I popped one last piece of roti into my mouth.'

'Sure.'

Popping a hajmola, I sat quietly as Ramesh let out a squeal.

'What happened?'

'Shit man! The bill is 35,000 bucks.'

'Must be a typo. Send it back.'

Ramesh motioned to the waiter who ambled over readily.

'How can I help you Sir?' he asked.

Pointing to the bill Ramesh raised it up towards the waiter's face 'This bill says its 35,000 rupees. I think there's a mistake'

'No mistake Sir. It is 35,000 rupees.'

'But we had only 19 rotis, 4 cutlets, 1 paneer makhani, a mausambi juice, and a lassi!' I said. 'And Ramesh had just 2 cutlets!'

The waiter replied 'Yes Sir. One roti is 1000 rupees. Paneer makhani costs 10,000, a plate of cutlets is 5000, mausambi juice is 3500, and chocolate milkshake is 4,500. Local taxes, VAT, and service tax extra.'

'Please go fetch your manager.'

Ramesh scanned over the bill for the umpteenth time wearily and said, 'Let's just pay and leave yaar. You're a freakin' multi billionaire. Why are you even concerned over a paltry sum like this?'

Ramesh's question surprised me. Chewing the last bit of Hajmola I replied, 'Ramesh, the stock market has taught me a very important thing and that is the power of valuation. Never pay for a share more than its value unless it's going to be worth more in the future. It's the same here. I could pay even 35 million instead of 35,000 for this meal if it was worth it. I eat the same roti on the street for 30 rupees made with the same ingredients and having the same taste, maybe even better than this.'

'True.'

'If the ingredients and labour that went into making this roti cost no more than 25 rupees then why should we pay 500 times its value. That's like buying a share at 500 times its normal value! I'd never do that.'

The manager, a conciergish looking dude who looked a lot like Ramakant minus the flashy embellishments, of course, appeared. A name tag pinned to his chest spelt 'Angelo'.

'Good evening Sir. My waiter said you wanted to discuss the bill with me,' Angelo smiled as the waiter stood next to him.

'Yeah. I only want to know why these dishes cost so much.'

'Did you not like them Sir?'

'Of course I did. But why does a roti cost 1000 bucks? And why does the paneer makhani cost 10,000? Have you used some special ingredients?'

'Yes Sir. We make tandoori zaika lahori roti with farm fresh Mountain wheat.'

'So this roti is made in Lahore from wheat grown on mountains?'

'It's made here Sir but the recipe is lahori and the wheat is definitely farm fresh mountain wheat.'

Ramesh and I exchanged glances as I asked Angelo this time, 'Which mountain?'

'Excuse me sir?'

'Kaunsa mountain bhai? Roti ke liye gehu kaunse pahaad se laate hain aap?'

'I...I don't know Sir,' mumbled Angelo as the waiter blinked. The fact that I was insisting to know which projected landmass had borne the agrarian produce which had gone into making my stomach heavier and my wallet lighter left the dynamic duo in a mound of doubt.

'Please can I get back to you on that, Sir? I will find out which mountain,' Angelo blinked haplessly.

I let him off the cliff...err...hook and asked him, 'OKAY, tell me why the paneer makhani costs 10,000 rupees.'

'Because we boil the paneer in specially imported Swiss Alpine aqua.'

'Aqua? You mean water?'

'Yes Sir, water.'

'So you use swiss water to boil this?'

'Yes Sir. It's packaged cooking water specially imported from Switzerland.'

'What's so special about it?'

'About the water you mean?'

'Yes.'

'The water is rich and flavourless. Perfectly neutral.'

'So basically its water which tastes like water?' Ramesh asked.

'Umm...yes.'

Ramesh chuckled under his breath. The waiter was confused.

'Please swipe my card and get me a bowl of tomato sauce,' I said giving Angelo my card.

'With pleasure Sir.' Angelo rushed off with my credit card and the waiter rushed off to get me the sauce.

A minute later, a bowl of red tomato sauce gleamed at me from the table surface. The waiter was now taking some other order. A guest at the next table was talking rather loudly, 'Saffronized pathan cauliflower and rose pakodas,' he screamed. It reminded me of Arnab. Grrr…

Angelo returned with my card. As he walked toward me, I opened my wallet, took out a crisp 1000 rupee note, dipped it in the tomato sauce and put it in my mouth. Slowly, rhythmically, like a donkey I started to chew down the paper as the taste of tomato and banknote slipped into my mouth.

'Sir! What are you doing?' an astonished Angelo asked. 'Nothing yaar. Just eating,' I answered very calmly as I continued to chew.

'I mean why are you eating a thousand rupee note?!'

'I'm hungry.'

'But why are you eating currency notes, sir? The kitchen is still open! I can get you anything you want!'

Ramesh was also a bit taken aback. I reopened the wallet, took out a five hundred rupee note, and placed it squarely onto another crisp 1000 rupee note. Folding them both like a cheese slice between two slices of bread, I shook a little salt from the shaker onto the rupee sandwich, dipped it in the sauce, and started munching.

Our waiter had reappeared. The sudden spike in Angelo's voice had also attracted two other waiters. They were awestruck as I quietly munched away on the currency notes.

'Sir! Please. Let me get you something. Anything!' pleaded Angelo unable to fathom my well-noted diet.

'Don't worry yaar. Instead of eating a few more thousand rupee rotis, I've decided to eat 1000 rupees itself. Ah delicious!' I exclaimed.

Quite annoyed Ramesh blurted, 'SAALA NAUTANKI! Khade khade drama karta hai!'

A bewildered Angelo scratched his head as the waiters stood next to him with jaws dropped as I proceeded to dip and digest another 500 rupee note.

'You've proved your point. Let's go now,' Ramesh authoritatively got up and dragged me towards the door by the collar.

Angelo sighed and said, 'Err...err...I'm sorry sir but you still need to pay the bill. Unfortunately your credit card broke the machine.'

'What?!'exclaimed Ramesh. 'What the hell are you doing, mote?'

Eh! Don't call me mote, you jerk. I'm not a mote. I'm just blessed with extraordinary thickness!' I yelled after catching a glimpse of the card in Angelo's hand. 'I think I gave Mr Angelo here my Visa gold credit card. It's made of actual gold. It must have broken the machine.'

'Moron!' an exasperated Ramesh panted.

'Don't blame me! The visa company gave it to me.'

'You aren't supposed to use it, dumbass. It's just for show!'

'How was I supposed to know that?'

'By reading this, you dick!' Ramesh pointed to an inscription on the card still in Angelo's hand, 'THIS GOLD CREDIT CARD IS ONLY FOR SHOW. PLEASE DON'T USE IT LIKE AN ORDINARY CREDIT CARD.'

'Oh!' I coyly grunted as Angelo and his waiters stood by wondering to high heavens just what the bloody hell was going on.

'Anyway, enough of your drama for today,' Ramesh proclaimed as he continued to drag me out. 'Mr Angelo, please charge it to my card and give me the bill. We'll be in the lobby.'

Ramesh stormed out pulling me by the ear. Angelo disappeared with Ramesh's card as we made our way to the lobby.

As we waited for Ramesh's card to be returned, I burped loudly. A few hundred rupee notes fell out. My stomach was burping change.

RIKHITPUR FACTORY

'Jhunjhunwala bhai, welcome! Let me introduce you to stage 2 in the Nothing revolution—NOTCO'S VERY OWN CONSUMER PRODUCTS DIVISION!'

A grey warehouse, bigger than a football field, loomed eerily behind Ramakant. His funnel crown tingled under the 11am sun. A gentle breeze nudged the brown fur coat hugging him. The golden chains and rings of course sparkled away. I alighted from the chopper and made my way to him, shielding my eyes as the flurry of the jet's wings viciously powder-coated me with dry sand. I hurried through the dust and the smoke and halted in front of an amused Ramakant.

The jewellery shop began to talk as the sound of the plane receded in the background. 'This is the world's largest Nothing processing factory. A 35-acre facility with state-of-the-art funnel sucking technology to absorb, refine, package, and transport Nothing to the everyday consumer. What a beauty! Marvellous.'

I had decided to head down to Rikhitpur to see and experience the ground reality for myself. Last night's debate and last morning's golf course confrontation was still ringing in my head. I had flown in to see if the situation was as bad as it was being made out to be.

My jet had landed on a huge, dusty open area in front of the warehouse. A stone compound wall enclosed the entire facility, making the Notco factory appear like a fortified adda run by crime master Gogo that could only be destroyed by the combined super team of Agent Vinod, Shahid Kapoor, Nana Patekar, John Abraham, Dharmendra, and their kidnapped love interests aka India's Avengers aka the *Badla lene wale Mahapurush*.

As I surveyed the scene looking for a hole for Shahid Kapoor to crawl out off and out-dance the bad guys into submission, Shastri explained, 'Please don't mind if you find me groggy. I've just arrived this morning from South America after negotiating a supplier deal with an Argentinean firm. We will start supplying Nothing to them from next week. When I heard you were coming here, I decided to fly in as well so I could personally introduce you to our biggest factory. We are here in the middle of Nowhere. I hope you enjoy it.'

Rikhitpur was about 250 kilometres from home. I had flown here by Air Jhunjhunwala—my private jet service. Like Shastri, I was also groggy since I had to leave at daybreak. Another jet, smaller and less grandiose than mine (obviously), stood next to the warehouse on my far right.

'Is that yours?' I asked Ramakant, pointing to the aircraft.

'Yes Sir! I've rented this one. Soon, I will buy my own jet just like you! Businessmen like us must be ready to fly anytime,' he replied.

Ramakant looked like he was intent on telling me more about his rented plane. I was uninterested and jumped right onto the issue at hand. I asked grimly, 'So tell me Ramakant, did you watch last night's newshour debate? How long have you known the people here have been getting cancer and why didn't you tell me sooner?'

'Jhunjhunwala bhai, it's all nonsense!' he insisted with the air of a self-assured defence lawyer. 'The people in this area have been getting cancer for years now. It's hereditary. They are genetically prone to getting butt cancer because their immune systems have been weak for generations. Also, the water in this area is polluted, it is carcinogenic. The bloody government doesn't want to take any responsibility! Worse, they want to dump their problems on us. They want us to bear the medical costs of these people. That's why they are doing all this drama! Otherwise how can Nothing cause cancer? Tell me! Nothing is in fact being approved for cancer treatment from next month by the United States Food and Drug Admininistration. It isn't public yet, that's why I am keeping quiet. Bloody government bastards!'

'But the Environment Ministry has said in its notice that they tested the water in this area and haven't found any carcinogenic substances in it.'

'Again Jhunjhunwala bhai they are lying. Why do you worry? We will prove it in court that they are lying. So what if they tested the water? For every test they have done, I can show you ten tests to say the exact opposite thing. If they say they tested the water and found cancer we will say we tested the water and found no cancer. The water got cancer because of them! We will, in fact, prove that the water become cancerous *because* they tested it. They put the cancer in the water. *Their test causes cancer*, not the water or my factory. We will prove this!'

'Eh! The water got cancer?'

'Yes, because of them.'

'What is the truth?' I asked impatiently as sweat soaked through his fur coat. 'Has this factory here been responsible for the cancer of the people in this area? Come on yaar. The media is going to town on this. As it is we are being sued on the patent issue. Doesn't look good for the company.'

'Don't worry, Jhunjhunwalaji. Everything will be fine. This is just the government taking advantage of Notco's success. It is obvious! People were getting cancer here even before Notco started building a factory in this area. I swear! We will prove it in court!'

'Who are those people?' I asked pointing to a crowd of about 30 standing outside the gate.

Removing his glasses and wiping the sweat off them with a white handkerchief, Ramakant replied, 'They are jobless protestors from some local NGO here in Rikhitpur. They are on a protest demanding we shut down the factory. As if! I can't just shut down 35 acres in one day and exit just like that. Idiots! Ajay Agarwal has paid them to protest outside my factories under the garb of the cancer issue.'

I shouted to a burly protestor standing at the head of the gate 'OYE! WHY DON'T YOU FELLOWS LEAVE FROM HERE?'

He shouted back, 'WE ARE PROFESSIONAL RIOTERS! WE WON'T GO TILL THE POLICE COMES AND DOES LATHI CHARGE ON US.'

'YOU WANT A LATHI CHARGE?'

'JI, EK DIN ANDOLAN KA PAYMENT LIYA HAI,KUCH TOH DIKHANA PADEGA, RIOT MEIN RECEIPT NAHIN HOTI. JAB TAK BAITHNE KI JAGAH BANDAR KI TASHREEF KI TARAH LAL–LAL NA HO JAYE, TAB TAK HUMEIN PAISA NAHIN MILEGA!'

'EH!'

'ALSO, PERSONALLY I DON'T GET THAT FEELING OF "JOB WELL DONE" UNLESS POLICE BEATS THE SHIT OUT OF ME! I LOVE LATHI CHARGE!'

Stumped, I tried to make my mutterings comprehensible. Ramakant hollered, 'Kameena haraamkhor…Ajay Agarwal. Usi ne in logon ko yahaan pe beja hai!'

'How do you know this?'

'Because I know Ajay. When we were selling agarbattis, I could smell the treachery on him. He is fully capable of pulling a stunt like this.'

'So you are speculating.'

'No, I am commenting without proof.'

'That is speculation.'

'I disagree. If anything, it is journalism.'

I paused and began to grit my teeth in frustration. Sensing the apparent animosity, Ramakant quickly reassured me, 'But I will prove it in the court no that he *is* motivating these protesters. Why you worry, Jhunjhunwala bhai?'

'Whatever dude,' I said peeved off as the sun beat down mercilessly.

Sensing that he had to cool the situation, Shastri said, 'Anyway, please come inside Jhunjhunwala bhai. Let me take you on a tour of the factory and introduce you to Notco's line of consumer products. It's very exciting! This will easily triple our profits, quadruple our growth, quintuple our manpower, and sextuple our production.'

'Your knowledge of incremental numerical elemental *tuples* is amazing!' I said in genuine amazement but immediately remembered the purpose of my visit. 'However, I am here to see some of the cancer patients, Ramakant. I will see this factory later.'

'Jhunjhunwala bhai, can you ever go to Agra and not see the Taj Mahal? You are at the entrance of Mecca here; the holy of holies lies just beyond. Why don't you visit the patients on your way back? Come with me! I insist!' Ramakant muttered as he pulled on my sleeve, catching me off balance, and yanked me suddenly into the warehouse with me whining all the way. 'Oye, get your hands off me! Now! You are molesting me! I'm a married man!'

Soon, we were inside. Feeling glad I was no longer in his death grip, I recomposed myself as Ramakant screamed to a worker, 'Bhai saab ke liye thanda laana!'. A bright yellow shiny hummer stood to my left and yonder was Notco's production facility. An insanely large floor this was. Somewhere in the middle was a huge machine with metallic tubes protruding out like an octopus. Glued to this black circular contraption was a much bigger, probably three times bigger blue orb. The whole thing looked like an igloo with metallic tubes pouring out of the entrance.

On top of the blue orb was a slit for the roof. I asked Ramakant, 'What's the hole in the roof for?' pointing at the gap as if it were a star in the night sky.

'That's where the funnel attaches to the machine, Jhunjhunwala bhai.'

'So there's a motor in the blue thing?'

'Yes. The blue circular structure is the main motor. It's the one sucking the Nothing. The black unit is the refinery. Impure Nothing is sucked into the blue machine from where it's transferred to the black machine which is fitted with millions upon millions of microfibres which trap the dirt and pollutants. Clean Nothing then comes out of those tubes from where the packaging begins.'

I stared closely, zooming onto a setup of conveyor belts. Each tube from the igloo was *'filling'* neatly lined up empty boxes with Nothing. That's a weird thing to say but it's the only way to describe it.

Factory workers dressed in a blue cotton shirt and pair of trousers stood beside the moving belts, guiding the boxes towards a sealing machine with their gloved hands. Once the mechanical robotic arm had sealed off the opening, another set of workers stacked the 'filled' boxes one on top of the other, waiting for a forklift to transport them to a loading dock nearby. From here, they would be transported into the hands of suppliers who'd eventually ensure its distribution into the friendly neighborhood retail shop.

As I observed the strange set of events, one worker ran towards us frantically, stopped in front of Ramakant, and blurted, 'Sir, this product is broken. What do we do?' The man gripped the air as if holding something, clutching the emptiness between his hands, an invisible 'item', as though his life depended on it.

Ramakant thrust his left hand into the empty space between the guy's hands, picked up the Nothing, and lifted it over his head. I tilted my head upwards as did Ramakant, peering at whatever he seemed to be holding. Inspecting it in an expert-like fashion, Ramakant then commanded, 'Yes it is broken, dispose it off', the worker *'received'* it and ran off eagerly to a nearby dustbin as I stood there scratching my head in complete and utter bamboozlement.

Yes, it is broken, dispose it off.
NOTCO nothing handle with care

'We never deliver defective merchandise to our customers. Quality is supreme,' puffed Shastri as the worker 'dropped' the Nothing into the bin.

'How did you know it was broken?' I asked trying to decode the mystery. 'I couldn't see anything. I mean I can't see anything anyway! How could you see something broken in something which can't be seen.'

Shastri smiled and explained, 'Jhunjhunwala bhai,when you dedicate your life to Nothing, you sort of become experienced to every nuance. I can simply FEEL if Nothing is broken, damaged, or needs to be replaced straight away. Even these workers are gaining experience in feeling Nothing. The more they work here the more they feel.'

'BUT! YOU...COULDN'T HAVE...'

'Jhunjhunwala bhai, why you worry?' he said trying to comfort me as though I was the only kid in class who hadn't understood the lesson while everyone else had moved on to the next chapter. Sensing my exasperation, he implored, 'Just relax. Come, let me introduce you to my son Ashok.'

Ramakant screamed 'Ashok' as I remembered the same-named intern at the studio who put the mic on me last night. A scrawny looking boy dressed in a black T-Shirt and a pair of jeans, looking barely fifteen, waded towards us from somewhere near one of the conveyor belts.

'Yes daddy!' he greeted Shastri as he stopped in front of us.

'Ashok, I want you to meet someone very special. This is Dr Sir Sri Sri Professor Godfather Mr Jhunjhunwala. He is the baadshah of the stock market. Say hello to him,' instructed Ramakant.

The boy, enamoured like everyone else at my staggering reputation, exclaimed, 'Hello uncle!'

'Don't call me uncle yaar! Call me Sir.'

'Oops! Hello Sir!'

'Hello Ashok. So what do you want to do when you grow up?' I asked.

'I am planning to do my MBA.'

'Why?'

'It will help in taking care of Notco after I graduate. My father has given me a 5% stake in the company. So I am easily worth about 100-200 million dollars. I think at my age I should equip myself with the skills needed to run a multi-billion dollar operation like Notco. I want to help my father, so I am joining Wharton Business School next year.'

'Very good, young man! Your father must be proud of you!'

Ramakant beamed, 'I am, Jhunjhunwala bhai! You see that yellow Hummer there? I am gifting it to him for his birthday next week.'

'Nice. You have a wonderful sense of hummer…'

'But daddy!' Ashok pleaded. 'Can't I take it out now only? Please! I can't wait one whole week. It's so unfair!'

'Don't worry beta, you can have it next week!'

'But all my friends have their own Hummers. I feel so left out driving just a dabba Mahindra Scorpio!'

'How old are you Ashok? Do you have a license?' I asked.

The beaming father hummed, 'Ah! He turns 16 next week. He doesn't have a license but no problem, Ashok is a very good driver. He drives my Ferrari even better than me!'

'Papa please! Give me the Hummer no! I'll drive only for a little! It'll look so good when I drive in it to the Young Achiever's party tomorrow with my good friends Virat Kohli, Saina Nehwal, and Kangna Ranaut! Please! Please!'

Ramakant began to ponder. Sensing his father was tilting, the boy pleaded even more, 'Please daddy! After the party we are all going to Pankaj Advani's house to play snooker! Please daddy! Even Yo Yo Honey Singh and Mika Singh will be there to sing the soundtrack of *Singh is King*! Please daddy! Let me take the Hummer, no!'

Ramakant broke with an eager sigh and shuffled into his coat and brought out a pair of keys, 'I can't say no to you. Take it.'

'Yay! Thank you daddy! I love you! Yay!'

'Oh, but wait beta. Before you go don't forget to take this also…'

Ramakant slid his hands once again into the fur, his chains jangling away as he rattled his hands from one side to another. The boy stood distracted, looking on with anticipation wondering what his father was so eager to give him.

'Dude. Don't shake so much. The funnel is falling down,' I implored.

'Dammit!' Shastri yelled as he adjusted the funnel back into position. 'I need a strap for this crown! Ah! Found it.'

Ramakant pulled out a bundle of folded papers from his coat pocket. 'Take this beta. This is an anticipatory bail signed by a local magistrate in case you run over someone walking on the road or a family of below poverty line people sleeping on the pavement. If the police come to arrest you, just show this to them.'

'WOW! THIS IS SO COOL!' the boy cheered.

'Yes. And this is a list of all policemen in every police station in a 50 kilometre radius who know me. Just ask for them and tell them you are my son. They will make sure they take care of you.'

'Dad! You rock!'

'Take this also,' said Ramakant fiddling with his phone. 'It's my lawyer's number. His personal cell phone, home telephone, and office telephone. I am forwarding them all. Also his mistresses home telephone in case he isn't at home with his wife. And this is my media advisor's phone. He will talk to the TV people in case there's a problem. But remember Ashok, this is for emergency use only. Don't drink and drive.'

Ashok was jubilant. Thrilled with the many gifts the Czar of Nothing had bestowed on him, he looked at his father with gratitude. 'I love you daddy! This is the greatest birthday gift ever!'

'I love you too son! Now go. I have important things to discuss with Jhunjhunwala Sir. Don't forget to take your anticipatory bail.'

'I won't,' said the boy as he rolled the papers tight like his father's nemesis—the lawyer Pankaj Mishra. 'Love you daddy. Bye Jhunjhunwala Sir!'

'Bye' I said as Shastri smiled contentedly at his son.

'This country, Jhunjhunwala bhai, is going to dogs. The roads are so small and full of potholes. Bloody population expansion, no place for people to live. They simply come and sleep on the pavements. If young people like Ashok run them over by mistake, this bloody media also creates so much ruckus! Chee, chee, chee! That is why we have to take precautions. When I imported this Hummer as a gift for his 16th birthday, that day itself I told my lawyer to get an anticipatory bail done in my son's name.'

Waving at Ashok who had started the Hummer, Ramakant continued as a few workers looked distractedly at the car. 'Your lawyer Ratmalani on the other hand, he really is a genius. He once represented an actor who ran over and killed four people in a drunken state.'

'So why is he a genius?'

'Because he sued the families of those four pavement dwellers for causing irreparable damage to the actor's car.'

'Wow,' I said, unaware of this particular feather in my lawyer's cap.

'Yes. He also sued the alcohol company and proved in court that their drink was far too strong and made the actor lose control. That Ratmalani is a legend!'

'I know,' I said, uninterested in listening about Ratmalani's achievements. Anyway, don't you think it's a little weird giving a hummer to a 15-year-old?'

'You think I should have given him a Bentley?'

'No, I meant isn't he young to drive?'

'But next week he'll turn 16 na! Moreover, things are changing so fast today. Youth is getting more restless. But in a certain sense you are right. That's why I have only given him one anticipatory bail. If he is involved in another accident then he has to spend at least 3 days in lockup. I can't arrange for bail over and over again. That's just bad parenting,' Ramakant declared.

Nodding lightly, I sarcastically pouted and said, 'I agree.'

The Hummer vroomed away. The powerful engine despite its ferocity was a drop in the ocean of noise compared to the suction motor below the roof funnel. The workers were stacking boxes, clearing boxes, holding the Nothing, passing the Nothing and even *throwing* the Nothing as they moved across the floor. I wondered how could so many people be this oblivious? Were they all just pretending? Clasping and maneuvering this invisible emptiness as though it were a real thing because they were being paid to 'act' or did they actually feel something? And if they did, then why didn't I?!!

The assembly line operations were meticulously panned out. Each worker was like a drone bee. Each drone had a function. Many drones came together to form a hive. An entire hive in the pursuit of profit.

Ramakant tapped my shoulder as I observed, lost in thought. 'Jhunjhunwala bhai, please come this way!' We sat on a factory vehicle which took us to the far right of the factory. A small yet wide entrance beckoned. This part was a lot quieter than the main factory floor.

I relaxed my eyes and alighted. As I adjusted my frames, I saw a…WAIT, NO WAY! This can't be true!

It was a supermarket! Aisle after aisle of neatly stacked items hanging under boards titled 'Home Needs', 'Dairy and Milk', 'Electronics', 'Grooming', 'Food' and many more, just like a regular supermarket. A single cashier's counter stood unmanned with a computer and a bar-code reader as I wondered if the opening I had come through was Alice's rabbit hole.

Surprisingly or…err…unsurprisingly, the supermarket was deserted. There were no customers in sight. Just kilometre long aisles stocked with items but no salesmen, no cashiers and no customers! The whole place looked like a ghost town.

'Jhunjhunwala bhai! Meet Frank Jones, the world's number one branding and marketing advisor,' squeaked Ramakant. I shifted my face from the supermarket as Ramakant's dentures flashed brighter than the diamond rimmed glasses on his eyes. To my right stood a foreigner, a fellow in his 40s, dressed in a grey suit and red tie. Smiling widely, he outstretched his hand.

I shook it, surprised he had popped up seemingly from thin air and crept up on me.

Ushering him forward, Shastri boasted, 'This guy is the genius behind rebranding pencils as "Writing Sticks" in Japan. He generated 100 million dollars in revenue just from that'.

'It's a pleasure to meet you Sir!' the man said in an American accent.

'I'm sorry I didn't catch your name.'

'It's Frank. Frank Jones. Mr Shastri here has told me all about you! We weren't expecting you today, but we're prepared to give you a tour of our new products anyway! Please join me!'

I had travelled 250.2 kilometres. 250 km by Air Jhunjhunwala and walked 200 metres by foot in this factory. For someone with awesomitis, I had already walked more than the medically cleared limit. Yet another example of my staggering physical endurance. However, out of respect for the doctor at JK, I asked, 'Hmm. Will this involve walking?'

'Yes. A considerable bit. It's a multi-acre facility and the supermarket alone is about 4 acres,' Jones replied. His face had become tanned under the Indian sun. I observed the streaks of white generously running through his scalp.

'I can't walk that much!' I complained.

'We'll get a vehicle for you Mr Jhunjhunwala. Don't worry.'

'Don't bother. I'll get my jetpack.'

HELL YEAH! I'm one of the few people in the world with his very own jetpack. Indra Nooyi from Pepsi has a similar jetpack but mine is bigger than hers. It's an XPKT 9000S with phosphorus thrusters! A machine strapped to your back, light as a feather, as quiet as a water cooler yet powerful enough to lift an entire army of elephants or pre-weight loss Adnan Samis into outer space. Also, it costs a million dollars. 3,50,000 dollars more if you get the accessories. Mine cost an additional 40,000 dollars as I paid to get my initials laser embossed on the nitro-propane fuel boosters.

I quickly relayed the instruction to Captain Topinath who promptly fetched the jetpack from the private jet and onto a factory vehicle. When he arrived and strapped it to me like an enthusiastic mother fitting her child's school bag, Ramakant's jaw dropped to the ground. Anyone can buy a Hummer but to get a jetpack…now that's STYLE.

'Chalo bhai. Show me jaldi,' I said adjusting the buckles and giving them one last tug before liftoff. 'I have to see the cancer patients also.'

The jetpack flared up and fumes sprang out accompanied by a burning noise. The plume tingled Frank Jones' nostrils as the poor dude started coughing.

'Easy there Mr Jones. This is nothing compared to the smoke from an autorickshaw running on kerosene. I am sure you will experience it at least hundreds of times as you experience Indian culture on the roads,' I said raising my voice as Jones tried to unsuccessfully ignore the ignominious fumes from the jetpack's ignition.

'Now then my friend, tell me why a well-dressed man such as yourself is stuck, stark in the middle of nowhere in a sleepy little village in western India.'

'Mr Jones is the expert among experts,' Ramakant answered as Jones coughed into a handkerchief. 'There isn't a finer mind when it comes to product packaging and branding than his in the whole world. He has graciously accepted my offer of working as a consultant with us on our consumer products division.'

'Tell me, Ramakant, why is there a supermarket in this factory?' I asked shifting my attention from Jones who was trying to get his breath back. 'This thing looks more out of place than L.K. Advani at a rap concert.'

Ramakant said unflinchingly, 'Because Jhunjhunwala bhai, I don't want the workers to forget their end goal and that is to enhance

NOTCO-Nothing
SALE
DISCOUNT DISCOUNT
NOTCO
40% off
JJ
Ice Cream
Shampoo

the customer's quality of life by providing him a superior product made by Notco which can be bought right in the supermarket or the local kirana grocery store! That's why they must never lose sight of what it is we are trying to create. Our company vision. Our ultimate goal. That's why I have built this supermarket right in my factory premises, so that every single day when these people come here to work, when they pass by it, they are influenced—just as Frank is—to believe in the power of Nothing. To submit to the superiority of a Notco product and dedicate their lives to making it with their heart and soul!'

Floating in the air and clutching the controls, I readied myself for Ramakant's elucidation. I had grown so accustomed with his long-winded speeches and explanations that I could almost sense them coming a mile away.

'Notco has started successfully selling bare Nothing to the people. We are earning good revenue thus far and have been paying off our debts as well. Obviously this has allowed us to take more debt to build more factories so that we can expand further.'

'Expand by taking more debt to build more factories to generate more revenue which will allow you to take further debt to expand?'

'Exactly'

'O…K…A…Y.'

'The next phase of growth is to enrich everyday products with Nothing. People will be able to experience their favourite goods and services *with* Nothing wherever they can! We will achieve this with strong production, solid distribution, and super marketing.'

'What do you mean by *"enrich"*?' I asked looking at Jones who seemed much better.

Shastri replied, 'Nothing is a very versatile product. It's like water. It can be used in anything. We've set up a 90,000 square feet innovation lab in Hyderabad which tests various products and how they can be combined with Nothing. I have hired the world's brightest PhDs and scientists to innovate new products for the public. They could have been working to find cures for AIDS and malaria, innovate hybrid seeds that can grow anywhere and end world hunger, find bacterial strains which can clean water at a millionth of the cost of the chemicals which do it, but instead they have dedicated their lives to innovating Nothing because this is more important in today's era. This is the power of Nothing. Also, as a wonderful employer, I pay them really well, and give them huge big offices with flat screen computers and mini bars. Notco has the best hiring practices in the country today!'

Shastri and Jones exchanged glances. Jones was still trying to come to terms with the fact that I was floating in space right above his head.

Looking up at me as we slowly moved the length of the aisles, Ramakant continued, 'Two of the scientists we hired—Dr Zahira Shah and Dr Vishwanath, have in fact just innovated a wonderful new product—NOTHING FLAVORED POTATO CHIPS!'

'Err...what?'

'You know, a potato chip—thin, wafery, crunchy, spicy, delicious! Made even more delicious by flavouring it with Nothing. It's the world's most delicious potato chip. Here, have a bite!' said Ramakant flippantly as he tossed a bag from one of the aisles to Jones.

Frank tore it open and held it up. The initial blast of aroma from the sealed packet promised a treat. I put my hand in and pulled out a chip.

'Nice! This is not bad,' I said crunching the chip.

'Yes it is fantastic. It is South American mango paprika Nothing flavor. We have introduced Notco chips in 5 different flavours from 5 different parts of the world—all made in India. We are competing directly with Lay's and Bingo. Since our chips are flavoured with Nothing, they taste better.'

'Hmmm...I am curious, how do you flavour something with Nothing?'

Jones replied, 'We use a technology called Nothing Molecular

Binding Technology or NMBT. With these chips we first make the chips then we leave the chips in a room full of Nothing. The Nothing molecules attach themselves to the chips and next morning voila! You get Nothing flavored chips. The good thing about NMBT is that it can be used to attach Nothing to almost anything.'

'By leaving the product in an empty room?'

'Not empty. *Full of nothing.*'

'Huh! How can you say that Nothing molecules are attaching themselves to these chips?' I asked experiencing a strange binding of nonsense and sense in my head.

'By taste. The chips taste better after leaving them in a room full of Nothing.'

'But...that must be because of some other reason! Not Nothing! There's no technology here!'

'It's there, Sir. NMBT is awesome. Even Lay's and Bingo are making mango paprika chips the same way, yet our chips are much better because they are flavoured with Nothing.'

'Yaar, dimaag mat khao,' I said sternly as Ramakant and Jones looked at each other.

Biting on a chip from the open packet, Shastri spoke spewing chip remnants all over Frank's boots. I was happy I was up in space and not in a place where fried potato projectiles launched ferociously from Shastri's mouth were landing on me.

'You yourself said its pretty good and this is only the beginning. We are currently selling 10 grams of chips at 50 rupees per packet. It costs us 5 bucks to make it with packaging included. We are netting a profit of 900% per packet.'

'And that's just phase 1 of our *grand chip strategy* or GCS. In phase two, we plan an increase of 50% per packet. This will lead to peaked consumer interest which will in turn lead to increased revenue,' Jones said, eager to join the conversation.

'So you are gonna be selling 15 grams of chips instead of 10 at 50 bucks?'

'No.'

'But you said you'd increase the quantity by 50%?'

'We are. This is where our innovation kicks in. *We are gonna be making the packet bigger.*'

Ramakant crunched on another chip and spoke as Frank stepped away, hoping to avoid falling on NMBT enhanced potato debris 'We make the packet 35% bigger and increase the quantity of air in the packet by 10%. So there will be a 35% air increase +10% packet increase + 5% chips increase. Ho gaya na 50% increase.'

'Hold on, so you're saying the exact increase in the chips is a mere 5%?'

'Precisely.'

'But...but...you said there'll be a 50% increase in quantity in phase two! But all you're doing is making the packet bigger and filling it with more air!'

Frank smiled and said triumphantly, *'We've been making the packet bigger for years now. That's innovation.'*

Ramakant continued, 'If we actually spend money on increasing just the quantity of chips alone, we suffer a significant loss in revenue because we need more potatoes to fry.'

'So why should we waste money on potatoes when we can make more money by making bigger packets and by filling it with more air?' Jones said wondering what the big deal was as the Indian and the American explained how best South American chips were to be sold.

'But that's false advertising. When you say 50% the customer believes that he is getting 50% more for the chips not for a bigger packet and definitely not for freakin air!'

Shastri insisted 'But Jhunjhunwalaji please understand no. We never specified to the customer that we are increasing the chips. He is assuming. We are letting him assume. His assuming is making us more money. What is the problem?'

'Errr...'

Sensing that I was once again getting exasperated, Shastri

courteously pushed forward, 'Don't worry, Jhunjhunwala bhai. Come let me show you a few more products.'

We moved through the aisles from the food section to the detergent and home needs section. Line after line of washing products lay in front of us. The strong smell of perfumed detergent and soap was mildly intoxicating. As I glided through the air, all I could think was that the next time I ate chips I had to make damn sure I was paying more for actual chips, not just bigger packets and air.

'This is our detergent powder,' Jones said pointing at a glossy 1 kilo packet neatly tucked on an aisle. 'It is a compound of sulphate. It's a powerful cleaner, has a hydrocarbon base, and is easy to prepare. Most importantly, it's cheap to make.'

'So is it a washing powder?'

'Yes Sir. It cleans.'

Shastri explained, 'In phase 1 we introduce it in the market. We'll give it some fancy shmancy tagline like Notco washing powder with 'Active bubble technology' or Notco surf with 'Action rubbing molecules' or SRS (stain removing system) or 'white microgranules'. The guys at force marketing under Frank will come up with something like that.'

Frank nodded.

'In phase 2 we will...'

'Make the packet bigger?' I interrupted.

'That only works with chips.' Frank emphasized, 'This is detergent so we can't make bigger packets but what we can do is change the colour of the packet. In phase 1 we will use a White colour packet. In phase 2 we will repackage it and use green or orange or blue or a combination of all three.'

'So a bunch of drivel and a change in the colour of the packet will be innovation?'

'We can also change the colour of the powder itself,' Shastri added, strolling like a king in the aisles. 'Basically it's the same powder doing the same job but because we change its colour or the colour of the packet, customers will think we are selling them a new product when we aren't!'

'So it's old wine in a new bottle.'

'Of course,' Jones said looking as if he were about to punish me for not knowing something that obvious 'Washing powders have not changed since they were invented in 1875. All that's changed are the packets they come on or the colours of the packets. Every company is selling the same powder under different names, different colours, and different prices. Let us also do the same thing and make money!'

'When we launch phase 2, we will increase prices. This will lead to higher growth,' Shastri declared. 'And in phase 3 we come up with more names like active Nothing molecules, white Nothing spreaders, dirt reversing Nothing particles, Nothing hydrogen power boosters etc. Every few months we introduce the same powder with a new tagline in a different coloured packet and run ads. We'll make crores this way!'

A young worker saluted us as we moved beyond the home care aisle and into the personal care section.

Waving his hands around, Ramakant began introducing another part of the supermarket. 'This is personal care. Everything from bathing soap to shampoo to fairness cream, hair dye, hair gel, toothpaste, toothbrush, shaving cream, sanitary napkins, cotton buds, cotton swabs, even condoms are here.'

'Head to toe products for men and women, all manufactured by Notco,' Frank added.

Looking at the two of them, as I oscillated my gaze from Shastri to Jones and back to Shastri, I asked, 'So what are you going to do now? Make the packets bigger and change its colour and spend millions doing that?'

Rightly sensing my attitude, Shastri answered, 'Sirji, I don't know why you are so against packaging tactics. Inn cola companiyon ko hi dekh lo. 50 saalon se cola nahin badla sirf bottle or colour badalte aaye hain. Naya cola chodiye, yeh log apna sara paisa sirf naya bottle banane mein lagate hain.'

'Hmm...'

'Take this toothpaste for example.' The bright blue box with glittering letters 'Notcodent' stared at me as Jones picked it off the aisle and gave it to Ramakant.

Both Jones and Shastri smiled first at each other and then at me as though they were advertising the toothpaste's wonderful ability.

Shastri explained, 'We'll start by saying it provides 24 hour round the clock germ protection.'

'Does it?'

'No.'

'Isn't that lying then?'

'Err...Let's just call it marketing.'

'But...'

'We need to tell people what they want to hear if we want to make money selling toothpaste. It's never true, it doesn't matter. They'll never sue us because the cost of suing us is significantly higher than the cost of toothpaste. Our courts have no time to test if the toothpaste protects 2 hours, 12 hours, or 24 hours. It's a toothpaste not a security guard.'

'But...but...'

'Few years ago, we had one toothpaste and one toothbrush. Aadmi ke mooh mein 32 daant hain, lekin market mein ab 300 toothpaste hain. Hum bhi usme shamil ho jaate hain. We have a 1000 different toothbrushes. We have toothbrushes which look like baseball bats and hockey sticks. Teeth still look the same so why are there so many different toothpastes and brushes?'

'I don't know,' I replied looking at Ramakant resigned to my fate. 'I guess I never really thought about toothpaste as much as you have.'

'Because people want variety, even if it's for something as mundane as removing stuck food particles from their mouth.

They need a story, we give it to them with these campaigns '24 hour protection', 'active salt', 'for sensitive gums', 'Whitening technology', etc, etc. We have an entire office in Chennai only to discover newer problems. Once you tell people there is a new problem—like their teeth aren't white enough or their breath isn't perfumed enough, they will then pay for a product which we have made to get rid of the problem they didn't even know was a problem! I love toothpaste.'

As I paused in mid-air to take a look around, Jones delightfully exclaimed 'We now come to my favourite! Everyday food items.'

'Here we have Notco choat,' Ramakant immediately said holding up a small, sealed packet.'

'What's choat?'

'It's instant noodles in chicken and goat flavour. Chicken + goat = CHOAT because sometimes you eat chicken and go ah! I wish this chicken tasted like goat or you eat goat and say ah! I wish this goat tasted like chicken. Now that problem is solved with choat! Add it to anything and get chicken and goat flavour! Two flavours in one! We spent 100 million dollars to develop this taste in our research lab.'

'Why?' I asked, not even astonished anymore at the way money was being spent.

Jones replied, 'Well we tried to get the chicken to have sex with the goat. If the chicken had laid an egg, we'd have taken the resulting hatchling, killed it, and used it to flavour our products. But since chickens don't fu*k goats, we had to extract their DNA, put it in amoeba, wait for it to multiply, and then chemically clean the amoeba with protein synthesis to create choat.'

I stared down at Ramakant. Quickly he rattled off 'Sir, hum kya karte? Bakra is not celebrating suhaag raat with the murgi…'

Ramakant added, lifting up the packets, 'We also have something for vegetarians. This is turlon. Same noodles with turnip and water melon. This is beetya matlab beetroot + papaya and this is orto equal to Orange + Tomato…'

'I get it, I get it!' I pleaded. 'Its like Brangelina. I get it. Did you make this also in the lab or did the turnip have sex with the watermelon?'

'Haha! Lab Sir.'

We moved to the next section.

'Enough of this Sir. Let me take you to our export area. We also have a cowshed here. Please come!' Shastri said realizing I was getting impatient.

'A cowshed! What's that doing here? Is this a dairy also or are you secretly doing a PhD in bovine genome sequencing ? You my friend are moo-ving in strange and mysterious ways.'

'Ha! Ha! Genome sequencing! I honestly haven't herd that before.'

'Thank God you have udder things to do Ramakant.'

'If I may interrupt, the faster we go the moooo-re ground we can cover,' Jones interrupted, wanting to pun-ish us for wasting time.

Shastri pushed a wooden door aside as I glided into an open area. A tarpaulin roof stretched over a wooden frame. Surprisingly not many cows were around but there was a hell of a lot of dung!

'Where are the animals?' I asked naturally surprised.

'Sorry Sir. It's still under construction. We built this place only last week. The cows, bulls, and buffaloes are being bought by our staff from the neighbouring farmers,' Jones replied.

'What do you plan to do here?'

'We plan to set up an adjoining dairy and next to that a slaughterhouse and leather processing unit. We should be getting regulatory approval to start the leather workshop here soon. We will also have a fake leather workshop for those who don't want to use real leather because of animal cruelty and all.'

'So there is no animal cruelty here?' I asked looking intently at both Shastri and Jones.

Jones fiddled a little and stuttered, 'Depends...on...what... you...mean...by "cruelty"... Its not economically...viable to adopt procedures and measures… which have not been proven… completely to comprehensively reduce animal…'

'Whoa! Whoa! Are you going to be causing pain to these animals?'

'Err…'

Looking at the expressions on their faces and getting the feeling they had no intention of answering truthfully, I focused on Shastri, then Jones and Shastri again, waiting for a reply. After a few seconds of blind staring I said grimly, 'I'm sorry. I can't accept that. Please shut this down.'

Ramakant immediately broke into action and started explaining in stark contrast to the silence before, 'Sirji please understand. Notco has tied up with European partners. We are making Italian leather here.'

'So what?! The cow is Indian no?'

'Actually Sir…it's not. We are bringing Italian cows to India. We are spending 500 crores on flying cows from Italy to India on Lufthansa Airlines. They will come here and eat Indian grass. I've already hired one minister from Bihar to do a fodder scam so we won't spend much on the grass and all. Most importantly, their skin will still be Italian. We will then make leather from them. Make bags and belts from that leather and send it all across Europe. Then we will import those bags again at 30 times the cost and sell it here as a luxury product for massive profits! It's how we turn 500 crores into 50,000 crores!' Ramakant proclaimed.

I responded, 'You can use Italian cow, Indian monkey, Chinese donkey, and American cat for all I care. I can't have you killing these animals under so much pain. Least you can do is adopt a pain-free method and then we will discuss how to exit this leather business.'

'But we can't exit Sir! We have signed a 20-year deal to supply Italian leather! And as far as animal cruelty goes, that's why we are making fake leather also here just for people who don't use real leather! This is also lucrative as it's a bit costlier than real leather.'

'Whoa! Hold on. Why is fake leather costlier?'

'Because making it involves a procedure which is costlier,' replied Frank, who finally broke his silence and jumped into the conversation.

Shastri quickly added 'See Sir that's why it's best to use real leather because its cheaper. It's especially cheaper because of the methods we adopt to make the leather.'

'So you're saying I am paying more for fake leather just so that you don't kill an animal in a painful manner?'

'*Obviously Sir*. We are killing it painfully just so that it's less painful for you, so that you can pay lesser. In that sense, the animals here are martyrs. Sacrificing themselves for us.'

'Why dude? You're already making so much money selling Nothing. Now with the chips and paste and creams and whatnot, you'll make even more money. I know that killing for leather will stop only when the buying stops. You need to exit this business as well but you have to start with adopting pain-free measures. It's the very least you can do. I am sure you can afford it.'

'Yes Sir we can afford but it will hurt our revenue. One bottle of euthanasia medicine is more than the cost of an entire buffalo. As Frank said, its simply not economically viable.'

I was irate. Hopping mad. Flawed logic, bullshit everywhere, literally. I had had enough. Thumbing down the joystick, I yelled, 'I'm leaving Ramakant. DO NOT START THIS LEATHER OPERATION. I repeat, DO NOT.'

Jones and Ramakant exchanged glances and looked at me with a, *'Why are you so upset? They're only cows'* expression as I angrily jet packed myself back to the front of the factory and packed off from Rikhitpur in a bad mood.

DAVOS

'Sirji! Kutte ko ek jagah baithne ko boliye, please! Kutte ka passport banwana hai toh photo leni hogi. Lekin who bhagta rehta hai, Sirji!' the travel agent appealed in frustration, sweat dropping off his brow like a wet hanky being wrung.

'Princy! Princy! Come here!' I ordered.

A frustrated Princy was scampering across the Persian marble floor of my weekend home like a ball rolling off VVS Laxman's bat. The barking humans at the golf course had sent my poor little mutt into a state of melancholy.

In a bid to cheer her up, I was taking her along with the wife and the kids to Davos. Yes, I had decided to go, afterall and no, I wasn't going because Anil Ambani had insisted.

Most people think that Davos is a town in Switzerland where the 'World Economic Forum'is held once a year. That's only partly true. You see, the Davos that most people have heard of is a lodge town in the Swiss alps where millionaires, heads of state, and government leaders go once a year, wrap themselves in fur coats, freeze their asses off, learn a little skiing, pee in the snow, get frostbite, and then return, having convinced themselves that the ~~trouble~~ vacation was well worth it because their net worth demands such a sacrifice.

There is, however, another Davos—the real one—which is of a mythical stature like Minas Tirith or the Hogwarts School of Magic. It's not some boring town in snow-capped hills; it's a magnificent magic island which reveals itself to only those whose wealth has crossed all possible limits. In other words, you have to be really, really, really, really, really, really, really, really, really, really, really, really super rich to set foot on it... Really. Davos is like that island from that TV show 'Lost' that can change its location. Sometimes Davos will also dive into the sea just like that. That's in fact how the legend of Atlantis started. Eons ago.

Of course you can't go around telling the common public about the real Davos, so they are led to believe that the Swiss Davos is the only Davos where something called the World Economic Forum is held, which is supposed to be 'a developmental conference between industry leaders and heads of state to foster economic cooperation, foreign ties, and strengthen relationships in the global marketplace.'

This year Davos had appeared in the Arctic Ocean close to the 0 degree Prime Meridian. To reach it, I would have to fly to Norway, then fly again to a group of Danish Islands called the Faroe Islands and from its northern coastline, board a submarine, journey underwater for 7 hours, and then resurface somewhere near the shoreline of Greenland where the island would be waiting graciously to receive the Jhunjhunwala family.

There would be enough stuff for the wife and the kids to do while I discussed important issues with fellow billionaires, like finding newer ways to avoid paying Value Added Tax.

Davos also has fun games like the paper boat race where you make a paper boat out of your favourite global currency note and race it against note boats of other billionaires in rivers of liquid silver. I won this race last year when my Chinese Remnimbi defeated George Soros' 1000 pound British note boat in the final. Soros, being the dick that he is, accused me of boat-fixing. I sued him for defamation in the International Court of Justice and won. Poor Soros had to polish my shoes for one whole day as punishment. Justice is awesome!

Speaking of justice, the court date for the patent hearing was to begin next week. Ratmalani had briefed me about it. I would be recording my statement at the beginning of the hearing itself. My impeccable integrity was necessary to sway the judge's sense of reasoning. My magnetic personality, Shakespearean eloquence, and clandestine demeanour were necessary to squash Agarwal's patent by presenting my testimony for Notco. I had taken this under advisement.

Sudhakar, the travel agent, was getting Princy's passport made. No living creature can enter the Faroe Islands enroute to Davos without a passport. The Danes are stupid like that. Last year they detained Priyanka Gandhi's puppy for over 24 hours because the pup did not have a passport.

This was going to be Princy's 25th trip abroad. Though she's just 7-months-old, she's already flown with me to Singapore, Berlin, New York, Cairo, Estonia, Sydney, Beirut, Frankfurt, Istanbul, Amsterdam, The Galapagos islands, and my cottage on the planet Venus. She also flies every fortnight to her therapist's office in Luxembourg where she de-stresses and barks out her daily problems.

Princy is the youngest of my 11 dogs. In addition to this cuddly Dachshund, I also have 10 Golden Retrievers. They're made of actual gold. After petting them, my hands get dirty with gold dust.

Shortly after lunch, we packed up and jet setted by Air Jhunjhunwala to Norway. Princy was in a much better mood now. The kids played with her on the Jet while I read out love poems to the wife who giggled and blushed, coyly exchanging glances with her handsome prince, her very own knight in flabby armour.

A few hours and a passport check later, we were on our way to Danish Faroe. A couple of hours later, we built sand castles on Faroe beach while waiting for my whale to arrive. It would serve as our transport to Davos.

You must be confused (again). When I say 'whale', I mean my submarine. It's a Russian nuclear submarine I purchased extensively for underwater travel. Sometimes when I need to inspect my underwater money vaults, I instantly hop on to the sub and dive many kilometres below sea level where I count my money in peace, away from the simmering tension of the world above.

It's called the whale because it looks like a whale. No really. Back when I purchased the sub from the Russians, it was plainer than a loaf of untoasted bread from Subway. About 50 million dollars and countless man-hours of aquamarine engineering later, it looks cooler and more extravagant than the USS Triton in its heyday. There's even a plasma heat ray in the whale's snout to burn away any irritating icebergs in its way. I often lend the whale to the Indian Navy to hold training exercises for the brave young men and women of the naval academies. Once, out of gratitude, they made me an honorary captain and gave me a cool 'I LOVE NAVY' T-shirt. Yay!

When we finally boarded the whale, night had set in. Marine commodore Iglesias Patrick Charles, the third from the house of Saxe-Coburg and Gotha in Portugal, sailed the sub. He's my officially designated submarine chauffeur. After saluting Pat and the rest of the crew, we crashed into our five star suite in the whale's abdomen. Soon all of us were asleep as the whale plied through the Arctic ocean.

The next morning we arrived at the island of Davos. After breakfast, I headed to the conference area as the wife and kids took Princy and headed for a day of sightseeing and fun.

Walking on one of the roads leading to the conference hall, I ran into Anil Ambani.

'Jhunjhunwala bhai! Wow! So you finally decided to come! Excellent! Excellent!' he said, his eyes glittering with excitement as though Mukesh had signed over his share of KG Basin gas to him.

'Yeah. I like the way these Davos people appreciate rich people like us.I realized I had nothing better to do, so I might as well do it here where I get tons of free stuff.'

'Speaking of nothing! Thanks a lot for bringing Ramakant along as well! I just met him sometime back. He's very interested in partnering with us.'

'Eh! That fellow is also here?' I yelped unhappily. 'Bloody Davos. Ever since that fellow became rich, billionaire ka standard hi gir gaya.'

'He's a genius, Jhunjhunwala bhai! All of us in the billionaire club are big fans of Ramakant. We have decided to make him our key note speaker. He will be giving an inspirational speech to close the event.'

'Hmmm…'

'Anyway, it's always good to see you Jhunjhunwala bhai!' Anil said with a sense of urgency as he began to walk away. 'Let's talk soon in the conference hall.'

'Okay. Have a good conference Anil,' I said as the Ambani walked off.

I was frankly irritated that Shastri was here.

Thinking about the factory in Rikhitpur, I headed into a nearby coffee shop for a hot drink. The weather was chilly like the other Davos. The sun had receded behind the clouds.

As I entered the coffee shop, I was taken back. There was Ramakant sitting on a cushioned chair with a gorgeous blonde sitting in his lap, the two of them smooching away to glory. Lips interlocked, they were getting more snuggly than a pair of horny koala bears in a eucalyptus tree. A bevy of watchers chattered among themselves as the two orally examined each others' tonsil cavities.

'Oye! What do you think you are doing? Stop sucking each other's faces!' I shouted.

Taken aback by my thundering voice, Ramakant pulled away from the blonde. The moustache was gone and he was now sporting a goatee. The blonde in his lap turned towards me. I recognized her immediately! It was part-time journo and full time skank, Shruti Sharma. Shit!

Shastri was clearly surprised to see me. As the blonde smiled mischievously, Shastri blurted, 'Oh Jhunjhunwala! So nice to see you here of all places! I never thought you would also be in Davos.'

It was the first time he had addressed me by my name alone. No prefix, no suffix, nothing. Not minding it, yet irate he was sucking face with none other than Ms Sharma, I picked up a cupcake from a passing waiter's plate and threw it at him, aiming directly at his forehead. Like a missile it struck.

'Oww! Why'd you do that?' he complained, massaging his forehead as though I had assaulted him with a frying pan instead of a cupcake. 'Don't you know I am against all forms of cake-based violence?'

'Shut up!' I shouted and stared at the blonde, ignoring the peeping crowd at the café.

'What are you doing here? Most importantly, why are you publicly displaying affection especially with her! Don't you know who this chick is?'

Gently brushing his goatee with her thumb, Ms Sharma answered seductively, 'Oh! He's gotten to know me very well over the past few days. Haven't you Ramu…'

'Ramu!' I cried, exasperated.

'Hehe!' Shastri laughed looking amorously into Sharma's eyes and declared like a bold Jehangir in *Mughal-e-Azam*, 'It's her pet name for me, Jhunjhunwala, and I'm not scared of publicly declaring or displaying my love for the woman of my dreams. Isn't that right, honey?'

They headed to smooch again but just as their lips were about to touch, I threw another cupcake at Ramakant.

'Oww! Stop hitting me with cupcakes man! Jeez!'

'Why are you doing XXX work in this wonderful coffee shop? Don't you realize how many khap panchayats are unhappy because of people like you?'

Ramakant and Shruti looked at each other and back at me.

'Aren't you still married, Ramakant? Why are you generously exchanging saliva with another woman, let alone her of all people!' I asked loudly.

'Mr Jhunjhunwala! What is your problem with me!' a flustered Sharma asked, unable to take my condescension anymore.

'Problem! Ha!' I laughed and extolled gladly. 'Everyone knows who you are. You are a one woman escort service. How many times and with how many men have I seen you these past few years? Every time I see you, you're cozying up with another man. You change men faster than a baby changes diapers!'

'Look, I'm quite choosy when it comes to my love life.'

'Oh, I'm sure woman. I bet Ramakant can taste every man in town everytime he kisses you.'

The hoochie fumed vigorously as Ramakant started to look riled.

Unwilling to back-off, I hollered, 'YOU are a gold-digging whore and you know it! Leave this guy alone. Go find someone else's pocket to steal from!'

Ramakant responded furiously as Shruti's face smudged into an appalled expression, 'Mr Jhunjhunwala. I demand you speak to Shruti with respect. I don't appreciate your tone.'

'Thank you Ramu dear! And let me tell you very directly Mr Jhunjhunwala, I fell in love with Ramu for the person he is. He just happened to be a billionaire when I fell in love with him.'

I sneered, 'Do you even know who this woman is Ramakant? Trust me dude, you are a billionaire now. If you continue hanging around her, you are gonna become a millionaire and after that you are gonna fall in value faster than the Indian rupee. She will suck your money faster than she's sucking your face. In no time you'll be back to selling agarbattis. Be grateful Davos has welcomed you. This is a place for capitalists to brainstorm and find ways to outsmart the tyranny of democratic governments, not a weekend getaway to canoodle with your mistress! Go to Bangkok if you wanna do that.'

'Excuse me!' interrupted Shruti vociferously insisting, 'I am not his mistress.'

'Yes Jhunjhunwala,' Ramakant added in agreement. 'I think you have some serious misgivings about Shruti here. We are planning to get married. She will be my second wife.'

'Why can't you just divorce your first wife?' I asked.

'Because I don't want to hurt her feelings. She is my public wife. Shruti will be my private wife. This is my side setting. That is my main setting. Please understand.'

'Don't you have a kid, the one to whom you gave the Hummer to the other day?' I asked trying to comprehend the man.

'I have two, Jhunjhunwala,' he replied. 'And Shruti is willing to become a mother to them both. She is taking care of a puppy to hone her maternal instinct just for this purpose.'

'Where's the puppy now?'

'With the servant of course, being raised just the way kids these days are.'

I paused, took a deep breath, and solemnly sounded off sincere advice, 'Dump her Ramakant. This woman is nothing but trouble.'

Shruti flew into a frenzy and shot out of Shastri's lap, screaming, 'Mr Jhunjhunwala! I DEMAND THAT YOU TREAT ME WITH RESPECT. You have done nothing but offend me and Ramu ever since you entered.'

'Hey lady, the way this guy dresses he should be in a mental hospital and the way you're sucking his face like a leech, you should be in a veterinary hospital.'

'GRR...'

'Aap dono yeh Sunny Leone wala kaam kahin aur jaake kariye na! You were sucking his face like a thirsty kid sucking Tropicana from a tetra pack. Saara paani nikal diya uska!'

'You are acting like the Taliban, Jhunjhunwala. I don't understand what your problem is!' Ramakant fervently countered.

'The problem Ramakant is that you should be back in India taking care of business, not making out with her in Davos,' I retorted. 'Your priorities are all over her face...I mean place. We are facing the biggest company lawsuit in recent history. There's a patent violation charge of epic proportions hanging over Notco. People are dying in Rikhitpur from cancer and investigations into that are still going on. Can you imagine the ramifications if the final report says Notco's factory is poisoning the people there? You have a duty to the hundreds of Notco shareholders, instead you are here with barely a week left, amply demonstrating phase 1 of the human reproductive cycle, that too with this bimbo!'

'HOW DARE YOU!' the angry bimbo blasted. 'Ramu is a genius. He's even giving the keynote at the event this year. Maybe thats why you're so jealous of him. Ramu can deal with the case with his eyes closed. Who else but he could have become the world's fastest billionaire? Who else could have sold nothing?? He's a magician!'

'Listen woman, just because he made your underwear disappear doesn't make him a magician.'

'THAT'S IT! I AM LEAVING. You, Mr Jhunjhunwala have no respect for women!'

Unmoved, I looked at Shastri and ordered, 'You better get yourself tested Ramakant.'

'For what?' he asked puzzled.

'Sexually transmitted diseases of course,' I replied. 'This bimbo might have mutated some new varieties of Chlamydia, Herpes, and God knows what else and passed them on to you. She's been with more men than a pornstar at an orgy.'

'ENOUGH! ENOUGH! I WILL NOT SIT BY AND LISTEN to you insult us! Come on Shruts!'

'Shruts?!'

'Come Ramu.'

The couple stormed out, banging the door on their way out. I motioned to the waiter, pointed to the seats formerly occupied by 'Ramu' and 'Shruts', and gave him specific instructions.

'Get your strongest phenyl, insecticide, pesticide, and every other germ removing chemical and clean this entire area, and if you don't have those then a bottle of Pepsi will do. A couple of monkeys have just been screwing here. I am afraid another new AIDS virus might breakout as an epidemic.'

The waiter scanned his eyes over the chairs and said, 'We have Notco's new phenyl with Sexy germ removing technology and activation molecules.'

'DAMMIT!'

I quickly ordered a hot chocolate and left.

Later in the evening I dragged myself reluctantly to the amphitheatre to hear Ramakant's keynote speech. I was hoping to perhaps even say sorry to him for what some might possibly conceive as an insult to him and his lady friend.

Correction… Shruti Sharma was a woman, yes, but a 'lady', HELL NO! She had been on more manhunts than the Crime branch of the Mumbai Police and had slept around with so many men that she should have been conferred the honorary title 'Kurl On mattress'. This is no exaggeration. Her modus operandi was to attach herself to an upcoming multi-millionaire and serenade him with her charm till he succumbed.

She was a WMD—Weapon of Mass Distraction—and had successfully distracted whoever she was with so far. Ramakant had fallen prey to the best seducer in all of Mumbai. He did not even regret cheating on his wife openly.

The amphitheatre was a large ballroom hall laid with circular tables. Everyone from Heads of State to billion dollar company CEO's to World Bank administrators to Industrialists were in the room. Right in front was a raised stage with a giant glittering electronic canvas screen. A glass podium made by Swarovski stood on top of the stage and glittered under the light from the giant chandeliers.

As I pulled up a chair at a table, ready to partake on a nibble of asparagus and mushroom with a glass of champagne, Ratan Tata sat down beside me. I like him, he's a little older than me and tends to get irritated when I mention Mamata Banerjee's name.

Anil Ambani, his wife, Adi Godrej, and Rahul Bajaj took the other seats at the table.

'Cigar, gentlemen and lady,' I asked as I pulled one out from my cigar box. The people around politely refused.

Anil smiled as we waited for Shastri to begin his keynote speech. 'Jhunjhun, you really must come to my new house in Ibiza. I've just bought a brand new palace where we can spend our summer vacations. It'll be my 5th summer home ...in Ibiza alone,' he said inviting me over with an air of brashness.

Rahul Bajaj added, 'That's great Anil. You should buy a summer home in Los Angeles atop the Empire State Building like me.'

Feeling left out, Ratan Tata quipped, 'I don't want to buy another summer home. I'm still frustrated after buying the Duchess of Kent's mansion in London last year. I use it to store all our unsold Tata Nanos. I'm too sentimental to part with them.'

'Well, you can always buy a new Rolls Royce or a Bentley or combine the two and buy a Rollsley. What do you think Jhunjhunwala?' Bajaj asked intently.

'Hmm. Hold on,' I replied and began texting away on my phone. Soon, I clapped my hands and stuck the cigar in between my lips.

The table looked surprised. A few minutes later, the sound of a helicopter whirred furiously outside, reverberated for a couple of seconds, and stopped. Seconds later, a gentlemen clad in a butler's outfit ran into the amphitheatre through the crowd carrying the Olympic torch, halted himself in front of me, prostrated, took out a candle from his front shirt pocket, and lit it with the Olympic torch in the other hand.

Another butler arrived and took away the torch. The table dwellers were confused as the first butler lit the cigar pursed between my lips, saluted me, and took off. As I blew a puff of smoke, Godrej asked, still reeling from the sudden spectacle, 'Who was that Jhunjhunwala bhai?'

I answered, 'Oh! That was Vijay Singh, my personal lighter attendant. He lights my cigars with the official Olympic Torch that I purchased from the International Olympic Association.'

Godrej gulped some champagne as the others smiled nervously. They wouldn't be trying to show me up anymore for sure.

The lights dimmed and a spotlight beamed onto the stage. An anchor in a shimmering red evening gown got on stage, mic in hand, and announced with a smile, 'Ladies and gentlemen, please welcome on stage our keynote speaker for the event, Mr Ramakant Shastri from The Nothing Company! He is the world's fastest billionaire! Give him a huge round of applause, folks!'

Ramakant walked up on stage and stepped into the spotlight as applause drowned the amphitheatre. The lights shone on Shastri dressed in a navy blue fur coat and with more gold chains around his neck. The feather in the funnel still remained untouched though the crown itself twinkled brighter with rubies redder than the anchor's velvety gown. He had more precious stones on him than a Turkish Princess or a smuggler walking through Airport security with a diamond store up his ass.

As the anchor descended, the applause quietened. Ramakant laid his hands on the slim dias. Keeping his hands on the edge of the table, he took a deep breath and began:

'Good evening fellow billionaires!

'My name is Ramakant Shastri.

For most of my life I've been an individual without focus or motivation. However, I've always been smart. I've always known that I've been a genius by birth but lazy by choice. Earlier no one took me seriously. People thought I was a joke but now that I have a billion dollars I have managed to prove once and for all that I am indeed the great man I always knew I was.'

A stray cough interrupted Shastri. Sipping some water from a glass, he quickly readjusted his fur coat. No one in the audience had moved. They were eager to hear what went on in the mind of the man who had sold Nothing and became a billionaire. Shastri resumed keeping the glass aside.

'I wish my father was here to listen to me today. He always said that I was good for nothing. He stressed repeatedly that I was good only for doing *nothing*. He always reminded me of how fantastically awesome I was at doing nothing all day...especially when I was young. I'm happy I've been able to make his dream come true. He always believed in me. Thanks Dad!

'My critics often argue that I'm selling emptiness, that the Notco revolution is just a bubble inflated by hype, clever marketing, and managing public perception. They say that if you can create enough interest, then people will eventually be persuaded to buy anything—maybe even Nothing. But let me ask you, is it so easy to pull the cover over your eyes ALL at the same time? As that saying goes "you can't fool all the people all the time" and you definitely cannot fool them for billions of dollars. I am certainly not the government, my friends!'

The audience roared with unsteady laughter.

'As a young boy growing up in Patna, I had a simple dream of becoming filthy rich so that common people problems like powercuts, petrol rise, water shortage, school fees, etc. would never bother me, simply because I would have way too much money to buy my way out of any problem that could possibly affect me.

'In my childhood itself I realized that I was not blessed with the talent other people had, like the ability to work hard or the ability to plan ahead and move towards accomplishing set goals.

'But what I was blessed with was definitely the capacity to avoid any and all forms of actual work. A talent most people deride but one which I believe is the key to my success—laziness. I have also been blessed with the remarkable ability to dream really big and conjure wonderful visions of the future I wish myself to be a part of. I am a visionary in every sense of the word.

'My life has mostly been about finding a way to avoid working so I can have enough money to buy whatever I wish for, so I can lead the life I always imagined.

'During my 1st stint as an entrepreneur, I started to sell agarbattis, not because I really cared about how houses smelled but because I needed to pay for the shitty life I was leading back then. I was so poor there were cobwebs collecting in my bank account.'

Shastri took another deep breath as the absolutely engrossed audience stretched their necks forward to absorb every tidbit Shastri was dropping.

With the air of a master he spoke slowly, 'Selling agarbattis taught me two things:

'1. Jasmine perfumed agarbattis are the most popular agarbatti in India. They sell a whole lot more than any other type of agarbatti, even rose perfumed ones.

'2. People will always buy things. As long as they do that, there will always be people to sell it to them. No one can buy anything for free. Everything costs money. In one sense, the act of buying and owning is even more important than what is actually bought.'

Ramakant paused and waited a few seconds for the audience to absorb what he had just said.

'That's why Nothing is the gigantic hit it is today because it is the only "product" which truly delivers a complete sense of ownership without commitments like *form* and *substance* and *colour* and stuff like that. It is the purest form of business transaction anywhere. Sell Nothing—Buy Nothing—Own Nothing.'

He paused again and waited a few seconds. The audience squinted their eyes in rapt attention.

He resumed, 'I am happy to say that at the age of 45 I have finally achieved my dreams...because I never gave up. Unlike others who shun laziness, I embraced it and kept trying to make lots of money without actually working too much. All I needed was one really solid idea. I am today a phenomenal success and the fact that I have a billion dollars is proof of my genius.

'My message folks is simple—*I have succeeded because I know the value of money. I could tell you that money isn't everything but if I did, I'd be lying. Money isn't everything, it's the only thing.*'

A solitary clap sounded off from the back of the room and quickly faded. The audience didn't know whether they were to applaud or shun what he had just said.

'I don't really care about democracies or dictatorships, about culture or heritage, about God for that matter or about atheism as well. I have no philosophy to follow nor any science to believe. The only thing I believe in wholeheartedly is the power of cash. *I am someone who honestly and deeply believes that money is everything and the only thing.*

'Frankly, I don't even care if the economic system which I am a part of is built on a concept of created wealth or shared wealth—so I've thrown out capitalism, communism, socialism and all that junk out of the window too.

'The secret of my success ladies and gentlemen has been to simply adopt the means best-suited to allow me to get what I want. I don't care if it's capitalism, god, godmen, science, democracy, socialism, politics, sports, entertainment, research, military, nature, it really doesn't matter. All these are just…options. Different choices combining in different permutations to give me what I want.'

'…And what I've always wanted in life is money, lots of it, so that I can buy cool stuff—like king-sized beds made out of sandalwood and mattresses filled with albatross duckling feather, Benzes and Porsches, private jets, champagne and caviar, bling, and flings. Money allows me to wear these funky fur coats of "endangered" but useless animals which have no real place in a world of humans because let's face it, if they were really that smart then they'd be wearing our flayed skin on their bodies instead of the other way around, right?

'Money allows me to come to cool places like Davos and Jet Ski on rivers of liquid mercury with my fellow billionaires! Abundance is not a crime. It's what we want, what we strive for, and the good thing about abundance is its never enough, and so it keeps us going to want more…even for someone as lazy as me!

'People may argue that I am evil and selfish. Selfish—yes, evil—HELL NO! I'm being honest and upright enough to tell all of you the truth. There can be no greater testament to my character than this. I have the balls to accept and embrace at my very core what type of a person I am and want to be and for this I must be appreciated.

'Hey! Thats why I'm here giving this speech because my actions powered by my beliefs made me a billionaire faster than anyone else in the whole world! I'm truly awesome.

'Bless you all folks and thank you!'

As Ramakant walked off stage, the shell shocked audience stayed silent for a few seconds till a slow clap broke out. In a few seconds, raucous applause filled the amphitheatre. Some people grimaced, others booed and some cheered. He had just unloaded a brutal missile of his world view. I left the hall confused and intensely analyzing every single word he had spoken.

Had he spoken the truth?

RIDING WITH THE KING

After returning from Davos the next day, I got back to work. Shastri's speech had become the King's Speech. Speech critic Kamal Nahta (aka Lotus Bathing) gave it 5/5 stars and speech therapist Taran Adarsh called it *'exceptional mind-blowing shit'*. It was a speech which reeked of Shastri's raging ambition, his extraordinary success, and a sleeping hubris that had awakened into an explosion of words. He had exploited the never-ending cycle of people's wants and needs and had used it to make big money. Perhaps that was the secret of 'Nothing'. According to him, it was the secret of business in general. One thing, however, stood out—despite the overflowing buckets of pride that accompanied Shastri when he addressed the Davos conference, there was also a blatant honesty in his words that I had never encountered before from any entrepreneur in all my years.

Back at the office, after an ordinary day in which I made 600 crores in 3 hours of trading stocks, I sat on my throne smoking a Gurkha. If you're imagining a night watchman of Nepalese origin burning away like a Vatican chimney after a pope's election, you'd be wronger than wrong. A Gurkha cigar is a special cigar made from tobacco leaf so smooth and so fine, it would put the silkiest of imperial silk to shame. It's a texture so soft that it crackles with the first hit of saliva like papyrus crumbles in vinegar. And it's so balmy, it pretty much feels like wiping your nose with a fluffy monsoon cloud. A leaf like that is so rare only 500 of them exist. They were unearthed by South American archaeologists in a clay pot while excavating a Yucatec Mayan tomb.

The 700-year-old leaf is then soaked in a Cognac from the drinking cabinet of King Louis the X. One drop of the drink and you'd be out for a month with your head in the clouds. A 700-year-old tobacco leaf soaked in 350-year-old whiskey, rolled with crunchy tobacco potent enough to get a freakin' dragon high. That's a Gurkha, a cigar so damn fabulous that stuck between my lips, I huffed and puffed away like a steam engine.

It's a cigar fit for the Gods.

Before we proceed, I am required to tell you that cigarette smoking and consumption of tobacco products is injurious to health. It's some new government rule or whatever. Anyway.

As the smoke rose up like a petal in the breeze, I dozed ever so slightly, ready to rest in my garden of Gurkhas, and wander away into the blissful shade of the tobacco plant.

At 4 pm, the soft vibrating ring of the mobile on the table awakened me from the siesta. Stirring back into awakening with the stub of the burnt out Gurkha still stuck in the corner of my lips, I lazily intercepted the call without even caring to know who it was and pressed the phone to my ear.

'Hello.'

'Hello Jhunjhunwala! It's Ramakant. Can you please meet me downstairs? I'm waiting for you at the entrance of Jhunjhunwala chambers.'

'Dude! How dare you disturb me!' I yelled sparking out from my slumber and discarding the cigar stub from my mouth with my free hand. 'What the hell do you want? I was going to smoke an entire box of Gurkha cigars. If you keep interrupting me like this, Al Gore and Rajendra Pachauri will never get the opportunity to save the planet from chain smoking environmental hazards like me!'

'I'm sorry to have interrupted you, but I just thought you could spend an evening with me. I think there might be some misunderstanding between us after our encounter in Davos. My head still hurts from all the cupcakes you threw at me…'

'Screw you! I don't want to get to know you better! I'm a bloody multi-billionaire stock mogul, not some flunkey you picked out from shaadi.com to have an arranged marriage with.'

'But Jhunjhunwala! I insist! Please! Please! We can also iron out the details of our court case. I want you to spend just a few hours with me, so you get to know my personality a little bit better. Please!'

Despite my repeated attempts to escape the unplanned encounter, Shastri's insistence won over. Dusting the cigar ash from my shirt, I dragged myself to the elevator and reluctantly headed out to the lobby.

Still groggy, I exited the lift and moved towards an eager looking Shastri waiting by the side of the same black Mercedes he had first emerged from at this very spot as *funnelhead*.

'Thank you for coming,' he greeted as I walked towards the car.

'Let's get this over with. Kya karna hai jaldi se bolo,' I said impatiently adjusting my glasses.

'Sure, please get into the car with me Jhunjhunwala. Let's go to my house.'

We got into the car and Shastri instructed the chauffeur, 'Ghar leke jao'.

As the car started, I looked at Shastri and parking my fabulous tashreef a bit more tightly on the brown leather seat said, 'Bolo, why did you call me?'

He replied, 'I think you did not like it when you saw me with Shruts in Davos. I'm not who you think I am. That's why I thought we could spend an evening together so you get to know me a bit better.'

'Theek hai but finish this quickly. Is sightseeing trip ke baad mujhe Kumarmangalam Birla ke saath Xbox pe Call of Duty khelna hai.'

Ramakant nodded with a smile. The vehicle pulled up at a traffic signal in Bhayandar.

I heard a gentle tap on window. It was Chandu!

'Oh ho! Kaise ho Chandu bhai,' I exclaimed and rolled down the window. Shastri looked surprised and Chandu, smelling of gutkha as usual, grinned like Manish Tewari at a Congress Party press conference.

'Ek dum bindaas sahab! Bahut khushi hui aapko yahaan dekhkar,' he replied.

I noticed a shaggy beard on him. It was thick, dense, and contorted. It looked like a beehive.

'Solid beard, man! You look like a total Badshah!' I commented sticking my nose out of the open window.

'Thank you Sirji!' he said and proudly confessed, 'I am going for Narayan Sai hairstyle. His beard only inspired me to grow my beard.'

'Who is Narayan Sai?' I asked. I was sure that I had heard this name earlier.

'Arre! You don't know Narayan Sai!' Chandu exclaimed. 'He is son of Asaram Bapu. He is my role model Sirji! He has not paid income tax in 125 countries across the world!'

'Isn't he that guy who raped a girl and went on the run from the cops?' I asked.

'He is a very genius criminal Sirji! Ten years back itself he was voted "20 most talented criminals to watch out for in the next decade by *Time* Magazine".'

'Really?'

'Yes Sir. I used to supply girls to him. Waise I know you are married and love your wife and all that…but if you ever change your mind then you can always contact me. I AM NUMBER 1 SUPPLIER OF GIRLS IN THIS REGION…maybe if…you are wanting…bedroom…hotel room book karwake…I can arrange five star…girls…Russian…American…Philippines…

Thai…Canada…Brazil…matlab…any country…More than 1… FULL SECRET…long night…happy ending for you…'

'You're trying to tempt me with a few girls…seriously?'

'Not few girls…many girls sirji. Even guys if you like…'

'Chandu!' I uttered. 'The world's hottest women throw themselves at my feet every single day. I'm being stalked right now by Katrina. Priyanka and Anushka are pulling each other's hair out because they both want me. Kareena wants to leave Saif and come live with me. Outside India, everyone from Charlize Theron to Scarlett Johansson to Jennifer Lopez are visiting India on the pretext of shooting a film just so that they can spend one night with me.'

Chandu conceded with a smile, 'Woh toh hai Sir, you are sexy and you know it!'

'Toh kaam kaisa chal raha hai?' I asked shifting my stare from Chandu to Shastri and then at the wallet my hands had automatically fished out of my pocket as soon as I laid eyes on Chandu.

Taking the crisp, freshly minted 100 rupee note from my hand, he replied, 'Business super hai Sir, I have decided to enter the Nothing business as well. I am also going to start selling Nothing from next week.'

Shastri's eyes immediately pricked. Leaning forward and turning towards the window, he stared at Chandu and asked rudely, 'What do you mean you are entering the Nothing business? Nothing is the copyrighted material of Notco industries. You cannot make or distribute Nothing without Notco's permission. Hadd hai!'

Jolted by the sudden restraining order, Chandu waved the folded note, touching his shaggy beard with it, and thundered, 'OYE BHAI SAAB, KAUN HAI AAP!'

'Main Ramakant Shastri hoon. Jis Nothing ko tum bechne ki baat kar rahe ho uska inventor hoon main!' he answered with an air of authority and leaned forward some more, squeezing me towards the door.

'Oh! Toh aap hain Notco industries ke maalik. Nice to meet you,' a surprised Chandu exclaimed. 'Myself Chandu, CEO Chandu begging company. Kabhi bhi black money ka laundering karwana hai toh please contact me. I will give you discount. We have seamlessly integrated money laundering business with our begging business. I am also owning many hawala offices with international network of branches. Best rate in industry. I AM NUMBER 1 MONEY LAUNDERER in metropolitan area!'

'No thanks, I get my money laundering done by a chartered accountant who handled the Commonwealth games account. Aapka koi zaroorat nahin,' Shastri rudely declined.

'Okay,' a visibly hurt Chandu sighed and then made a counter-proposition as he moved even closer to the door. 'If you want pirated DVD, also you can let me know. I am NUMBER 1 SUPPLIER OF PIRATED DVDS in west India! Any film before release, *I can get for you. I can get you pirated DVD of the film even before the film has been made*. Right now there is Akshay Kumar film festival going on, I can get for you all 5 films in the *Akshay Kumar Khiladi pentology*. In fact just for you I will also throw in *Khiladi 786* free! Khiladi pentology ho gaya Khiladi Hexology! DOUBLE TRILOGY BOSS!'

Shastri fumed and rushing his hand past me towards the open window, pointed at Chandu who was just millimetres away from having his eye poked out by Shastri's finger. 'NO! I AM NOT INTERESTED IN YOUR BLOODY CHUTIYA PIRATED DVD BUSINESS! YOU WILL NOT BE SELLING NOTHING!' he shouted.

'BUT WHY YOU DON'T WANT AKSHAY KUMAR KHILADI PENTOLOGY? In *Khiladiyon Ka Khiladi*, he defeats Undertaker and becomes World Heavyweight Champion!' Chandu pleaded.

'NO! GODDAMMIT! Bloody BHIKARI!' Shastri raged on.

'No need to abuse boss!' Chandu said in a conciliatory tone. 'DVD nahin chahiye koi baat nahi. I am also NUMBER 1

SUPPLIER of ecstasy, cocaine, and heroin in Maharashtra. I have many satisfied customers. You can go on my website and read satisfied client testimonials from Rahul Mahajan and Fardeen Khan. I specialize in rave party; if you ever want farmhouse home delivery of drugs for New Year rave party, please let me know.'

'OYE! I DON'T WANT YOUR DRUGS, YOU FILTHY BLOODY JUNKIE DRUG DEALER!'

'Oye! Tameez se baat kijiye! I am not a drug dealer. I am a well-known and well-respected narcotics supply chain management professional!'

'YOU BLOODY FILTHY STINKING BEGGAR! I WILL HAVE YOU ARRESTED AND DON'T YOU DARE SELL NOTHING WITHOUT MY PERMISSION. IT IS MY INTELLECTUAL PROPERTY! JAIL BHIJWA DOONGA MAIN!'

'YEH MERA BUSINESS HAI. AAP JOH CHAHE KARIYE. I will sell Nothing. I can't afford your licensing fees and franchisee charges. I will make Nothing from home only. I have sold off all my furniture and items. There is only open empty space in my home now, and I will collect Nothing from there and sell!!!! I WILL NOT STOP!! YEH MERA PET KA SAWAL HAI!'

'TERE MAA KI! ONLY I MAKE REAL NOTHING. ONLY I! I! I!' Shastri yelled pointing at Chandu who had now moved back for fear of having his eye poked by Shastri's outstretched hand had he stayed in the same place.

'I WILL MAKE NOTHING!' Chandu taunted Shastri and leaning into the window hissed angrily 'FAKE NOTHING IS COMING TO INDIA FROM CHINA, I WILL MAKE HOMEMADE NOTHING, THE REAL NOTHING THAT PEOPLE WANT! *MY NOTHING IS BETTER THAN YOUR NOTHING!*'

'BLOODY BASTARD, HARAAMKHOR! I AM A VERY POWERFUL PERSON, DON'T MESS WITH ME, I WILL SEND YOU TO JAIL FOR SELLING DRUGS AND NOTHING!'

'MAINE ALREADY BOL DIYA MUJHE JAIL JAANE KA DARR NAHIN HAI! Jail teri maa ki aankh! Even Narayan Sai is pen pals with me. When I go to jail, I can share a jail cell with him. I wish he autographs my FIR!' replied Chandu.

Ramakant burst out of the car from his door in a flash as the signal finally turned green. Chandu took flight immediately. Flabbergasted, I stuck my head out of the window and yelled at Shastri to get back as vehicles zoomed past us, almost knocking my head off.

Shastri had bolted out and was now chasing Chandu who was running through the gaps in the moving vehicles like an Olympic hurdler jumping over obstacles. From a distance, all I could observe was a scrawny, bearded, shaggy, disheveled beggar being chased down by a decorated Christmas tree which was yelling, 'YOU CANNOT SELL NOTHING! NOTHING IS MINE! NOTHING IS MINE!'

Twenty minutes later, we arrived at a sprawling, palatial compound. A courtyard as large as a football field lay in front of a giant three-storied mansion. The 5 pm sun was glistening in the swimming pool on the courtyard.

'We have arrived,' Shastri announced tiredly as a couple of security guards parted the cast iron gates and made way for the car to enter.

Shastri was puffing and breathing heavily. He had swallowed two bottles of mineral water after having unsuccessfully chased Chandu into the moving traffic. Tired and more exhausted than Anna Hazare after 14 days of fasting for a Lokpal Bill, he had returned to the car and simply sat quietly, trying to regain his composure in an air of resignation and fatigue.

'Nice property,' I remarked looking out of the window.

'Thank you. This is my house. It used to be Ramesh Sippy's house. He put all the money he got from making *Sholay* into buying this house. Unfortunately for him and fortunately for me, he put it up for sale and ran off into the jungle as soon as Ram Gopal Varma threatened to make another *Sholay* remake.'

'Oh!'

'This house is 14 acres big. Currently there are only 3 floors, but soon I will add 14 more floors above it and each floor will be 14 acres long. It will be taller than Mukesh Ambani's "Antilla",' Ramakant groaned clutching an empty bottle of mineral water by its cap.

'How many people are staying with you here?' I asked pointing to the big house as we moved along on the driveway.

'48.'

'48! Kitne log bhai! "Balika Vadhu" serial mein bhi itne log nahin hote!'

'Yes, myself, Shruti and our 46 servants. We are busy people as you know Jhunjhunwala. I work hard for my money and so when I come home at the end of the day, I want to relax. That's why I have hired all the people to assist me. In return I pay them well.'

'What about your kids? Where do they stay?'

'They stay with their mother,' he replied grudgingly.

'Accha, can I ask what her name is? Your wife's?'

Ramakant exploded and crushed the bottle in his hand 'Her name is BITCH!'

'Whoa dude, calm down. What's her real name?'

'HER REAL NAME IS *BLOODY BITCH*! I HATE HER. GRRR. KAM HAEMOGLOBIN WALI PYAASI KHOON LABAKNE WALI CHUDAIL!' Shastri frothed battering the crushed bottle like electrons at the Swiss Hadron collider.

The car pulled up in front of the main building. Sensing the anger in his tone, I hadn't pressed the name issue further. The air was disturbed and dust was flying about as I disembarked from the car. The noise of metal clanging and earth being drilled hit my ears. It was obvious there was some type of construction happening inside.

Raising my voice, I pointed to the house and asked loudly, 'What's going on here? Are you putting another light beam in your house as well?'

Dismissing the driver, Shastri replied loudly, 'No! No! I am building a Café Coffee Day in my house.'

'Huh?' I blinked in surprise.

Shastri explained, hands tied behind his back, as we began moving toward the entrance of the house. 'I love fresh coffee and feel like drinking it often. Waise, there is one Café Coffee Day across the street. There's another about 200 metres from here to the left side and another about 500 metres to the right side, but I don't want to walk that far just to get a cup of coffee. That's why I decided to build a Café Coffee Day in my house itself!'

All I could think was 'WOW'. 'Bandh karo! Bandh karo!' shouted Shastri to a passing worker who ran up to clarify the instruction.

'Aaj ke liye kaam bandh karo. Bahut sound aa raha hai. Rikhitpur factory mein bhi itni awaaz nahin aati,' he said pushing the door ajar.

The worker ran off and alerted the others. The noise from within stopped immediately. Taking a sip from a fresh bottle of Notco mineral water, Shastri looked at me and said, 'Come Jhunjhunwala, let me introduce you to Hukum Singh. He is making a film which I am producing.'

'You are producing films also now?' I asked in amusement, tucking my hands into my trouser pockets.

'Yes of course, films are a very lucrative business. I want to increase my revenue. Come,' he said as we moved past the outer hall into a more discreet inner hall.

Moving past the debris and construction material scattered about the open marble flooring, we witnessed at the far corner of this ground floor shaadi-mandap sized hall a strappy looking Sardarji dressed in a dark blue shirt, dull black trousers, and a dark blue turban. He was seated on a plastic chair in the otherwise empty room.

The Sardarji was angrily shouting into his cellphone. He looked to be in his late 50s but didn't have a single white hair on his beard. Either he was a contributor to Super Vasmol kesh kala's topline sales growth or was the product of some real robust genetic material in the facial follicular region. A slight paunch protruded as he rustled on the cell.

A nearby worker pulled up a couple of plastic chairs next to Hukum Singh and we proceeded to seat ourselves. Disconnecting his phone immediately he looked at Shastri, then me and introduced himself with a forced smile.

'Hello! Myself Hukum Singh,' he said leaning forward to shake my hand.

'This is Mr Jhunjhunjwala,' Ramakant said introducing me to the Sardarji.

'Of course, inko kaun nahin jaanta! How do you do Sir?' he genuflected.

Before I could reply, a short, fat, 40-ish something gentleman clad in a safari suit with a leather pouch tucked below his left shoulder ran in from seemingly nowhere and facing Hukum Singh, panted loudly like Shastri from a few minutes ago and uttered the words 'Sirji! Rapper mil gaye!'

'Shabhash Khurana! Unko bolo bahar wait karein,' the excited Sardarji ordered and grinned satisfactorily.

'Ek minute, Sir,' Khurana obliged and instructed somebody on his phone, 'Rappers ko waiting room mein bitha do.' His moustache was thick and oily and shook under the force of the words he had just barked into the phone.

Shastri butted in and said, 'Hukum Singh is a very big producer. He has produced such classics as *Khopdi—The Skull.*'

'I have also produced dubbing of *Iron Man* films in Hindi called *Lohpurush Mahapurush*,' Singh added and sat back down into the chair with a huff.

'So what film are you making now with Ramakant?' I asked.

'It will be a super duper duper hit. With Shastri Sir's budget and my expertise in films, we will definitely give competition to Yashraj and Dharma productions! Film will be superhit.'

'What is the film called?'

'Not yet decided.'

'What's the story?'

'It can be any story. That is not important.'

'What do you mean? I asked perplexed and declared, 'A story is the most important part of the film!'

'Aiji! Kamaal karte ho aap! Yahaan pe Ramakant bhai is making money without even a product! After all, I am making a film… story, screenplay sab baad mein dalenge. It's the important things which I am now concentrating on,' said the aggravated Sardarji.

'Like rap music?'

'What can I do? All the young people only listen to this yay yay yoyo rap things. If I don't put that in my songs, they will never watch, no! Varna Bollywood film mein inn bees rupay ke Kayne West ke saath kaun kaam karna chahta hai? '

Khurana supplemented 'Even well-known bhajan singer Narendra Chanchal ji is doing next Jai Mata di bhajan album with foreign rapper Pitbull. He will appear on the album with Chanchal ji and fellow Indian rapper Galli Ka Kutta.'

'Mata ki kripa se album hit ho jayega,' Ramakant said and looked at Hukum Singh assuredly.

'Hmm,' I muttered.

Singh continued, 'One good thing is we announced the film yesterday with a production budget of 100 crores. Today we have already recovered 65 crores. Now after the film releases we will make another 100 crore easily. Profit hi profit hai!'

'Hold on. How have you recovered 65 crores?'

'Very simple boss. Out of 100 crore budget I have already sold TV rights for 40 crore. Music rights for 10 crore. Merchandising deals for 10 crore, and DVD rights for another 5 crore.'

'But the film hasn't even been made yet!' I pointed out.

'Yes but it will be made no soon. And when it is made, its TV rights will be worth 40 crores. Its music 10 crores and wagera wagera.'

Ramakant added, 'The film business is extremely profitable Jhunjhunwala. We will book 3500 screens in multiplexes and single theatres and charge 300 rupees per ticket. In the opening weekend only we will cross 100 crore aaram se!'

'But doesn't that depend on viewer occupancy? People have to fill seats and watch the film to make it a hit or a 100 crore thing as you say,' I countered.

'So they will go no!' he emphatically declared. 'That's why we are doing heavy marketing and promotion for the film. Hero and Heroine are going to be on everything from *Promotion Nights... err...Comedy Nights With Kapil* to *Comedy Circus* to *NDTV* to *Headlines Today* to *India's Got Talent* to *Bhatinda has Talent* to *Dance Tiruchirapalli Dance* to *Masterchef Pondicherry* to *X Factor Rohtak to Nirmal Durbar Samagam Jalandhar*!'

'But what about audiences liking the film?' I reiterated making my confusion more apparent and spread my arms out.

'So they will like no! That's why newspaper fellows will give my film 4 and 5 stars the moment I make a cheque to them with 7 to 8 zeroes. The public will be influenced and watch the film. It doesn't even matter if the film is bad! Aaram se 100 crore ban jayega sirf promotion aur ticket price se. By the time they even realize, we would have made 100 crore. And if the film turns out to actually be good then word of mouth hoga and we'll make more money. Film business is solid boss!' the Sardarji grinned and looked up at his smiling assistant.

Taking a deep breath, I declared unhappily, 'I still can't believe there isn't even a story!'

Turning back from Khurana, Hukum Singh insisted comfortingly, 'Aiji, story nahin hua toh kya hua? The important things like I said are there: 4-5 fight scenes, 2 item numbers,1 bikini scene, 4-5 songs where one will have rap music, 2-3 kisses,1 sex scene, action climax, interval, aur anth mein happy ending.' Pausing for a moment he added, 'In between, jahan jahan ho sakta hai hum story fit kardenge.'

Khurana interrupted and looking at Shastri said, 'By the way Ramakant Sir…dus crore ka cheque aaj milega toh…waise hum abroad shooting kar rahe hain. We are putting 2 acre sunflower ka khet in Times Square in New York. Title song ka shooting wahi hoga…isiliye…'

'Haan, haan, de doonga,' Shastri replied and looking at Hukum Singh directed, 'Just make sure the characters all use Notco products in the film…'

'Zaroor, zaroor. Isi liye hum yahaan baithe hai Ramakant bhai!' the Sardar gladly obliged.

'Sirji, heroine ka phone hai,' Khurana interrupted again, this time covering the mouthpiece of his black mobile with his palm.

'Ek minute,' Singh smiled awkwardly at both Shastri and me and plucking the phone out of Khurana's hands, placed it to his ear.

'Hello! Yes how are you?' he greeted and after a few seconds of listening to the other end spoke animatedly.

'3 inches bikini…it's too long. I am telling tailor to design 2 inch bikini for you…aise minimum coverage maximum impact hoga…Yes madam, don't worry. It will be sexier than Kareena and Katrina. We will have you coming out from the beach in slow motion…saraa jagah sirf paani hoga…aapko lagegaki pralay ho raha hai… Arvind Kejriwal bhi itna free paani nahin deta hoga Dilli mein…It will be super sexy!'

Shastri tapped Hukum Singh on his knee and whispered, 'Tell her to go to the gym regularly. Dubbing aur acting class baad mein, lekin gym pehle.'

'Yes yes,' Singh nodded.'Shastri sir says you have to concentrate on your figure. Please go to gym regularly. See…this film will get you noticed and even if you don't get any more films after this, you can make an entire career from just doing magazine cover shoots. *Vogue, Elle, Cosmopolitan, Verve, Nerve, Stuff, More Stuff, Sex Stuff, Femina*...sab magazines mein aapka photo aayega. Aaram se you can make lakhs per photoshoot. You can become the next Sonam Kapoor of India!'

Singh then looked at Shastri who nodded in approval. Happy with his producer's approval he declared into the phone

'Talent hai aap mein, isi liye humne sign kiya aapko... Also, koshish karo hero ke saath public mein photo khichwane ka... promotion ke samay kaam aayega... Maine bola hai usko six-pack ab banwane ke liye... Songs mein bhi aapka dancing bindaas hona chahiye... As it is we are paying so much to get background dancers from Ukraine, Russia, Spain, and Australia. Chalo, ab main phone rakhta hoon. Happy gymming.'

Returning the phone to Khurana, Singh said, 'Haan, so where were we?' and uncomfortably got up. Looking at Shastri he asked, 'Oh Sirji, mujhe thoda bathroom jaana hai. Kidhar hai?'

Shastri replied pointing to the eastern part of the house, 'Go down the end of the corridor. You will see a lift. Take that lift to the first floor. First floor mein ek aur coridoor aayega, wahaan pe escalator milega. Escalator ke end mein bathroom aayega.'

'Thanks,' Hukum Singh said and immediately set off to relieve himself.

Looking at Ramakant I asked, 'You have an escalator in your house?'

'Yes, kya kare. Ramesh Sippy ne 1st floor pe bedroom dala aur second floor pe bathroom...pishaab karne ke liye hum itna chal nahin sakte...iss liye maine do crore ka escalator lagwa diya...'

'So if there's nothing else, I'll leave,' I declared 20 minutes later. Hukum Singh and Khurana had left, so had most of the workers.

'Arre! We've just got started. I'm sorry so much construction is going on. Please come with me to the Lakme Fashion Week. I have been specially invited by the Fashion Council of India. They are honouring me with the Style Icon of the Year award.'

'Hmmm, well. Go ahead. I'm not interested.'

'But please Jhunjhunwala! You promised to spend the evening with me.'

All of a sudden, a male servant ran in from behind us and blurted to Shastri, 'Saab, minister aaye hain aapse milne.'

'Haan, leke aao unko humare paas.'

'Theek hai saab.'

After a few minutes, a 60-year-old, chubby man in a politician's khaki walked across the floor flashing a wide smile. Behind him were two younger men who seemed like his chamchas.

'Namaste Ramakant bhai!' he greeted.

'Namaste Yadav saab, kaise hain aap?' Ramakant replied getting up from the chair and proceeded to shake hands with the minister who folded his palms in a Namaste.

'Jhunjhunwala, this is Shivlal Yadav, Minister for Rural Welfare and MP from Chotanagar,' he said turning towards me. 'And this as you know is Jhunjhunwala.'

'Of course, of course! Namaste Jhunjhunwala bhai! So nice to see you finally. Aapke charche duniya bhar mein hote hai. I hope you don't mind. I came to meet Shastri bhai,' he said seating himself down on the chair opposite to the one Ramakant had got back into. The two men stood behind the minister's chair with arms folded behind their backs. They were obviously too shell shocked to utter a word after encountering my greatness.

'Ramakant Shastri is a great man. Invented Nothing and all that. Government is thinking of awarding him a Padma Bhushan for making Nothing,' the minister said as he smiled at Ramakant.

'Well, the government has been rewarding people who have done nothing for India for years now. Ek aur se kya hoga?' I commented.

'Hehe! You are really funny,' the MP laughed. He then turned to Shastri and appealed, 'Ramakant bhai, see the thing is we want you to put up a factory in my constituency...bahut fayda hai isme...aapka bhi...aur desh ka bhi. I have tried to talk to you earlier, Ramakant. Even our party President has spoken to you. We even promised you a seat in the State Cricket Board and since you know absolutely nothing about cricket, you would be perfect for the job...bas Lalit Modi ya Srinivasan ke damaad ki tarah kuch mat kijiye...issliye I thought I could maybe ask you to ...thoda... humare taraf se baat ho jaaye toh...'

'Accha, toh yeh baat hai,' Shastri grinned.

'The thing is that ever since Notco became so famous and well... important...everyone wants a Notco factory in their territory. I also want his factory in my constituency. I think it will be good for the people, the state, and all of India if we can contribute to the economy. In fact, Chotanagar is ideally suited to have a Nothing factory.'

'Why do you say that?'

'Because Ramakant bhai, honestly there is nothing in Chotanagar. *ABSOLUTELY NOTHING.* It is as naked and as empty as a malnourished adivasi baby. It's fit for a Nothing factory. Everywhere you look, there is nowhere for miles on end!'

The minister paused for a second and continued, 'There was nothing there when I became MP and even after 10 years there is nothing. In fact, there is more nothing now compared to when I first became MP. From the past fifty years there has been nothing.

'I have worked relentlessly day and night, night and day to ensure that no development takes place in Chotanagar because we know how valuable the Nothing there is and how dangerous development can be. We know how development is the enemy of nothing.

'For years we have endeavoured. Not built any schools, hospitals, or even temples there. We want the nothing to be pure fresh, and unaltered—just the way Mother nature intended for us.

If we build roads, infrastructure, and do development work in this area, then all the nothing will become something.'

The minister sipped on a glass of water a servant had brought in. The chamchas stood motionless. Shastri's face had not wavered, I was the only one in the room itching to get up and punch the MP in the face.

'Year after year there is drought in Chotanagar. The land is baked like a piece of hot pav on a tava. In time nothing will grow there. The people will eat nothing, they will drink nothing. Only nothing will remain there. Our party and I personally will make sure that nothing remains there.'

'So what do you guys do with all the funds?' I asked.

He replied 'We donate to our party fund of course so we can give good governance to the people, continue winning elections, and make sure that our rich natural resources of nowhere are protected. *We will work hard day after day to give the people nothing.'*

Squinting my brows I asked, 'But isn't that corruption?'

The MP smiled and hissed 'Arre what you are saying Jhunjhunwala bhai. Corruption and nothing are related. The more corruption we do the more nothing there will be for our children.

'Huh!'

'Corruption is very important Jhunjhunwala bhai. Corruption is a very good thing. I want to do so much corruption that they should one day name a Swiss bank after me! It is the ultimate tribute!'

Too shocked to utter a word, I looked at him with a stone cold stare. Mistaking it to be a sign that I wanted to hear more, he continued.

'I will oppose all types of development to make sure that Chotanagar remains empty and filled with nothing. For years the political class of this country has been accused of doing nothing for its citizens. Today the same citizens applaud us when we do nothing, all thanks to this great man Ramakant Shastri.' Yadav motioned towards Shastri.

I stared back in disbelief.

'Jhunjhunwala bhai, I want Ramakant to put up his factory in our area. Our people will do jobs in his factory. Even the labour is cheap. They are so dedicated to nothing that they will do the job for nothing! This is my constituency. What else does one need for a factory?

'I will move a bill to make sure there is no infrastructure development in this area for the next 20 years. The vast hinterlands of nowhere containing Nothing will be preserved. We will make it a protected industrial zone. The bill will incorporate punishments for anyone who does anything that destroys the Nothing by planning to make something.'

'That's a lot of things.'

'Exactly!'

'Hmm…'

'The political class has more or less adopted doing nothing as a matter of policy.

'What do we do when prices rise—nothing

'What do we do when bomb blasts happen—nothing

'What do we do when farmers kill themselves—nothing

'What do we do when riots happen—nothing

'What do we do when women are raped—nothing

'What do we do when kids die after eating mid-day meals—nothing

There are hundreds of more instances of us doing nothing. Would you like to hear?'

'No, no please. I believe you.'

Exchanging glances with Ramakant, I turned back to the MP and declared 'Look, I'm gonna ask you the same thing I asked Ramakant once. How does Nothing help anyone? It has no utility. It serves no purpose.'

Pat came the reply, 'That's where you are wrong Jhunjhunwalaji. In a democracy, we must respect the choices people make. If people are buying Nothing, it is obviously because they have a use for it no? Of course if they misuse it, it becomes a law and order issue.

We will frame laws and send police after them. Law will take its own course.'

'This is an interesting perspective' I said and got up.

'Hehe! Please come and listen to my election speeches. I am sure you will enjoy them. I have released a 5 DVD set of my speeches during the general election campaign.'

'Theek hai. Well, nice to meet you Mr MP. I need to get back to important work like internally filtering carbon products produced by combustion of organic matter.'

'I...don't understand...'

'I meant, you continue talking to Ramakant. I will smoke a cigar in the balcony. Nice meeting you.'

'Dhanyawaad Jhunjhunwalaji! Many thanks. Please come to Chotanagar sometime. I hope you will convince Ramakantji to put up a factory there. I will personally give you a tour of all the Nothing and nowhere in Chotanagar. Please do come!'

'Sure, I'll look forward to seeing it in Chotanagar though I'm used to seeing such "nothing" pretty much in many Indian places thanks to the efforts of great men like you!'

Yadav and the cronies smiled, folded hands and waved. I pushed the balcony door ajar as I headed out. I moved a plastic chair into the balcony and looked at the Ashoka Pillar bust towering in the distance atop the State Legislature building. The sea yonder was raging silently. Night had set in.

The minister had left 10 minutes after I had moved to the balcony and Shastri had since ~~dragged~~ ~~kidnapped~~ brought me to the fashion week fashion show.

It was being held at the Blue Jasmine showroom. We were seated by the ramp. The room was slowly filling up. It was 9 pm. I was still thinking about everything the MP had said. Shastri was basking in the glow of his Style Icon award. He would be felicitated at the end of the show which was supposed to start in about half an hour.

The runway ramp was blue. White lights glittered above. Chairs arranged all around the room were tightly packed into arrays, like Dominos about to fall. There was a separate press enclosure near the top of the ramp. The photographers were still filling in. At the start of the runway was a bejeweled, translucent curtain which hid the backstage area. Atop the curtain in bright red letters were the words 'Lakme fashion week 2013' and 'the Rohan Khosla show'.

As I stared at the empty ramp, the noise was gradually rising. Shastri seated next to me, turned towards me and said, 'So Jhunjhunwala, why don't you fight the case with me as a partner instead of representing yourself alone against Agarwal?'

Turning my head to him from the ramp I replied, 'I am not alone, dude. I have a very good lawyer handling the litigation for me. He hasn't lost a single case in his life. In fact his record is 13,785 :0. He's so good that Tarun Tejpal wants him to prove that he isn't a rapist but an aspiring lift inspector, bellboy, and a sexual scientist.'

'Awesome!'

'OYE! Don't say "Awesome"! That's my word. It's copyrighted material.'

'Hehe! Sorry. By the way, do you think Ratmalani will work for me? I am suing *Forbes* Magazine—in their new issue they have said that I am worth 900 million dollars though in reality my net worth is 1.3 billion dollars!'

'Hmm...'

'Anyway, getting back to our case, I am just saying two shareholders should fight together on the same issue instead of alone especially when we are on the same side...is all I am saying.'

'Look, I need to protect my interests and I don't know you that well so I am going to have to say no but thanks for offering. When the case begins, I am sure you will be okay as will I...that is if you say are speaking the truth.'

Shastri smiled, 'I see you still don't trust me fully and that's understandable. But don't you at least know me a lot better...after today...I mean...I'm not a bad guy. I'm just different...I'm also famous now...Like you. I am doing a *Walk the Talk* episode with Shekhar Gupta before the case next week.'

'Just make sure he knows who you are. That guy has a habit of mistaking people,' I replied.

Suddenly, a screeching sound blasted from across the curtain. The lights showed a couple of shadowed silhouettes against the cloth. One was male and the other a female.

'IT'S MY DESIGN YOU BASTARD!'

'NO IT'S MY DESIGN!'

'IT'S MY DESIGN YOU BHENCHOD!'

'OYE!'

'DON'T OYE ME!'

'I came up with the idea of the model wearing Nothing!'

'No I came up with the idea of the model wearing Nothing,'

'Saale, my model is wearing real Nothing. Your model is just plain naked! Look at you, you have no class or shame!'

'Bastard! My model is the one who is wearing Nothing. Your model is the naked one. I know naked when I see it since most of my models are more or less naked in all my fashion shows anyway! You copied my design!'

'No, you copied my design! My model is wearing Nothing! You just copied that and made your model also wear Nothing!'

'YOU BASTARD!'

Suddenly, the curtain fell to the ground. The cameras went wild with excitement like hyenas having laid eyes on fresh meat. The guy and the girl had been de-silhouetted and were fighting in the flesh.

From the corner, two topless women,completely nude above the waist, darted across as the photographers clicked away furiously. It was a free show for all.

'My costume is worth 5 lakhs and its much better than your design!' the guy screamed.

I looked at Ramakant, arose, and simply said, 'I'm leaving. Bye.'

'Bastard! My model is the one who is wearing Nothing. Your model is the naked one. I know naked when I see it since most of my models are more or less naked in all my fashion shows anyway! You copied my design!'

MARKETING MEETING 2

'So, what's the strategy for the case, buddy?' Ramesh asked over the phone as I fidgeted in the car seat.I was on my way to RK Studios to meet Shastri who was shooting an ad for some Notco product there.

'My strategy is to listen to my lawyer,' I replied.

'And what is Ratmalani's strategy? I know he's a great lawyer and all, but how good is he when it comes to patents and intellectual property rights? I heard Ajay Agarwal's lawyer is a specialist at these types of cases.'

'I know that, but I am confident Ratmalani will get me off the case. His strategy has never failed him and me...till now.'

'Oh yeah, what exactly is his strategy?' examined Ramesh perhaps doubting that I had misplaced my belief in my excellently sneaky weasel of a scumbag lawyer.

'Confusing the fu*k out of the judge,' I said without hesitation.

'Excuse me!'

'You heard me. Ratmalani's strategy is simple yet highly effective. It involves wasting as much time as humanly possible and quite simply confusing the fu*k out of the judge. I can't put it any other way.'

'You're joking!' Ramesh howled in disbelief.

'No!' I asserted.'This is *actually* his strategy. Even the Chief Justice of India is scared of this guy. He got so petrified at the prospect of having to preside over Ratmalani's cases that he almost sentenced himself to ten years in jail. He gets a skin infection everytime Ratmalani is even in the same pincode as him!'

'If Notco loses this case, won't it be good for you?' Ramesh asked, still doubting my lawyer, and added as an afterthought, 'You can make that exit you're always talking about.'

'I thought that too but the prosecution is holding every single member on Notco's board criminally liable for the patent violation. If Notco loses, I do too,' I replied.

'Well, at least you won't go to jail.Why don't you just pay this Agarwal fellow, no?'

'Are you crazy! He's asking for a 15,000 crore settlement.There will be no payout. I'm not losing crores over Nothing! Bah!'

'Okay, but what about the Rikhitpur wala case?'

'We'll see. I expect they will accuse me of eating baby foetuses yet again.'

'What now?'

'Nothing. Purana joke hai.'

'O...k...'

'Chalo.I'll go and meet that idiot now.'

'Theek hai. Talk to you later.'

I disconnected the call and lazily dropped the phone on the seat. It was 6 pm and we were driving towards the studio. I was missing bingo night at Geoffrey's to meet Shastri and his marketing morons after he had texted me an hour earlier. *This better be good*, I thought to myself.

The first SMS read: 'Please melt me after 5pm, rk studies, shave to discuss import ants.'

Delighted to melt Shastri, I got ready to shave thinking it was a pre-burning requirement and simultaneously wondering if Notco had now ventured into importing ants, when another text arrived immediately:

'BLOODY HELL! I hate this cellphone text, I meant—please meet me after 5pm, RK Studios, have to discuss important things'

Disappointed, I continued working till 5 and left the office with my bodyguard escort in my Batmobile. Yes, it's the actual Batmobile. The tumbler vehicle used by actor Christian Bale as Batman in the *Dark Knight* trilogy. I bought it from the Warner Brothers studio for 35 million dollars.

When we arrived at the studio, the guards manning the gate were frightened by the tumbler. We stopped in front of studio '9' which was one of 11 acre-sized enclosures on the large RK Studios complex. Number 9 looked similar to the Rikhitpur factory from the outside—grey and dull painted. A number of vans were parked out front and the place was bustling with energy.

As I walked in through the entrance, I saw a small signboard that read 'Notco ad film shoot'. Paying no attention to what was around me, I walked ahead.

About 10 metres away from the entrance, propped against the wall, was a linear table. Sachin and Bipasha were seated at it on one side, tapping away on their laptops. I spotted the sales head Nitin on the opposite side as he lifted his head from the computer. Immediately he arose, ran over, and shook my hand as I laid it out for him to clasp with admiration.

'So great to see you again, Sir!' he exclaimed running towards me. 'Please come! Ramakant Sir will be here shortly.'

'He isn't here already?'

'No Sir. He'll be here in 5 minutes. I just spoke to him.'

Sachin and Bipasha walked towards me and shook my hands as well. We walked to the table they were seated at. I pulled up a simple looking metal chair and sat down. Wiping my glasses, I surveyed the area. Spotboys were all over the place.

'Paani Sir?'asked a young teenage spotboy holding a tray of white plastic cups filled with water.

'Nahin bhai. Thank you,' I said and requested, 'lekin ek khali glass milega?'

'Bilkul Sir,' obliged the lad.

He smiled as he laid a transparent cup in front of me. I smiled, thanked him, and removed the concealed whiskey flask from my shirt pocket. I may have missed bingo at Geoffrey's but not the whiskey. If Jhunjhunwala cannot go to the whiskey, the whiskey must come to the Jhunjhunwala.

Pouring myself a drink, I quickly gulped two shots of Black Label whiskey.

'How come the drink is still cold, sir?' asked Sachin looking at the condensation droplets on the side of the cup.

Waving the flask in front of him, I uttered, 'Its cold because I store it in this special pocket-sized aluminum flask. I had it made in Ireland. It keeps whiskey cold for centuries together. It's made from the same technology used to store dinosaur DNA in refrigerated condition.'

His eyes lit up and bedazzled in absolute awe. 'Sir, I've got to hand it to you—whatever you do, you do in absolute style!'

'Yes,' I acknowledged with humility.

A nearby TV set displayed a recent face. The charged news anchor screamed, 'Rural development minister and Chotanagar MP Shivlal Yadav has been arrested after an evening raid on his home premises found him to be hiding crores worth of Nothing boxes. Box after box full of Nothing have been found stored in a hidden room. The minister has denied any wrongdoing and has claimed it is an opposition conspiracy to hurt him. He has since been rushed to a local hospital after complaining of stomach pain which developed after he was told that he was going to be arrested. Stay tuned for more.'

I snickered silently, '*Good news at last,*' I thought to myself.

Suddenly, a big, jarring metallic sound exploded into the air. We turned around to see that a ladder had fallen to the ground by the side of the entrance. Ramakant was helping up a spotboy. It seemed like he had knocked it down.

'Dekhke seedhi nahin laga sakte kya?' scowled Ramakant at the panic-stricken spotboy. 'Bloody low income fellow! No education, no class! Jao yahaan se!' Shastri shouted pushing the lad away with his palm.

'Sorry Sir. Dekha nahin aapko,' the boy replied apologetically as Ramakant shooed him and waved at us.

'Purple, hmm,' I said.

'Sorry, what Sir?' Nitin asked having been caught off guard.

'Purple,' I reiterated.'He's wearing a purple fur coat. Do bears come in purple?'

'No Sir. I don't think so, unless they discovered a new species.'

Thumping away on his feet, Ramakant marched towards us. It was amazing how he managed to move so quickly with so much... equipment...on him all the time. The thud of the metallic aurum boots went clackety-clack as he moved towards us.

Ramakant was huffing and puffing like a temperamental contestant at the 'Bigg Boss' house who had just realized that a fellow participant had used his toothbrush.

'Holy shit! Did you guys see this? What the fu*k? How? How the fu* k did this happen? How, How, How? How? How? Tell me bloody how!'

An irate Ramakant had screamed the word 'how' so many times as though he was a dog howling 'how-how' instead of barking 'bow-wow'.

'The minister was being corrupt. He got caught. Simple,' I said.

'I don't care about him!' Shastri shouted.

I gestured my hand towards Ramakant who, having realized only then that he was at a movie set, quickly tried to regain his composure. Adjusting his feather, he placed one hand on his funnel crown, removed it from his skull, and placed it on the table. He then pulled himself an empty chair next to Nitin and sat down.

'I'm sorry. I was panicking,' a tired looking Shastri apologized. 'The sales of Nothing have gone down this month.'

Nitin looked at me and explained, 'It's because of the lawsuit. People are beginning to think Notco stole Notcorp's idea. The bad press we are receiving is not helping either.'

Bipasha stated in a distressed tone, 'I also want to say that the novelty value of Nothing has worn off, you know? I mean when it first came into the market a few months back, it was new and exciting! It was current and awesome. People couldn't wait to buy it. Now its being viewed as old and boring!'

'Also everybody's making it. Bloody pirates! Stealing my idea. Footpath fellows are selling fake Nothing from China! Some low quality shit. How can they call it Nothing? Its just crap! The government should crackdown on them,' Shastri complained.

Sachin, who had till now remained silent, blurted out in shock, 'Arre! What are you saying, Sir! China is making fake Nothing!'

'Bastard fellows!' Shastri abused angrily. 'Thanks to my company, this country has become the largest manufacturer of Nothing in the world. WORLD, I tell you! India makes more Nothing than the USA, UK, Russia, and China put together. All because Notco has lead the Nothing revolution. This bloody government should realize that the GDP of India is growing because *WE* are making Nothing in our factories and employing thousands of people. Instead, they are suing me for a few bloody votes and allowing these footpath fellows and small shops to sell Nothing. The worst part is that it's not even Nothing! IT'S FAKE NOTHING MADE IN CHINA. Bloody useless, colourless, odourless, invisible, horrible shit!'

He quickly lowered his voice and whined as the unsettled table folks listened on. 'Where would all these workers be if it weren't for Notco? They'd be bloody unemployed or be selling vegetables on the road like other poor people; tomato for 30 rupees a kilo, beans for 45 bucks. Haggling with people over the price of pumpkin and lemon. What lives can they lead with such meagre incomes? Instead, my company hired them, trained them, paid them a meal allowance and a salary.

'Now look where they all are. All self-sufficient and easily able to apply for a bank loan. Maybe if they work hard, then they can also buy a car in 5 years on loan. In 10 years, they can apply for a small housing loan also. See how much we have helped them! See!

'I am telling you right now, Jhunjhunwalaji. Doing something good in this country is a bloody crime. You should never help anyone! What was my problem, afterall? I could have easily gone off to America after my MBA. By this time, I would have got my green card also. I could have voted for Obama. Instead, I am stuck here dealing with two-bit *kantri* bureaucrats and uneducated ministers—every single day—to get approvals for my factories. And now they are suing me for some bloody ass cancer in some god forsaken graveyard of a village. Bloody hell!'

Shastri was clearly livid with anger. The purple coat was drenched in his sweat. Out of a need to abate his anger or perhaps genuinely discuss the issue, Nitin said, 'I don't mean to interrupt you Shastri Sir, but I think we need a strategy to deal with falling sales numbers.'

'Yeah…' acknowledged Ramakant hesitantly.

The people at the table looked at each other trying to grapple with the situation. I observed intently when Ramakant blurted,'Maybe we should introduce a new line of products. New Nothing!

'Huh!' I expressed, jolted by the sudden announcement. 'How will you make new Nothing, man? I don't even get how you make the present Nothing. Plus you launched it just a few months back. Then you launched those Notco consumer products. What is the need to launch a new product now?'

'Sirji, you know we can't keep waiting for the consumer to want something. The consumer is very unreliable. That's why we have to *make* him want it! That way he wants what we want him to want.'

'But isn't your job to satisfy the consumer's need? Instead you seem to be intent on creating more needs. Then you offer products to fill that need. That way the consumer's needs are never fulfilled because every time his need is fulfilled, you guys end up convincing him that he needs more and more but actually he doesn't.'

'Thats right Sir! Bravo. This is why you are a genius. Write this down, fellows. I couldn't have put it better myself!'

I muttered irritatingly, 'I wasn't praising you man.'

'No Sir, I get that,' Shastri insisted, eager to placate me. 'What I am saying is that in business…like you know…we have to keep fulfiling needs or else we will go out of business. We will go broke. Then even we have to sell vegetables. I can't sell vegetables, Jhunjhunwala! As it is pyaaz se bahut darr lagta hai mujhe.'

Disregarding his fear of onions I pointed out, 'I understand that. But why are you creating needs which don't need to exist? *If this is what you do, then all your life you will keep creating needs instead of better products* and when the consumer tries to fulfill that need from…let's say your competitor…then you have a problem. You helped create the need in the first place, right?'

'But that's business no Sir?'

'This is not business! THIS IS MADNESS!' I hissed angrily as a rattlesnake.

A defiant Ramakant nodded his head in disapproval. '*I believe that the quickest way to make money is to create a need.* We cannot possibly wait till the need arises on its own and then monetize the solution. We'd rather create it ourselves and ensure a constant demand. Notco's entire business model is based on convincing people they need to buy Nothing. These marketing guys are there to convince them they need Nothing. Everyone is making money. What is the problem with that, Jhunjhunwala?'

'Are you going to start a war tomorrow just because you want to sell more guns and bullets?' I uttered coldy.

Realizing that the discussion was getting a bit out of hand, Shastri declared, 'Hmmm… Let's all take a break. We'll discuss this further after 15 minutes.'

Break ke baad:

6 empty tea cups rested on our table. The ad crew had also taken a break. The shoot was over, the set wore a deserted look. A few spot boys were running around cleaning up the set. It was the first time I had actually observed the place and by god, it was huge!

I had been reading in the papers that Notco's newest campaign was the costliest advertising campaign in history and by the looks of the set, those rumours seemed damn real.

I still didn't know what the set was supposed to be. Maybe it would become clear when I saw the final ad. It seemed like a palace. Fancy stuff generously strewn all over the entire floor—glass chandeliers, Italian marble flooring, high quality teak doors, fantastic furniture, fine woolly carpets, silken curtains. Heck! It looked like one of those houses I had built for Princy.

Just beyond the set, in a not too discreet corner, our meeting continued. Ramakant had ordered a spotboy to bring another cup of tea for me. For someone who drinks whiskey like water, I was always amazed at how my palate could retain its taste for fine tea, and the tea I had just had moments ago was superb! A power-packed, bubbling, hot shot of tea leaves deliciously married to milk soaked with ginger and spoonfuls of sugar. Chai!

Nitin wiped his forehead with a handkerchief and spoke.

'Maybe we can increase revenue if we charge a convenience fee from now on.'

'Whats the convenience here that you are providing,' I asked sipping a little.

'Well, it's a convenience for us if they pay the convenience fee,' he replied.

Stirring a little, Ramakant leaned forward and said 'We need to redefine our pricing strategy. Let's make our prices more attractive.'

'What do you mean? Reduce our prices? Make nothing cheaper?' I asked.

'Yes maybe,' he replied.'That way demand will increase, no? More importantly, we need to make the prices attractive.

Customers these days like to see only good looking numbers on their price tags.'

'What do you mean? It's a number. Not Katrina Kaif molesting a bottle of mango juice.'

'I think I know what he means, Jhunjhunwalaji. Let's do that thing where we end all our prices with 99s!' Ramakant answered as Nitin smiled gladly and added, 'Yes! That's exactly what I'm talking about! Let's end all our prices with 9s like 99, 599, 699, 999, 9999 rupees! Like that.'

'Excellent idea, Nitin!' Shastri complimented. He was glad his investment in hiring Force Marketing was finally paying off. 'We can do a trendy ad campaign! Have a caption running on TV: *Brand new prices! Nothing now starts at only 999*.'

Bipasha squealed, 'Ooh! That would be perfect! Especially during a cricket match. We can make an ad just for the L-box!'

'Whats an L-box?' I asked.

'You know Sir, when you're watching a cricket match and then suddenly the viewing screen shrinks to 3/4th of the space and the remaining space is covered by an ad being run by the channel so you can't see the score?

'Yes Sir. That space which runs the ads is called the L-box. My friend invented it.' said Bipasha.

'So he's the reason I can't tell what the score is?'

'You should be happy, Sir,' she insisted looking at me like I was some sort of ungrateful step-child. 'He also invented a "P" shaped box. If that proposal had gone through then cricketers ke sar pe underwear ka ad aa jaata aur who bhi"P" shape mein. The ad agency disapproved that idea.'

'Thank god!' I said with a genuine sense of relief.

'I'll tell you a secret Sir. The L-box is growing at 1 cm per year. The channels are being paid by the companies to increase the ad display area. There is a popular myth that when the L-box becomes a perfect square then the world will end. According to my calculations the L-box should reach the top and right sides of an average sized TV screen in a about 15-20 years. Advertising is evolving.'

I was regretting the fact that I had been dragged into a marketing strategy meeting between Dumb and Dumber, Stupid and Stupider. Sachin could see that I was getting irritated with L-boxes and end of the world scenarios.

He nudged Bipasha lightly but the woman completely ignored him and continued, 'The good thing is Sir that now there are HD channels where there are no L-boxes. I am sure you can easily afford an extra 100 rupees/month. Then you can watch a cricket match without any ads!' Bipasha tried to explain as Shastri, Sachin, and Nitin looked on impatiently, waiting for her to cease talking.

'I am telling you Sir, these channel-wallahs are all thieves. They are increasing the APM rate just to irritate the customer into subscribing for the HD version of the same channel where there are no ads. It's the biggest scam in the history of television Sir! This HD nonsense is crap. HD pe live match dikhate hain aur SD pe highlights. Chaar-chaar channel launch karte hain yeh log ek match dikhane ke liye. Do par ad ke saath, do pe ad ke without. That day I was watching a HD channel and I saw a big huge pimple on Kareena Kapoor's forehead! I will never be able to look at Kareena the same way ever again! Bloody HD! Tera beda garag! You've spoiled all my fantasies!'

'What is APM?' I enquired like a school child listening to a complicated Physics lesson.

'It's short for Ads Per Minute, Sir,' Professor Bipasha explained.

Ramakant thrust himself back into the conversation with a high-pitched shriek.He was aggravated and stared down Bipasha like RR Patil staring at an open Dance Bar.'ARRE YAAR! WHY ARE YOU GIVING A LECTURE ON ADS AND HD? Keep quiet, no! Let's just focus on our pricing strategy. So we will end all our prices with 99s from now and we will have an ad campaign to advertise it.'

'One question Sir, if we have to make our prices end in 9s then we have to reduce prices by 1 rupee. All our products currently retail at prices ending with zeros like 500 or 1000, etc. So now they will become 499 and 999? We sell 50 million units of nothing in India alone per month. If we reduce prices by 1 rupee then we suffer a loss in revenue of 50 million rupees! As it is our sales have gone down because of the lawsuit and the product getting old. What should we do now?' asked Sachin.

Ramakant immersed himself in deep thought. The marketing trio too started to ponder over the pricing problem.

The din of the shoot was back. The set lights gleamed across the marble floor. A few metres away, the ad had commenced shooting. An actress lay seated on a throne dressed like a princess or a queen. The cameras were rolling. The royal helpers looked distressed that the princess was unhappy and waved their hands around with the charged frustration of a railway passenger trying to book his ticket on the IRCTC website. I couldn't make out what the idea was but it seemed like the princess was hungry and her court couldn't find something to kill off her hunger pangs. Out from one corner, a handsome fellow (not as handsome as me) rode in on a horse and gave the princess a box, a long, elongated one like a box of cornflakes.

She tore it open and turned the opened part towards her hand. Poof! There was Nothing inside. The hungry princess reached out for the Nothing from the box. In one swift motion she placed her hand over her mouth and began to chomp. Her frown had been replaced with a huge beaming smile. 'Delicious' she said seductively.

'CUT!' screamed the director. 'Ek aur retake!'

I turned my attention back to Ramakant and the group. Ramakant banged his hands on the table and yelled 'GOT IT'. The set was a little startled. Ramakant quickly brushed his hair and smiled at a passing spotboy.

'We need to pass on the benefit to the customer without our revenues coming down, so we can't cut prices even by a rupee so it ends in a 9 number right?'

'Yes,' agreed Nitin and the others nodded. I looked on.

Shastri grinned prominently with the satisfaction of an out-of-form batsman raising his bat after a long overdue century. Spelling out each word he enumerated,*'So let's increase prices by 100 bucks and then cut 1 rupee!'*

Nitin exploded with jubilation,'Oh ho! Waah! Genius Sir! Genius! This way you can increase revenue and still pass on the benefit to the customer! Awesome Sir! Awesome! It's a win-win situation.'

Sachin and Bipasha rejoiced with Nitin and Shastri as the four high-fived and congratulated each other.

It looked like I was the only party pooper in the group. I was stupefied and yelled 'What! Why are you increasing prices now? As it is Nothing costs so much and now you are increasing the price? How is it a win-win ? Only you are winning not the customer. He is paying more.'

Cutting short the celebration, Shastri answered, still beaming from ear to ear, 'But that's why we are passing on the benefit of 1 rupee no Sirji? He is saving one rupee and getting a 9 number price! He is also winning no!'

'Dude! This is absurd. You're increasing the price, don't you get it! Why will he buy a costlier product now?'

Shastri poked the funnel on the table lightly and scratched the goatee on his chin.'I thought about that as well.'

Trying to give me the full benefit of his knowledge Shastri illuminated, 'Notco is the number one maker of Nothing today. Even with this lawsuit we are still the market leaders. Other companies making Nothing don't offer such high quality as us. We have built up a very significant brand value all these months and business is all about taking risks as you yourself have said many times Jhunjhunwala! Now, this past month revenues have fallen and we need to address that problem. We also need to solve this issue of attractive pricing. People only buy things today if the end with the number 9. What can I do?'

I was still unconvinced and responded, 'It's only 1 rupee Ramakant. I am sure you can manage. What nonsense is this. You want to increase the price, then be frank about it. Why are you bullshitting me with this 99 business?'

This time Nitin answered.'The customer is an idiot, Sirji! What can we do if he is an idiot? If he wants to be an idiot then let him pay for the privilege of being an idiot. Let him be an idiot without us having to cut our revenues, no?'

A still beaming Shastri looked on at Nitin and then, switching his gaze towards me, questioned,'Why should I cut my price and trick him? I might as well increase the price and trick him. That way he thinks he is getting a good price and I am getting a good profit. Problem solved! It's a win-win!'

I answered, 'You are dependent on the customer Ramakant. Don't ever forget that. He is the reason you are here. If you shut shop tomorrow, he will easily go to someone else.'

'*True, but that someone else will also do the same thing no?* If I increase prices and make more money by making the customer think that he is getting a good deal by paying less for more, then another company will also do the same thing immediately. In fact we all do it. I am just doing it first. I am being smart. You should praise me for being innovative and proactive. Instead, you are pissed off with me for wanting to legitimately protect my profits?'

'But why are you unnecessarily increasing prices? There's no need for it. You just want more and more. The economy is fine. Your raw material—I'm still not sure what it is—isn't getting costlier. You're still paying your workers the same amount of money to suck emptiness from nowhere and put it in a box. How have your costs gone up?'

'But they will no, Sir? Inflation is at a 12% high.'

'Boss all along you were saying that you want to increase revenue and now you are saying you have to increase prices because of inflation. What is it? Profits or inflation? And don't say both!'

'But boss we are losing money already!' he argued like a dissatisfied auto-driver 'To increase my cash flow I have to either borrow more from a bank, sell more products, or increase the price. I can't sell more because the number of people buying is reducing everyday. I have already borrowed so much from the banks everywhere to open up factories nowhere. I can't borrow more. The only option left is to increase the price of Nothing. Afterall, I have cut one rupee no? I am giving the customer the psychological satisfaction that he is paying less and frankly I don't have to do that also!' Shastri sternly stopped.

Our discussion had become so engrossing by this time that we were completely unbothered by whatever was happening around us and hardly paid attention to the goings on.

'What Ramakant Sir is trying to say Jhunjhunwala sir' Bipasha explained, 'is that the customer does not want to pay less. He only wants to think that he is paying less. By ending our price in 9 we will get him to think he is paying less.'

'Even though he's actually paying more?'

'Yes, but *he thinks he's paying less* but because he thinks he is paying less he will buy more and when he does we also make more by selling less for more! Do you understand ?'

'More or less…'

'Great!' Shastri uttered pleased with Bipasha.

'How about developing a low-cost Nothing?' Sachin suggested 'Anything low cost sells in India. It should be easy to manufacture and should be of affordable quality. People with smaller budgets can also enjoy Nothing then.'

Shastri nodded his head approvingly and declared, 'Brilliant idea! We should introduce two low-cost variants. One which sells at 99 rupees and one which sells at 69 rupees. I really think the 69 wala Nothing will do well because it is very very low-cost. It is actually a low-low cost product. I am really looking forward to 69ing our customers.'

I spat my tea out. Shastri didn't seem to realize what his latest sentence meant. Ironically though, I did think he was really fu*king over his customers in more ways than one.

'You guys haven't even discussed the product yet and you have already decided the price?' I asked wiping my mouth with a hanky.

'Sir, it's not that hard,' Nitin insisted.'We will use everything low-cost to make low-cost Nothing.'

'So cheap stuff used to make cheaper stuff?'

'Cheap, yes, but good quality.'

'How do you make Nothing cheaper?'

'Most of our manufacturing costs go in cleaning and packing Nothing. So when we suck the Nothing from the nowhere, we'll not refine it that much. We'll clean it just once or twice. Pack it in much cheaper material and start selling it. We can then market it as a low cost product.'

'But how will people know its low-cost Nothing when it looks the same as high-cost Nothing? They're both bloody invisible!' I uttered loudly realizing that my BQ was increasing.

Shastri butted in, 'Arre! We'll just put that on the contents no like: Low-cost Nothing contains 40% pure Nothing vs premium Nothing which contains 90% pure Nothing.'

'But dude, you do realize that you are selling emptiness in a box? You've got emptiness in a small box which sells for less because you say is low-cost and you've got emptiness in a bigger box which costs more because you say is high-cost and pure and all that,' I said.

'Yes but we spend more time, effort, and money sucking and cleaning high-cost Nothing. Thats why it costs more. It's not just emptiness, *its costly premium emptiness*. They type of emptiness you really need to pay good money for.'

'But to make it affordable, we will also offer emptiness to lower income people so that they also experience the pleasure of feeling empty,' Nitin added.'The difference is that we will make it in a much cheaper way.'

I blinked haplessly as Sachin interjected 'Let's also introduce Nothing in rural India. We'll call it "KUCH NAHIN".'

Bipasha hollered, 'EXCELLENT! Rural India is where our next phase of growth will come from anyway. But since these villagers are so poor, it's unlikely they'll have money. We can have an exchange offer where they can pay in belongings for Kuch Nahin.'

Nitin smiled and rubbing his hands together sounded off 'We'll have a campaign called: Aap hummein sab kuch do hum aapko KUCH NAHIN denge!'

Shastri supplemented Nitin as I prepared to leave. I was getting bugged. 'The aim is to make the product less costly but it should give the same feel as a high quality product.'

'I don't understand,' I muttered pushing the chair back.

'In our country not everyone can afford high cost Nothing, but then why should they be robbed of experiencing Nothing nonetheless?'

Bipasha added, 'That's like saying you shouldn't wear shoes just because you can't afford to buy a pair. Its our job to make shoes for these people so that they can also run, but they will have to adjust because the shoes will be a lot cheaper, less sturdy and less comfortable, but then at least because of us they can run no?'

The patron of 'Kuch Nahin', Sachin, now forcefully emphasized, 'So low-cost Nothing might look similar to high-cost Nothing like a pair of cheap shoes standing next to a pair of costly shoes or an expensive sedan parked next to a cheap one but the customer will only buy the Nothing he can afford.'

Ramakant topped off the explanation, 'See my aim at the end of the day is to make Nothing affordable and available for everyone.'

Nitin erupted like a flowerpot of joy, 'Sir! You are great Sir! You are great! You are a social entrepreneur Sir! Please give me a xerox copy of your feet Sir! I want to worship them Sir. What high thinking sir! You are really a great man sir!'

'Always think of the customers my dear Nitin. Always!' Shastri responded with a smile.

I got up and quickly walked out before my head could explode.

A DAY IN COURT

For two out of the next three days, furious correspondences were exchanged between my office, Ratmalani's, and Ramakant's. The media coverage went into overdrive. The main focus was the beginning of the case proceedings between Notcorp Industries vs Notco Industries in the matter of patent number 961/ MUM/1997/27826.

The wife was worried that all the hectic preparation and stressful activity was putting my health in jeopardy. She rubbed my tummy for good luck but prayed to Ganesha to keep me safe.

Ratmalani was confident he had the case in the bag. He had assured me numerous times that I was a character witness and if anyone was in trouble, it was Shastri. I had no cause for worry. In any case, I was not thrilled about going to court especially under so much media scrutiny, but I had to.

The week crawled into a brand new Friday—the day of the case.

I finished my ablutions, said 'bye bye' to the wife, relayed instructions to the office guys over phone, and boarded my car. I wanted to present the impression that I was an obedient, law-abiding, down-to-earth citizen, which is who I am anyway. Ratmalani insisted that I drive to the court in a vehicle which indicated subtle humility, an unassuming nature, frugality, and simplicity. Hence I chose my Ford Mustang which only costs 10 million dollars.

As we pulled into the Court premises, the media congregated at my car door and drowned me in camera flashes and incessant questions. My bodyguards paved the way and I walked in rapidly into the Bombay High Court.

Ratmalani and his assistant immediately ran over and ushered me towards the courtroom. I was trying to prepare myself mentally one more time. Shastri wasn't coming since only my statement was going to be recorded today.

Ratmalani said with a sense of urgency, 'OKAY, it's 10 am. Justice Ramachandra will be our judge. The prosecution lawyer Mishra and his team are already inside. I've spoken to him. Sir, please enter the court when you hear your great name being called.'

'OKAY, go and make the opening statements. I just need a glass of water,' I said pensively looking around.

'Sure. I'll be inside,' he said and disappeared into the courtroom as I observed its interior from outside without entering. The walls were painted a pale white and a reddish looking roof covered the top. A big black desk stood atop a raised platform and a few sheets of paper were stacked on it. A name plate next to a still lying mallet and the accompanying sound block read 'Judge Hon. Satish Ramachandra'. Adjoining the desk was the witness box.

Opposite the Judge's desk and a few metres away were two parallely lined tables. Mishra sat with two others on the left table facing the judge's right. His desk was mostly empty save for glasses of water. I could see the back of his head as Ratmalani was talking to the court attendant on the other table.

The noise picked up. The packed courtroom was filled with reporters and people. Not a single chair in the room was empty. The reporters with their press badges rampantly texted on their phones as the others murmured.

'SILENCE!' screamed the court attendant. 'The Court is now in session. All rise for the Honourable Judge Satish Ramachandra presiding.' Everyone stood up like a high school assembly before singing the National Anthem.

The judge entered from a side door, climbed onto the podium, and took his place behind the desk. His fairly old, shrunken, clean-shaven face enveloped a sparkly set of eyes. 'Good Morning,' wished the judge. 'Please sit down.'

The attendant stated the case details for the official record. The Judge looked into a sheet of paper from underneath his thin, wafer-like spectacles and nodded to Ratmalani.

Ratmalani walked forward and made his opening statement.

'Good morning your honour and fellow people in this courtroom. We are privileged to conduct judicial business in this exalted, high honoured pedestal of gratuitous deliberated reasoning to *discern the truth*, *reward the honest*, *punish the guilty*, AND set an example for the upholding of righteousness and correctness of fair justice as enshrined in the fundamental charter of human rights extolled in the Constitution of India by our forefathers like Mahatma Gandhi, BR Ambedkar, Sarojini Naidu, Pandit Jawaharlal Nehru, Ironman of India Sardar Patel, Mulayam Singh Yadav, and others.'

The Judge gulped with a startled look. The prosecution looked nervous. Ratmalani smiled. The slimy bastard was just beginning. He had just begun a new innings with a four of the first ball.

'Ajay Agarwal's lawyer!' he mouthed off as his tone increased in volume and flair. 'Sitting right here on this Nilkamal brand court-issued plastic chair has on behalf of Mr Agarwal, *unfairly* and *wrongly*, accused Notco Industries Chairman Ramakant Shastri of Intellectual Property Rights theft and held every single member on Notco's Board of Directors *including* and *especially* my distinguished client...the multi-talented, the mega awesome, the super-duper sexy, the monstrously rich, the phenomenally intelligent, the extremely charitable, kind, venerable, pious, humble, handsome, great, cool, strong, dashing...I have literally, figuratively, directly, indirectly, outrageously, and metaphorically run out of adjectives to describe this great God of a man—MR SRI SRI DR DR HIS HIGH EXCELLENCY OF AWESOMENESS, THE JHUNJHUNWALA SIR SIR!'

The court went nuts at the sound of my name and began to clap hysterically. The applause thundered through the entire High Court. Two constables held the door ajar as I entered. I walked in slow motion, waving and pointing to the devotees seated in the room. It was evident from the Judge's expression that he was giving me a standing ovation in his own mind. I slapped a high five to Ratmalani, made my way across to the witness box, and sat down on the extra large chair placed there especially for me.

'Your honour! Look at this man,' a charged Ratmalani pointed with his palm. His pitch was loud. 'Does he look like a criminal? No!! Criminals have hair all over their bodies, especially their chests. Their faces look *mean* and *ugly,* with multiple scars, cuts, bruises and pimples, boils, papules overflowing with pus, sweat, mucus, grime, AND *the darkness of their hearts*. They carry *knives* and *guns* and *bombs* and stuff like that. They hurt women, children, old people, young people, foreigners, locals, nationals, internationals, and *especially* little tiny cute puppies!!! Tell me now your honour! Does my client look like a criminal?' Ratmalani questioned, outraged that the very idea was conceivable.

The judge shuddered and Ratmalani thundered. 'NO! Does he look like he could ever hurt a soft, cuddly, tiny, sweet, innocent looking puppy? NO!!! OF COURSE NOT!

Look at this picture of a criminal your honour and now look at this picture of Jhunjhunwala Sir. Look! Look!' he said thrusting a photo from his file right into the judge's face.

'I'm looking, lawyer saab,' said the Judge trying to avoid getting his face assaulted with the photo.

'Thank you my lord!' Ratmalani continued as he withdrew the photo and walked back and forth between the judge and the audience 'Mr Jhunjhunwala is the most law-abiding puppy-hugging citizen I have ever come across!!

'This lawsuit is illegal and unlawful. My client is only being sued because he is rich. *My client is being discriminated against because of his wealth*. This is the highest form of prejudice. Our country has slipped into anarchy and societal chaos! We are *crumbling, falling, shattering, spiking, demoralizing, and demonizing* into the festering maggot infested ABYSS OF DEMOCRATIC BREAKDOWN!!!!!

'By dragging his name into this lawsuit, Mr Agarwal and his prosecutors have shown they will fall to any level to hurt *puppy-huggers* like my client. This entire matter is *malicious, capricious, scandalous, disastrous,* AND *horrendous*! I therefore implore you my lord to immediately toss this case out of the window, out of the door, out of any open space so that the miscarriage of justice does not, will not, cannot, should not occur. Thank you my lord! JAI HIND! INDIA IS THE BEST!'

The court blew up like a Diwali atom bomb. The thrilled crowd screamed in adulation. A few whistled as the court attendant instructed them to keep quiet, reminding them this was a court room and not a theatre screening a Rajnikant film. Ratmalani puffed, smiling ear to ear, and sunk into his chair.

The judge gathered himself and shouted, 'ORDER, ORDER. We will take a 15 minute break and reconvene.'

The crowd exited as Judge Ramachandra walked out through the door he had entered from. I alighted from the witness box and sat down next to Ratmalani at his table.

'Don't worry Jhunjhunwala Sir. We will win this case with hands closed and eyes open. I know this Judge very well,' he said beaming with the success of his opening statement. 'Abhi Abhi transfer hua hai from sessions court of Daman and Diu. This is his first trial as a High Court judge in Bombay!'

'That was one hell of an opening speech,' I said giving credit where it was due.

Ratmalani blushed and tried to look modest. 'Sirji, I never prepare for cases with a lawbook. I always prepare with a dictionary instead. I have mugged up at least 25 Oxford dictionaries and 10 Webster's dictionaries in my career. I learn at least 20 new words daily.'

'Hmm.'

'Today I learnt the word "misoneistic". It means the fear of change.'

I grunted disapprovingly though I was secretly admiring the slimebag's theatricality and diction. 'What happens now?' I asked.

'Well, after the break we will begin examining witnesses. I will call you up to the box. You can give your statement and testimony. After that you will be cross examined by the prosecution and defended by me. Oh! By the way ...1 second...' he stopped abruptly like he had remembered something and pulled out his phone.

Ratmalani made a call, mumbling something incoherent into his phone as I looked at the open window. A few minutes later, his assistant walked in carrying something under her shoulder. I couldn't make out what it was at first but it appeared brownish golden and had a furry appearance. As she passed it to Ratmalani, he smiled and turned towards me with a loud, satisfied 'AAH!' sound. I could now clearly make out what the paralegal had brought to him.

'Whoa dude! What is *that* doing here?'

'Relax Jhunjhunwalaji. You're acting like you haven't ever seen a puppy before!'

'Of course I've seen a puppy you idiot. What's this adorable little thing doing here?'

'I want you to hold this puppy and cuddle it every 2 minutes when you are in the witness box.'

'Eh! Why?'

'Because I am trying to prove that you are not a criminal who encourages other criminals to steal patents.'

'And you are going to do this with me holding a puppy?!'

'Why are you freaking out? Look at this thing. It looks so innocent, so cuddly, so loving. It is a ball of goodness. It's absolutely, positively aww-inspiringly cute! This puppy is so cute! *Sooooo cuuuute*! This puppy was once arrested for being too cute. I got it released. In fact this is how we met.'

'Hmm.'

'Jhunjhunwalaji, no judge, no human being, or even monster can accuse you of any wrongdoing when you hold this. Butterflies will flutter in his heart! Violins will play in the background once he looks at this pup. It is a Weapon of Mass Cuteness. Look at it! One look at it and its soft, cuddly, ball-like fur encompassed body and the Judge *isn't even thinking about remotely associating anyone holding it with an inkling of criminal activity*!'

'But do you seriously want me to sit in front of a High Court Judge in the witness box of the Bombay High Court in the biggest corporate case this country has seen in the last 30 years holding a puppy in my hands?!!!!!' I yelled exasperated as the puppy squirmed uncomfortably in Ratmalani's hands.

'Would you like an alligator or an orangutan instead?'

Gritting my teeth, I snarled ferociously. Ratmalani looked at me with the confidence of a professional scumbag and muttered, 'In any case what do you want me to do now? I can't return him back to his owner. I have hired him for the whole day.'

'Hired him?' I asked as my outrage turned into surprise.

'Yes, hired him. This puppy is a professional cuteness artist. He is the puppy from the pedigree dog food ads. Per day iska charge ek lakh hai. He makes more money than me also!'

'Really?'

'No, of course not. He doesn't make more money than me, but he is definitely very rich. Those pedigree guys have him on a contract as their wholesale dog food model. It will be a waste of cash if we return him without even utilizing his full cuteness. Just look at his *adorable, small, cutesy-putesy* face and tell him you want him gone!'

Ratmalani held up the little fellow right in front of my face like he had held the photo in front of the judge. Our eyes met and it was love at first sight.

My heart melted. Begrudgingly, I agreed. 'Fine! He can stay but I am not holding him!'

'How can you not hold him, Jhunjhunwalaji?' he argued. 'I don't know why you are so surprised, considering the number of asses I make out of people every day in some court or the other. I am only asking you to cuddle a puppy after all. I once made a gorilla and a rhinoceros witnesses in a forest fire liability case. I even made a street dog a witness in a murder case to help my client.'

'Did you win?'

'Of course I won, Sir. Today, my client is out and that dog is in jail for murder.'

Looking into the pup's soft, dewy eyes, I said, 'Aww! But I can't have this awesome fuzzball in jail!'

'Of course not, Sir! He is here to assist you with his cuteness. Think of him as an excessively cute pooch professional. One look at him and the judge is bound to be floored. Now please take him. The break is about to end and the judge should be back soon along with the prosecution,' he said and placed the puppy on my lap without waiting.

The court settled down as the new session was about to start. Outside the din was just like before. I could hear the clicking of cameras from the window. The lime-covered white walls of the courtroom were being hit with the breeze from the windows all around and the air from the brown ceiling fan above. The judge entered and reseated himself on the dais.

'Order, order!' he shouted banging the mallet. 'Be seated everyone. Order, order.'

The noise immediately faded out as if the judge had activated the mute button on a loud TV screen. Once everyone was seated, the proceedings began.

'Mr Ratmalani. You may call your first witness.'

'Thank you, your honour. I would like to call Sir Sri Sri Sri Jhunjhunwala to the box please.'

As I stood up, puppy in hand, the crowd started cheering again.

'Order, order! This is a court,' Judge Ramachandra yelled banging the mallet even harder.

I sat down on the wooden chair and patted the little fellow who looked very calm and adorable as usual!

'State your name for the record please,' said the judge looking at me.

Immediately, Ratmalani interrupted frantically, 'Objection your honour!'

'Why?' the baffled judge asked.

'This man needs no introduction,' Ratmalani declared angrily as he switched glances between me and the judge. 'And the very fact that he has been asked to speak his name is proof enough that the prosecution is *misleading*, *misinforming*, and *misrepresenting*. Please declare a *mistrial* and immediately toss this case out before it becomes an absolute *misadventure*!'

'Objection your honour!' intruded Pankaj Mishra loudly.

'Why are you objecting?' the judge asked shifting his gaze from Ratmalani.

'I am objecting because he has accused the prosecution of misappropriation.'

Ratmalani shouted, 'OBJECTION YOUR HONOUR!'

'Now why are you objecting?' the confused and by now irritated judge asked.

'I am objecting to the prosecution's objection towards my very simple pointing out of facts.'

'OBJECTION YOUR HONOUR!' shouted back Mishra. 'We object to the defence's objection of our objection.'

'AND I OBJECT TO THE PROSECUTION's OBJECTION OF MY OBJECTION TOWARDS THEIR OBJECTION!' Ratmalani exploded.

The irritated Judge roared, 'ORDER, ORDER, ENOUGH! Gentlemen, I will not have you making a farce out of this case.'

'I apologize your honour,' Ratmalani continued. 'But by dragging my client's great name into this frivolous lawsuit, the prosecution has already made a farce by exposing their mischievous, misdirected, and misoneistic designs.'

'Err...what does misoneistic mean?' the judge asked.

'Allow me your honour. Misoneistic is the fear of change' I replied.

Ratmalani winked at me as the judge instructed, 'Mr Ratmalani, please don't use so many *M* words. Keep your arguments simple and straightforward.'

'Pardon me your honour, but this entire case is neither simple nor straightforward. I must therefore meaningfully make a demonstration of my disinclination to acquiesce to your acute observation of my legal interpretation to the subject under consideration pondered under litigation in this honourable jurisdiction of upholding executive legislation offering protection from the violation of fundamental rights...ation!'

'Uh...'

'He's saying "NO" in a very lawyerish way, your honour,' I interjected as the hapless judge stared with jaws dropped down.

'Oh!' the judge exclaimed finally bring his jaws back together.

Ratmalani glared at me as though my sentence had just shattered his entire defence.

The judge then looked at me and said, 'Once again I ask you please state your name for the record.'

On cue Ratmalani blasted, 'Objection your honour!'

'Again! He has to state his name. This is procedure Mr Ratmalani. I am once again instructing you to not turn this trial into a farce.'

'I beg your pardon, my lord. But Mr Jhunjhunwala, my esteemed and distinguished gentleman of a client, who pays me generously might I add, does not come under the ambit of regular procedure. He is a rich man and rules for rich people in this country are different. There is no need for him to state his name.'

'Objection your honour!' Mishra objected.

Ratmalani continued before the judge could even take note of Mishra's objection and argued vociferously, 'Let me complete my lord. It is obvious who this man...no...this superman holding a puppy sitting in the witness box is the greatest man in the world. I bring you to exhibit 1 of evidence.'

The court clerk handed a piece of paper encased in plastic to the judge.

'This is a birth certificate. What is it supposed to signify?' asked Justice Ramachandra who peered over the contents of the document handed over to him by the clerk.

Ratmalani replied triumphantly, 'Look closely your honour. This is not a birth certificate. It is *the* birth certificate. It is the birth certificate of Mr Jhunjhunwala. IT IS THE DAY GREATNESS WAS BORN.'

'O...KAY...' the judge conceded. 'But what does it have to do with the case and why are you disallowing his name to be entered?'

'This is the centre of my argument my lord. Mr Jhunjhunwala needs no introduction. He puts the "GOD" in "Godzilla"... One does don't walk into a boxing ring and ask who Muhammad Ali is. One does not talk about India and ask who Mahatma Gandhi is. One does not talk about playback singing and ask who Lata Mangeshkar is. One does not go to Metropolitan Ladies Centre Dandiya Festival expo 2013 and ask who Falguni Pathak is. Similarly...you do not ask this man for his name. *YOU simply know it.* I once sued two men for 40 crore rupees for just pretending to not know Mr Jhunjhunwala's great name.'

The puppy had by this time slumbered of blissfully in my arms. Nestled in my elbow he was off in dreamland. I was not so lucky on the other hand.

'Fine,' the judge said. 'I am asking you one last time, is your name Jhunjhunwala?'

'Indeed it is. Awesome without ME would just be AWESO,' I proudly replied.

'Objection your honour!' Ratmalani interrupted again.

'NOW WHAT!' screamed the irate judge who had reached the end of his tether.

'YOUR HONOUR, I would like to object to the fact that my lord has not addressed his greatness with the appropriate nomenclature.'

'I don't believe that is a legal requirement Mr Ratmalani, though I am well aware of Mr Jhunjhunwala's staggering reputation.'

'Objection your honour, but *it is* a legal requirement. I present to you exhibit 2 of evidence which is an order from the District court of Siliguri clearly pronouncing a binding verdict unequivocally and categorically stating that in all legal matters or otherwise Sir Sri Jhunjhunwala must be addressed only as Sir Sri Jhunjhunwala.'

'Seriously? Wow!'

Inspecting the document, the beaten judge looked at me apologetically and muttered, 'Well, O...KAY...Sir Sri Jhunjhunwala...'

Out of the goodness of my benevolent heart, I excused the judge and replied without a hint of smugness or pride, 'That's unnecessary your honour, but please call me 'Mr'. That order was for an unrelated matter.'

Ratmalani immediately broke into a loud, happy chorus. 'Wah! Wah! You see your honour, you see! This is the modesty of this man. He is a walking guardian of the Constitution of India. A pillar of uprightness, humility, and integrity. Even though the court says he should be called "Sir Sri" he walks among us as a "Mr" There is no greater evidence of his unimpeachable character than this... This and the fact that he's holding a puppy of course!'

'Objection, your honour,' bawled Pankaj Mishra realizing my awesomeness was taking the case away from him. 'Defence is twisting facts and wasting time.'

'I OBJECT your honour!' Ratmalani retorted and thumped the table. 'I have not even begun to waste time or twist facts! Trust me, I have specially prepared for those. My point is that this entire matter is *useless, hopeless,* and the prosecution is *clueless*. Mr Jhunjhunwala is the innocent victim of a grand conspiracy. This is a nefarious, notorious, and a *nuisance* of a design to cheat my client of his hard-earned billions of dollars.'

'Objection! Your honour! This case is about justice!' Mishra countered.

'I also object your honour! This case is not about justice. This case is about money. Cold hard cash, plain, and simple.'

An awkward silence broke through as Ratmalani paused. His eyes met Mishra's a few feet away. They were gladiators punching the daylights out of each other with words.

As Mishra sniggered, Ratmalani looked at the judge and continued, 'My client Sir Sri Jhunjhunwala is so rich he doesn't have the time to count his money. He has to weigh his money and there isn't a scale big enough to measure his fortune. Any earthly scale would literally break under the weight of even a. 01 percent of his stacks of notes and coins.'

Mishra chimed sarcastically, 'The scale would also break under his weight alone your honour!'

I erupted, ready to throw the sleeping pup at Mishra. 'SHUT UP, YOU BASTARD! DONT TRY TO IMPLY I AM FAT, YOU ASSHOLE. I'M NOT FAT, MY BODY JUST HAPPENS TO EXPAND FASTER THAN OTHER PEOPLE'S!'

'Wah! Wah! You see your honour, you see! This is the modesty of this man. He is a walking guardian of the Constitution of India. A pillar of uprightness, humility, and integrity. Even though the court says he should be called "Sir Sri" he walks among us as a "Mr". There is no greater evidence of his unimpeachable character than this... This and the fact that he's holding a puppy of course!'

'ORDER, ORDER!!' fired the judge. 'Prosecution will shut the hell up and speak only when allowed and Mr Jhunjhunwala, next time you use such language I will have you arrested for disrespecting the court. And please don't throw the puppy at the prosecution.'

'I'm sorry your honour but I was not disrespecting you. I was disrespecting him. He tried to call me fat,' I responded angrily as I apologetically cuddled the puppy and burnt a hole in Mishra.

Mishra, looking cocky as always, replied. 'I wasn't trying…'

'That's it! Step outside you asshole!! I'm gonna break you in half!'

'ORDER, ORDER! MR JHUNJHUNWALA, PLEASE DONT USE SUCH LANGUAGE. THIS IS YOUR LAST AND FINAL WARNING AND THE SAME GOES FOR THE PROSECUTION,' screamed the judge. 'If you make any comment about Mr Jhunjhunwala's weight, then I will throw you in jail as well. GOT IT?'

Mishra looked around, paused, and considering his options, said meekly, 'YES Sir. I apologize.'

'I demand he apologize to me as well! I am a victim of weight discrimination,' I said appalled that the judge had been unjust for not ordering Mishra to apologize to me.

'I am not apologizing!' retorted Mishra looking at me victoriously with an indignant smirk as he tried to get under my skin some more.

Ratmalani sprang into action and reeled off as I fumed, 'Your honour! If the prosecution does not apologize then under article 21 of the constitution and provision 499, section 21 of the Indian penal code, I will have no option but to initiate legal proceedings against the prosecution for defamation, libel, name calling, miscarriage of justice, contempt of court, and for generally being a douche who insults great people like Sir Sri Jhunjhunwala *sarcastically*, *directly*, and *indirectly*!!!!'

I agreed with Ratmalani and gave him thumbs up. The prosecution had tried to rattle me and this guy had rattled them right back.

The judge looked questioningly at Mishra who, after Ratmalani's threat, discussed furiously with his colleagues. Sipping a glass of water, he conceded grudgingly, 'I apologize sincerely, your honour. I meant no offense to Mr...err...Sir Sri Jhunjhunwala. It was an off the cuff remark and it will not happen again. I meant no offense to his generously impressive Body Mass Index or his wonderfully amplified sideways growth in general'

'Damn right!' I sounded off triumphant.

'Thank you Mr Mishra for the apology,' Nodded the judge eager to get on with the show and looking at Ratmalani from his perch ordered, 'Mr Ratmalani please continue.'

'Thank you your honour. Your fine quality of maintaining equality in this hall of decorum is *exemplary, exceptional* and *excellent*.'

The judge tried to smile but the poor lordship looked like he was getting a migraine. I was not going to be surprised if he packed his bags and took the next flight out back to Daman after this. Ratmalani can give a headache even to a Dispirin tablet.

The purveyor of headaches continued, 'Like I was saying before, Sir Sri Jhunjhunwala is so rich he has an ATM machine in every bathroom of his houses and each bathroom is bigger than a full-sized city mall your honour.

'Not only does he have ATMs in his house, he even has a fully functional bank in his verandah.

'Sir Sri Jhunjhunwala is so rich that he has three lotus ponds in his washbasin alone. So much so that BJP guys come and try to steal them.

'Sir Sri Jhunjhunwala is so rich that when he waves a 100 rupee note in the air, coins from all around him come and stick to that note. He is a walking, talking magnet for both money and babes.

'Sir Sri Jhunjhunwala is so rich that the Reserve Bank of India borrows money from him.'

'And the World Bank also your honour...' I interrupted as the judge looked ready to tear his silvery hair out.

Mishra stared seemingly unimpressed and sniggered some more. Ratmalani paraded on, 'Sir Sri Jhunjhunwala is so rich that when he files his IT returns, the Income tax officials go on strike because his taxes are way too high to even count!

'I get it! I GET IT! Okay! Mr Jhunjhunwala is very very very very rich. I GET IT,' Justice Ramachandra chimed as Ratmalani, taken aback with the sudden jolt from the judge, turned away from the audience and back towards the judge.

'Why are you telling the court how much money he has and how much money he makes? In this court all are equal poor or rich,' the judge declared.

'That's where I disagree your honour,' Ratmalani argued. 'Sir Sri Jhunjhunwala is being sued for his involvement with Notco and being held liable only because he is rich. There is no case here. The only crime he has committed is that he is rich and he is being punished for being rich and nothing else! Absolutely nothing else!'

Ratmalani sipped a glass of water. The little puppy who had woken up, thanks to the noise, looked even cuter and cuddlier than before with his sleepy eyes! Awww!

Placing the glass down, Ratmalani pulled up his coat, gently rubbed his bald head, and resumed. Eloquently, he summarized as the spell bound audience listened intently. 'Sir Sri Jhunjhunwala is the richest man in the world and he became richer after involving himself with Notco. The prosecution has alleged that he *encouraged, demonstrated,* and *delivered* falsities by encouraging Ramakant Shastri to take part in patent stealing. I fully intend to prove this is not the case.

'My client, as I have made abundantly clear, is extremely rich. He's so rich that you could touch him with one finger right now and your bank balance would immediately go up like mercury in a thermometer stuck in a sick kid's mouth!

'I'd also like to tell the court that Sir Sri Jhunjhunwala is a supremely respected member of society. Once Sachin Tendulkar, Nitin Gadkari and Bipasha Basu were all thrilled just to parade their smartphones in front of him.

'Sir Sri Jhunjhunwala did not even know of Ramakant Shastri till he had already set up his office and a small factory in Rikhitpur. Mr Ajay Agarwal is targeting the giant bull's eye on Mr Jhunjhunwala's back. A bull's eye which is sitting there only because he is rich.

'*Like I said this case is not about justice. It's about money.* A rich man is like a South Indian heroine. Everyone wants to take advantage if she's nice and fat but the moment she loses weight everyone loses interest. Sir Sri Jhunjhunwala is definitely not fat, he is fat only with money. Money he has worked hard for and created with years of genius, toil and torture.

'People like Agarwal wait their entire lives for rich men like Sir Sri Jhunjhunwala and then try to skim this money by *devious, devilish* and *defiant* stealing. Of course because they take the legal route, we can't call it *stealing* but rather *suing* but let me assure you your honour this is stealing. It is legal stealing. They are clearly suing the wrong person here and how do I know this? BECAUSE I CAN HONESTLY TELL YOU THAT IF THEY WERE SUING THE RIGHT PEOPLE THEN THEY WOULD 100% BE REPRESENTED BY ME!

'I, therefore, appeal to you to immediately excuse Sir Sri Jhunjhunwala and acquit him. He is in no way involved or liable in this case in any way. THAT'S ALL YOUR HONOUR.'

Ratmalani concluded and dropped into his chair. The crowd which was silent with rapt attention until now burst out into loud cacophonic applause. They were clapping for Ratmalani. I nodded at him with a satisfied, '*You were iffy in the beginning but stole the show in the end. Good job*' look.

'Order! Order,' the judge hollered banging his mallet down. 'The court will now break for lunch. The prosecution may examine Mr Jhunjhunwala after lunch. Court is now adjourned.'

During lunch at the court canteen I felt pretty good despite Ratmalani's many blades. The bastard seemed to know what he was doing. Once the prosecution's examination was over, I could relax and maybe go to Geoffrey's in the evening.

We walked back into the empty court room after discussing a few details and settled ourselves. I lazed around in the witness chair. The same paralegal who had fetched the pup arrived, and this time sat behind Ratmalani. She whispered something in his ear as the prosecution returned and seated themselves. Soon the judge also walked in. We were ready to begin our post lunch session. The crowd returned and filled the seats. The room was packed even more than before.

'ORDER, ORDER!' shouted the Judge banging the table with the mallet. The prosecution lawyer immediately stood up and looked at me. I hated this guy for ~~implying calling~~ accusing me of being fat and all. BASTARD!

'We now reconvene for the post lunch session,' said the judge. 'Prosecution may begin cross examining Sir Sri Jhunjhunwala.'

I smiled lazily at the fact that he had addressed me rightly.

'Mr Jhunjhunwala. I would like to start by once again tendering my apology for any perceived insult during my remark earlier,' said Mishra feeling satisfied he had displayed the appropriate ~~sportsman~~ lawyer spirit by re-apologizing. 'I'll begin by asking, do you know Ramakant Shastri?'

'Yeah,of course.'

'When was the first time you met him?'

'In my office a few months ago.'

'Are you sure? Can you be a bit more specific?'

'Well if I were writing a book I would say I met him in chapter one, on page 3, exactly 277 pages from this one ago.'

'Are you absolutely sure?'

'Yes. Ask anyone reading this. They've just counted and checked the page number as well.'

'O...kay. I would like to produce from evidence, exhibit "P" your honour. This is the original patent license for Notco's funnel sucking technology. It predates the patent filed by Ramakant Shastri. As you can see, it bears Ajay Agarwal's name, signature, and date of course,' pointed out Mishra reaching over to the judge's desk and handed over exhibit 'P'.

'Objection your honour!' an electrified Ratmalani sparked into action. 'This is forgery. How can we know it is the original? We must analyze this document in a forensic lab. We need to take hair fibres and DNA samples. We must test Ajay Agarwal's blood. We should take his BP, ECG, EEG, haemoglobin, and lipid profile. We should do Narco tests on him. Obviously this will take time. Maybe 5 or 10 years. So please adjourn the case. OKAY YOUR HONOUR! SEE YOU AFTER 10 years. BYE EVERYBODY!' shouted Ratmalani dramatically picking up his bag in a huff ready to march out like a school kid after the last bell of the year indicating the start of the summer vacation.

'Mr RATMALANI!' the Judge fumed, 'PLEASE DO NOT TELL ME WHEN TO ADJOURN MY OWN COURT! DO NOT INTERRUPT UNNECESSARILY! Prosecution may now continue.'

'Thank you your honour,' Mishra said as he looked at Ratmalani who had been forced to lay his bag back down. 'I was about to say that we have got DNA testing and document analysis done on this patent. I have here also affidavits from witnesses including the Chief Patent Officer clearly stating *this application was signed not only by Ajay Agarwal but also by Ramakant Shastri*.'

Ratmalani banged his fist on the table as murmurs spread across the room with each document being passed onto the judge by Mishra. I sat up startled.

'This patent clearly shows both Ramakant Shastri and Ajay Agarwal as signatories. The funnel sucking technology is *both* their idea. By using that technology to make his products and not giving due credit or compensation to my client, Mr Ramakant Shastri has violated the law,' Mishra pressed on smelling the first signs of an upstaged victory.

Giving the documents a thorough look over, the judge scanned the documents amid the jolted courtroom. Mishra smiled. Ratmalani scratched his bald head having been outfoxed.

'Your honour, we would like to have the document examined,' appealed Ratmalani as the court attendant waved his hands about like an orchestra composer telling the crowd to stop murmuring.

'You will get your turn,' the judge obliged. 'You can also examine these witnesses who have signed the affidavits when we reach that stage of the trial. Right now let us focus on Mr Jhunjhunwala's role in this affair.'

Mishra bowed and cast a quick glance at Ratmalani who had begun pondering his next few moves like a chess grandmaster.

'Thank you your honour,' Mishra said and turned towards me as the fever pitch in the room escalated. 'I want to ask Mr Jhunjhunwala if he instructed Ramakant Shastri to *steal* this patent and to claim all the credit for coming up with the funnel sucking technology. In other words, did you, Mr Jhunjhunwala, *order* Ramakant Shastri to claim to the world that he *and he alone* and NOT *he and Ajay Agarwal together* came up with Notco's funnel-sucking technology? Did you instruct him Mr Jhunjhunwala?'

'No, of course not. I never told him to claim anything.'

'Thank you Mr Jhunjhunwala. The witness is excused.'

Puzzled, I walked toward the empty seat and sat down next to Ratmalani. Giving the pup to the paralegal I sipped on water. The judge wiped his brow. Ratmalani smiled while an uneasy hint of nervousness spread across his lips. He had no idea about the patent that the prosecution had produced.

After waiting a few seconds and discussing with his team, Mishra pulled his pants up and proclaimed, 'PROSECUTION calls Ramakant Shastri.'

'Objection your honour! Mr Shastri is not here,' Ratmalani countered as the crowd grew even louder sending the court attendant into a flurry of 'shhh', 'keep quiet please'.

Mishra declared, 'True your honour… but he is in the building. He arrived just 5 minutes ago and is waiting to enter.'

Immediately, the court broke into a loud, unruly buzz. The murmurs had escalated into noise. The room had been thrust into the sudden unexpected knowledge that Shastri was in the building. The judge screamed haplessly, 'ORDER, ORDER' repeatedly banging the desk into a pulp with his mallet. I was surprised. Ratmalani immediately started to bark orders at the paralegal.

'Objection! My lord. Prosecution cannot call Shastri now. We are still in phase 1,' he whined.

Mishra asserted forcefully, 'Your honour, Mr Shastri will be asked only one question by me your honour and this pertains strictly to Mr Jhunjhunwala's role in all this which is what we are here to discuss anyway. Please let me summon him.'

The judge pondered for a few seconds. The courtroom flipped into silence and waited with bated breath. Time stood still.

Justice Ramachandra's eyes flickered. Satisfied with Mishra's assertion, he proclaimed in an authoritative tone, 'Call your witness.'

The gates opened. Shastri stood outside glinting of gold. Everything on him was gold. He looked like a mountain of gold. Eye frames, boots, the fur, the funnel—all gold. Bappi Lahiri would have killed himself had he seen him.

He walked in calmly, bristling in golden fur, sat across from me on the chair I was upon till a few minutes ago and looked demurely at the prosecutor. The crowd had been stunned into silence as he made his way across.

'State your name please,' Mishra said looking at Shastri who was practically glowing gold.

'Ramakant Shastri.'

'Are you the chairman of Notco industries?

'Yes.'

'Do you recognize this patent application here?' Mishra asked as he gave exhibit 'P' to Shastri.

'Yes it was a patent I filed in 1997,' replied Ramakant without as much taking a second look at the document.

'Let me ask you simply,' Mishra examined. The lawyer was hunting: 'We will examine your role soon. As of now can you tell me if Mr Jhunjhunwala *instructed* you to claim that this patent was filed not by Ajay Agarwal *and* you but *ONLY* by you?'

'Uh...'

'Please tell us...'

'Uh...'

'Tell us if Mr Jhunjhunwala *instructed* you to claim this patent as yours and yours alone?'

'Uh...'

Shastri stared at me. The outline of his eyes spilled out of his glasses as he mouthed something.

'What did you say? A little loud, please,' Mishra pleaded. His eyes were focused only on Ramakant. The transfixed lawyer hadn't moved. Neither had anyone else in the room.

'Yes...'

The court exploded. A nervous, rampant epidemic of excitement had broken out like a fever. Outside the media were stirring. I could hear them buzzing beyond the window. The journalists inside furiously texted away on their phone. I could pretty much read the headlines breaking live on every channel. With every text, a nail was being driven into my coffin.

Shell-shocked, I sat there staring at Shastri with my mouth hanging open.

Ratmalani gently poked me with his finger. I quickly tried to gather my wits. As if on cue, the phone in my pocket began buzzing. I jammed my fists on the table and screamed.

'ITS A LIE! A GOD DAMN LIE! RAMAKANT, YOU BASTARD! YOU KNOW I HAD NOTHING TO DO WITH THIS. BASTARD IS LYING YOUR HONOUR!'

Justice Ramachandra immediately shouted back banging his mallet. His face flushed with blood. 'ORDER,ORDER! SILENCE MR JHUNJHUNWALA. I HAVE ALREADY WARNED YOU NOT TO USE BAD LANGUAGE IN THE COURT ROOM. I HOLD YOU GUILTY OF CONTEMPT OF COURT AND SENTENCE YOU IMMEDIATELY TO ONE DAY IN JAIL AS PUNISHMENT FOR USING REPREHENSIBLE LANGUAGE DISRESPECTING THE COURT!!'

'WHAT?! You're sending me to jail!'

'YES. OFFICER, PLEASE ESCORT SIR SRI JHUNJHUNWALA TO THE LOCK UP.'

'YOUR HONOUR! THIS IS RIDICULUOUS. I OBJECT!' shouted Ratmalani.

The judge brought the hammer down and adjourned the court. The crowd roared. Jolted by the news they pulsated into a frenzy. I was about to become the world's first billionaire to go to jail for something other than fraud or sexual harassment.

THE MAN WHO BECAME GOD

Feeling more embarrassed and humiliated than Sunny Deol in a dance movie, I was MAD AS HELL.

Three hours later, we drove straight from the jail to court and then to Shastri's office. I was quaking fury. My blood pressure was so high it could be measured by a full-sized seismograph. My BP was high enough to register a 70.6 on the richter scale. I was ready to spew ash and fire. Inside my organs were fuelled by testosterone pouring like a waterfall. I was ready to pounce on Ramakant and whoop his ass into a bloody pulp.

Shortly after 6 pm, I arrived at Notco Towers. In the fading glow of the sunset, the Notco laser beam had just been switched on. The blue pillar of light burning through the atmosphere was a sight for sore eyes, considering I had been staring most of the day at dull white walls of the courtroom and the black insides of a jail cell.

I charged in with my bodyguards. I pushed the door wide open and without waiting for the receptionist to usher me in, headed straight to the lift.

'Sir! Sir! You can't go in. Mr Shastri isn't in right now!' she screamed.

Immediately my bodyguard pointed his AK 47 straight at her.

'Oh, oh! I'm sorry. He just appeared out of nowhere! It's a modern miracle,' she exclaimed in panic mode.

I instructed the escorts to leave. They were hesitant at first but left after my assurances that my fantastic martial arts skills were more than enough to deal with anyone who made an attempt on my security. I told them I would karate chop Shastri into a million little pieces if need be.

When I arrived on the 27th floor, a guard ushered me into Ramakant's 5000 square foot penthouse cabin. I closed the door behind me and slowly walked in, each step measured with the cold vengeance I was feeling.

Things had reached a breaking point and it wasn't long before Shastri popped into view.

He lay straight ahead at the far end of the room, holding a drinking glass in one hand, the other behind his back as he gazed out of the window. He turned around as he heard my footsteps.

Outside, the blue from the beam was bouncing off the window. The refraction of light looked as though a giant had playfully spilt neon blue paint all across Ramakant's office.

Ramakant stepped forward and removed his glasses. He was still glittering in the gold ensemble he had attended court in, though his funnel crown was gone. Our eyes locked in a cold stare. The tension was building. I was burning a hole through him but he didn't seem fazed. Calmly he drank the last of the whiskey in the glass, placed it aside on a small table next to his glasses, and started to talk.

'Can I offer you a drink Jhunjhunwala?'

'F*ck you.'

'Come on now. We may have disagreements but I must be a hospitable host. You're in my office after all. Have a drink first. We can chat in peace after that.'

'You're trying to act classy now after trying to burn me in court today, you bloody liar! I didn't come here to chat or drink, you asswipe. Why did you lie? Do you even know what you've done?

All my stocks are down solely based on what you said in court today. Why? Why'd you lie man? Why'd you do it? Why?'

'I regret dragging your name into this...'

'You didn't just drag my name into this. Your statement has made everyone think I am the kingpin here. I didn't have a damn thing to do with all of this and you damn well know it, punk!'

'Can you just calm down please...'

'NO! I WILL NOT CALM DOWN. I spent the last few hours in jail because of you asshole! I haven't had a bath in 24 hours and for the first time in my life I've missed a meal. Screw you! Stop beating around the bush and tell me why you did what you did!'

'FINE! FINE! YOU wanna know? FINE!'

I remained unmoved like a statue. Shastri gathered his wits and composed himself.

Realizing I wasn't going anywhere, he exhaled loudly and surmised, 'Honestly, it was the only way out for me. It was either kill or be killed and I am not going to be the victim here just because my jealous ex-partner can't handle the fact that I am a success and he's still rotting in failure.'

'So you decided to serve my name up!' I responded in amazement.'You just told the whole court I was behind this fiasco. That I told you to steal the patent. How dare you? How bloody dare you! This after the fact that you forged my signature so blatantly!'

'Don't blame me Jhunjhunwala. Hey, I invited you to fight this case together but no! You had to hire your own lawyer. You had to prepare your own defence. We could have found someone else to blame this shitstorm on. You sealed your fate the moment you decided to represent yourself independently.'

'That's what this is about? Revenge? You jerk! You screw me over because I didn't fight the case with you? I hired my lawyer to represent my interests and guess what, dickhead! He was doing it beautifully till you walked into that courtroom today and screwed it up!'

Beyond the window I could see that the grey sky had turned

into black. The dark had set in. Without flinching he said, 'You're wrong about one thing. I didn't do this for revenge. It was just business for me. I was only doing what was best for my company. I am in fact grateful to you. I still consider you a friend. But like I said, this is not about revenge...'

'Then what is it about!' I howled, flabbergasted.

Coldly, he replied, 'It's about what it's always been about. Money.'

'Money!'

'Yes. Money. Cold hard cash. Rupees, dollars, pounds.'

'So why drag me into this? Why lie? Why?'

'Boss, let me be very clear. I have waited an entire lifetime to climb the ladder of success. In a word, I simply don't want to lose the money I have made over the past few months. *I know better than anyone else how meteoric my rise has been.* I cannot...I will not...I will not lose. I WILL NOT LOSE! You hear me?' Shastri screamed with the agony of a caged animal.

Perplexed and unable to understand the true extent of his words I asked, 'Lose what?!'

'I REFUSE TO LOSE ANY MORE,' Shastri cringed aloud. 'At home, at work, with friends, with family, with the law, with... whatever. I will no longer *lose*. I will not go back to selling agarbattis.'

'So you're saying you are a winner because you have all this money for selling Nothing?'

Shastri sneered, 'How does it matter what I sold to get all this money? Fact is I have it today and I will no longer be a loser like I was...'

I declared with a hush of disappointment, 'You're a fu*kin amateur man. You wake up one fine morning; find out you are insanely rich. You learn that your plans worked and now you have tons of cash and all of a sudden you freakin' lose your mind! You dress like a clown, you've got these reality show dickheads following you everywhere, even to the bathroom to see if you as much as take a piss, you dump your wife and start romancing a slut like Shruti Sharma, you spoil your kid rotten, and you do nothing when your factory is causing life-threatening cancer to innocent villagers. Plus you disrespect your customers with one ridiculous selling strategy after another…'

'Well…' he interrupted.

'SHUT UP!' I yelled irritated more so by the fact that he had butted in. 'And now you've stooped down to breaking the law and defaming my great name by parading me as the architect of your patent fraud. I ought to bitchslap the fu*k out of you, slimeball!'

Ramakant took a long breath and adjusted the fur by pulling the ends near his chest. Curving his eyebrows and with a stone cold look, he gazed right into my eyes.

'Seriously boss, who are you without all this money?' he uttered in a dry tone.

And then it poured. Icicle spears for words fell from his mouth.

'You're just a fat man who sits all day, smoking and drinking. You eat more than a hungry elephant, drink more than a walrus, and look like a constipated hippopotamus, and you're telling me about how I spend my money?

'The only thing you can do is pretty much make money. It's the only reason people know you. To be specific, they only know you because you have *lots of it.*

'Now I too have money. *Lots of it.* In fact, I think I have more than you, and that's what bugs you. That's why you're here because you can't accept the fact that Ramakant Shastri has made this much damn money this damn fast. I AM SHITTING MONEY FAT MAN!

'Your big giant fat mutton chop head can't even imagine it! You're like like *Oh god! Why? Why did you make someone richer than me? Why? Why?!!*

'I have so much money…I am God now. I am the richest man in the world. People will remember me as…*the man who became God.*

'Cars, cash, gold, stocks, property...people. I OWN AND CONTROL THEM ALL. I AM GOD! GOD, YOU HEAR ME? GOD!'

My mind had stopped running. I had been jolted into a state of no-talking. No one had ever spoken to me like this. No one. Ever. Not even Airtel customer service.

Lost in silence, the realization dawned imminently. My dazed mind howled into reality. Collecting my wits, I switched back on and locking onto Shastri's remorseless eyes uttered, 'You've been living in the penthouse for far too long. It's time to knock your ass back to the basement...boy.'

Steely eyed, he retorted, 'What mistake have I made and what is this? A big fancy speech? You expect me to change the way I think and act because your somehow transformative words will have a Sri Sri Ravi Shankar effect on me? A sunrise of transcendental wisdom will dawn upon my soul with the sound of your voice and the moving power of your words? Ha! Bullshit. My eyes have been opened after years of struggle and I have finally attained enlightenment. *This world cares only about money.* Nothing else matters, fat man! People will tell you life is about "passion", "career", "legacy", "family". Ultimately everything only comes down to how much you sell, how much you save, and how much you spend. MONEY. FULLSTOP...BOSS.'

'Why are you doing this? Why are you talking like this? This is...insane. You've lost your mind dude. Don't act like this! We can still salvage something. Money is supposed to empower you. Instead you're using it to destroy yourself. Total personality flip ho gaya...'

Shastri paused for a moment. The ceiling lights played off the diamond rings on his fingers. Slowly, he scratched his cheek and walked to the bar. Pouring himself another glass of whiskey, he turned around and settled at the bar counter.

I walked to the bar unsure if continuing this conversation would prove any more fruitful. Perhaps sensing my frustration, the skinny agarbatti-seller I had first laid eyes on in a simple white striped shirt and a pair of dull grey cotton pants spoke up.

'My personality has not changed. For the first time in my life I'm really being who I've always been meant to be. Money hasn't made me worse, honestly it's made me…free.

'Two years ago I turned 43. Mid-life as they say. In today's age more than half my life was over and all I had done was to be an instrument in someone else's hands. I never got to be who I wanted to be or do what I wanted to do. I was simply never happy.

'I needed cash so I started working. Initially I was happy or relieved rather I could stand on my own feet. However, like all things in my life, even that was short-lived. I started as a chai wallah at a garage. Impressed with my resourcefulness and drive, the owner put me in charge of the supplies.

'Pretty soon I became an automobile accessories dealer. Given my ability to sell I was offered a job in an auto parts company. I was happy at first. It was also the time I got married. She was happy too. We were happy…

'In a couple of years the illusion shattered. I was no longer happy with the stuff I was selling or the woman I had married. I was working 15 hours a day like a Chinese kid at a sweatshop. Why was I working so damn hard selling bloody gear pistons, heating coils, and engine oils? This was not what I wanted!

'No matter how much I earned, it was never enough…never. IT'S NEVER ENOUGH! There's always this tax or that tax or this charge or that charge or inflation or recession or 'economic realities' or 'curse of the middle-class'.

'Anyway to cut a long story short, I was sick of making shit, slaving long hours for shitty bastard bosses younger than me, meeting one shitty company goal or business forecast after another, and finally going home to a shit wife to lead what was left of a shit life.'

The Czar of Nothing sipped and continued, his voice rhythmically belting out his life story.

'So... I started selling agarbattis with Ajay. I made some money but nothing compared to what others were making. Finally a few days after my 43rd birthday, I realized that I was sick of it all. I had done everything *"right"* my whole life and I was still unhappy and broke. Had to think a million times before going to a movie or buying a shirt or petrol. Had to eat less because rice and vegetables were too much. Had to talk less on phone because call rates were too high. Had to lead a sub-standard life while everyone else was having fun.

'I was at a crossroads. Either I had to turn over a new leaf or break bad and guess what I chose? *Breaking bad.* I was done being ruled. From now on I WAS GOING TO BE THE RULER OF MY LIFE! ME!' he thundered angrily.

'Okay, you made your choices,' I said beginning to feel sorry for him. 'You've made tons of cash simply selling a cock and bull story about something invisible and non-existent. Was that the right thing to do?'

In a flash he answered as though he was expecting the question, 'I've known what I was doing and what I was selling from day one.'

'You did?'

'Of course I knew. What do you sell people who already have everything they would ever need, Mr Jhunjhunwala?

'You sell them Nothing. A product. No. An idea actually, that what they are buying has immense value and will make a tremendous difference to their lives. I was selling hype. They're sheep. All of them.'

'I can't believe this. You're calling your customers fools? Those people who spent their hard-earned money to buy your stupid boxes full of emptiness and void?'

'Their own lives are empty. That's why they bought the emptiness I sold them. They chose to be slaves like I once was. *Customers are only good for having their money taken. I realized sometime back that business in its essence is just a fancy term for thieving.*'

The tide of understanding had turned again. My sense of feeling sorry for him disappeared. Angrily, I shouted, 'You're wrong!'

'Look around, you fat man,' the Czar boasted. 'Look what I've done with just a few boxes and a bunch of big-boobed bimbos delivering snazzy lines telling people to buy those boxes.

'I've had everyone from the media to politicians to fellow corporates to ordinary people kiss my ass. Any attempt to logically debate what I am selling was easily overshadowed by my tremendous success in selling it. *At the end of the day it didn't really even matter what I put in those boxes. They would still sell because all people care about is show, glamour, hype and peer pressure. Substance and utility died years ago.*

'I've created an entirely new universe. A universe where people no longer even need a product. They just need an idea. All I'm doing is taking money for selling them that idea. What's wrong in that?'

'You're a butcher slaughtering sheep my friend.'

'I am not your friend Jhunjhunwala!' he slapped back. His words whiplashed through the room.

'People are like sheep. Instead of grass they are fed money and they eat it up happily. It's what they work their whole lives for and when they get fat enough to part with their money, butchers like me are always around slicing chunks into their wallets so that we can get fat ourselves.

'I gave the people what they wanted. Something they thought could add value and meaning to their lives. They paid money for it and I got rich off that. I ask you again, why is that wrong? It's just business boss! It's the way the world works.'

My anger had reached boiling point. Unable to bear it any longer I shouted, 'ARE YOU DONE, YOU ROTTEN PIECE OF SHIT!'

'Why are you getting angry, boss?!' he immediately countered. 'Even you know what I've said is the truth. Okay, I blamed you in court wrongly, but why are you losing your mind over this? You are a rich man just like me. Your own lawyer I heard was fancifully elucidating how abundantly wealthy and deep-pocketed you are.

'Do the rich in this country ever get punished? No! The rich get away with absolutely anything and everything. They literally pay their way out of their problems. Even though I named you, you will still get away. You could kill someone right in front of the judge and you'd still get away with it because you are rich. For the right price even a policeman becomes a criminal.

'This world is about money. If you have it, you can get away with anything. You Jhunjhunwala have lots of it. Even though I took your name you will still get away with it. This is just a strategy for me to win this case, that's all. Tomorrow we'll bury our differences and come together. The market will rejoice. Stocks of Notco will go even higher. You and I will get richer boss! It's just business!'

'FU*K YOU! The difference between you and me is that I make money while on the other hand money makes you.'

Shastri finished the glass off and chimed sarcastically, his eyes tingling with an icy stare, 'Thanks for the philosophy lesson.'

'You're about to get a lesson in reality now,' I said meeting his cold stare with a burning look.

'What do you mean?' he asked.

'Look outside your window, God. Look beyond the glare of your blue beam. That is Dalal Street. It's littered with the bones of countless men and women... All who made the same mistake as you. All of them too thought they were Gods. All these Gods who adopt unethical means to make money are sooner or later discarded into the dustbins of History.'

'Are you threatening me?' he inquired beginning to grimace.

'Threat? Ha!' I countered. 'I make one statement and you wet your diaper? I thought you were God.'

'What are you trying to say?'

'You've lied to me. You've tried to hustle me. You've tried to implicate me in your wrongdoings. You've disrespected and conned your customers and now you've insulted me. I've tolerated your nonsense long enough and now...I AM PISSED OFF. You better prepare yourself!'

'For what?'

'WAR.'

THE RETURN OF THE BAND

When I narrated the events of the day to Ramesh that night, he was livid. Inflamed with a fierce loyalty for his best friend, he bellowed and balked at the very name of Ramakant. Now I know how important Uday Chopra is to Abhishek Bachchan in the *Dhoom* films. If not for him, Abhishek would never have had such an able bandana wearing, bike riding, right-hand man!

'Whoa! Dude! You have got to take this bastard down! How dare he?! I mean…' Ramesh sounded off unable to bear my indignation. He was at a loss for words and seemed puzzled at Shastri's behaviour.

'I know man…I know,' I said trying to calm him down.

'Great! So what are you gonna do? Teach him a lesson he will never forget! Usko chaddi mein nanga karke khada karne ka plan banao!'

'I intend to but I need your help.'

'You can count on it man!' Ramesh replied.

'I am moved by this display of friendship and camaraderie. Ramesh, go and get a motorcycle with a side car,' I said with tears in my eyes.

'Why?'

'Because I want to sing *Yeh dosti hum nahin todenge*. I will be

Dharmendra. You will be Amitabh. Your willingness and readiness to help me requires that we sing this song from *Sholay*.'

'Shut up! Where am I going to get a bike with a sidecar at 12 in the night! MORON!' Ramesh yelled, asking a very pertinent question.

'Let's go wake up Rahul Bajaj,' I replied as Ramesh looked disapprovingly. 'He must have one of those old Hamara Bajaj scooters lying around somewhere in his house.'

It was slightly after midnight. I had left Ramakant's tower shortly after 8 pm in a rage. Of all the things which had transpired since morning, what Shastri had said was what had enraged me the most. It had also hurt me. Sitting in the back of my Aston Martin, I had pondered the words that had come out of his mouth as I drove back home.

I didn't wanna get emotional about it. There was no point rationalizing his deeds because despite his motivations, other options were always open to him. I didn't feel like judging him either. People would make up their own minds about him and his deeds, but right now *I was sitting on a time bomb*. The next court date was in fifteen days. I had to control the damage before eliminating the cause once and for all before it made things hell of a lot worse.

Upon entering home, the kids and the wife hugged me. I looked into their eyes and felt grateful. I uttered a silent prayer to Ganesha and wished that despite our differences Ramakant would find happiness.

As I untangled myself from the family hug, a familiar voice railed, 'Sir! Sir! I am so glad you are out and back home. You don't worry Sir! As soon as the court opens after the weekend, I will file a defamation, fraud, libel, murder, burglary, fraud, illegal trespass, terrorism, medical negligence, treason, arson, animal cruelty, deception, criminal conduct, piracy, diplomacy, indecency, mental lunacy case. IPC, constitution, civil, criminal, international, national, gram, vidhan sabha, vidhan parishad, UN se lekar CNN tak jo bhi laws hai un sabka maar maar ke case file kardoonga against that dangerous criminal Ramakant Shastri! I WILL SUE HIM FOR HURTING RELIGIOUS SENTIMENTS AND CAUSING COMMUNAL DISHARMONY BECAUSE YOU, SIR, ARE GOD! DON'T WORRY SIR!'

I looked at the bald-headed, white-haired geezer who was sniveling like a nasty hungry hyena and said patiently, 'Ratmalani'

'Yes Sir!' he said like an enthusiastic waiter waiting to serve me.

'I've had a long and hard day. I want to take rest. Thank you for all your help today, especially for arranging bail in just 3 hours, but I would like to spend some time with my family now.'

Ratmalani rattled off, 'Of course Sir! Of course! Don't worry sir. We will sue that Shastri fellow so many times he will feel like a sewing machine. You don't worry Sir!'

'Thanks Ratmalani.'

'Goodbye Sir!' he said and immediately left.

A hot bath and 5 large pizzas with olives, jalapeno peppers, extra extra extra cheese, and some more cheese later, I was back and revving at full throttle. Bring on another jail vacation, I say!

Being in Chennai, Ramesh had been unable to arrange bail, so I had left the task to Ratmalani and the office staff. Ratmalani had swung into action as soon as I had been rushed out of the court through a bevy of raging media reporters and straight into the police van.

He had ambushed another judge in the court and had locked him up in the bathroom but not before stealing his pants, playing and replaying the 'Greatest Hits of Himesh Reshammiya' CD over and over again till the judge who had reached the point of suicide desperately signed my bail order.

The judge was then sent to the hospital (without pants) after suffering a heart attack and Ratmalani had rushed to the jail, where I was being held, in a bulldozer to run over any and all media people who had thronged the jail entrance. Terrified, they had parted like the Dead Sea before Moses. Ratmalani had thrust the bail order into the cop's face who resigned from the IPS the moment Ratmalani walked into the premises. Soon, he ushered me out into my waiting Aston Martin from where I drove to Shastri's Tower.

I was glad to be home. It had been a long and punishing day. The media were dying to talk to me but my commandos had kept them back. At 11 pm, Ramesh arrived back in Bombay and wanted to come home. I told him I needed a chill pill after a tumultuous day.

The best way to chill was to do it at our favourite haunt—the Bombay Stock Exchange.

Three hours after eating 5 large pizzas, I was hungry…so I ate bhel-puri from a paper cone as I sat in the cold night air waiting for Ramesh to arrive.

Around a quarter to midnight, Ramesh's car pulled up. He had arrived straight from the airport and looked famished. My poor hungry best friend! Mani quickly dished up more bhel and we started talking.

After he had rudely dashed aside my celebration of our friendship by crooning and making appropriately choreographed movements to the Sholay song in a motorcycle with a side car, we continued discussing how best to get rid of ~~Gabbar Singh~~ Ramakant Shastri.

'Do you have a plan?' he asked pensively.

'Of course I have a plan! It involves a long rope, black clothes, anti-gravity boots, a truck, a midget, a telephone directory, a flame-thrower, a box of farm fresh chicken eggs, and a packet of chewing gum,' I replied emphatically.

'What!'

'That is the plan.'

'Dude! Be serious. The moment the market opens on Monday, news of your arrest and the Notco case is going to impact every single company you've invested in. I don't need to tell you this!'

'I am serious! Look, go find me a midget. Go!'

'JHUN! GODDAMN IT!' an exasperated Ramesh thundered.

'Relax dude,' I said comfortingly.

'Jeez! They should have kept you in jail only.'

'So you won't help me find a midget?'

'DO YOU WANT ME TO KILL YOU!' he thundered again. 'IF YOU DON'T HAVE A PLAN, THEN LET'S AT LEAST THINK OF ONE.'

'I have a plan,' I said immediately, calm and cool as ice.

'What is it?' he asked as his irritation turned into curiosity.

'I'm still working out the finer details. I was thinking about it while having a shower before the pizza.'

'Do you think it will work?'

'I'm not sure...though my experience says it should and that's the thing about experience... It teaches you things. I know a guy who was shot 10 times and he still survived. Today he makes the world's safest bullet-proof jackets...and he's able to do that because of his shooting experience. I made a lot of money when I invested in his company.'

'Hmm, so how do we destroy this Ramakant fellow?'

'The problem is I don't just want to destroy him. *I don't think that will destroy anything. I want to destroy Nothing.*'

Holding the paper cone of bhel in one hand and palm outstretched into a questioning claw with the other, Ramesh asked, 'Huh?'

Like a Professor I elucidated, 'What we need to do is destroy this very concept of selling NOTHING. *I want to destroy this very idea itself.*'

'Why?'

'As you know I have never been a fan of this. It's time we brought an end to this. We have to destroy Notco Industries. That's how we finish Ramakant off.'

'But what about the patent case and the Rikhitpur factory and the other shitstorms?'

I grinned and replied, 'Chakkar chalana padega.'

'Kaise? And I don't want to hear about the midget!' Ramesh countered.

Taking a long, patient breath and gobbling bhel from my cone, I looked at Ramesh and mischievously grinned, 'This is a large scale operation…'

He pondered what I had said and a few seconds later, his eyes flickered with the sparkle of realization. 'Uh…oh…' he muttered.

'It requires a lot of things to happen at a lot of places…' I said again, this time with a nastier grin.

'Uh…oh!'

'We need help. Just you and me doing this will take a lot of time and that's a luxury we can't afford.'

'Uh oh! Uh oh!' he repeated nodding his head in disbelief.

Getting onto my feet, I held onto the horns of the Dalal Street Bull and declared, 'It's time.'

'UH…OH! JHUN! I KNOW WHAT YOU'RE THINKING. I AM SURE THERE'S A BETTER WAY! NOT *THEM* PLEASE! THEY ARE LUNATICS! EK EK NAMOONA HAI! AND DON'T EVEN GET ME STARTED ON SUBHASH!' Ramesh pleaded.

'Nope…There's no other way dude. I ran all possible ways to solve this problem in my head and this is the best one.'

'NO…NO…NOT THEM! NO…'

'THE BAND IS GETTING BACK TOGETHER BABY!!'

THE RETURN OF THE BAND 2

On the outskirts of the city, on a dusty road branching off the highway, Ramesh and I awaited THE BAND…

THE BAND©™ is a top secret organization consisting of mutual fund managers, bankers, stock exchange members, investors, traders, currency importers, lawyers, teachers, athletes, and mercantilists from every walk of life. The band has one main purpose—*to mobilize in an hour of need in order to protect the world financial system from descending into chaos.*

We fall under no regulations. We do not come under the purview of any government. We need nobody's permission. We do what we want when we want. We are the last line of defense against the collapse of the modern economic system. It was the band which saved the world's ass after the Lehman Brothers crash in 2008.

We protect the economy from invading alien currencies like the guys from *Men in Black*, we fight against evil communists like *The Avengers*, we restore faith in the capitalist system like the Justice League, and we investigate corporate fraud and heinous moolah criminality like ACP Pradyuman's CID Team. Officially we are CID IN BLACK. That's the writing on the letterhead at least.

More commonly we are simply called THE BAND and when we decide to run riot on you, you best believe we're coming to kick your ass...guaran-damn-teed.

To be a member of the band you must love the ideals of democracy and capitalism. Hate the communists and most importantly love ice-cream. The world's most intelligent people have wished to be a part of the band but have been disallowed because they hate ice-cream. Bastards!

The band is headed by a fearless leader with balls the size of watermelons dedicated to the highest principals of capital creation, preservation, and distribution. The leader is called the BANDMASTER and under his or her direction, the band bajaos everyone. The leader is a warrior elected in a brutal contest where 12 nominees fight each other to the death in a steel cage match with terrifying instruments of torture like chainsaws, axes, steel chairs, metal ladders, swords, iron clubs, and DVD's of Abhishek Bachchan's *Drona* hanging from the sealed roof.

They fight like Roman gladiators beating the living shit out of each other. The winner must eviscerate each of his opponents in front of a jam-packed arena full of shouting, screaming, blood-thirsty, salivating band members one by one... till no more are left. He must then cut off his final competitor's head and parade it around on a sharp wooden spike as a mark of victory.

The winner alights from the cage, stinking in the blood of the vanquished. Brazen and soul ravaged, he then takes his place on the throne where he is crowned and given a commemorative trumpet. After he blows his own horn, with the first blast of the trumpet, the winner is officially hailed as the bandmaster and he leads the band to one victory after another bajaoing the pants off everyone.

There is also another way of electing the leader which for the record I am strongly opposed to. It involves a simple ballot election where members vote for their own leader. By writing a name on a piece of paper or pressing a button on an electronic voting machine or more recently SMSing 'nominee name' YES to a 5 digit number. Each SMS costs 10 rupees and 2 rupees from each SMS will go towards feeding poor people who can't afford any food because they lost all their money sending 10 rupee SMSs.

For some strange reason the band has off late elected the bandmaster by the above election method instead of the steel cage match I am strongly in favour of. However, even with that, there is currently only one BANDMASTER, chosen with a clear and concise, comprehensive, and popular mandate—ME.

I was elected in a landslide victory at the last conclave; there were literally landslides of jubilation in the world markets when I won. The ground beneath every stock exchange—from New York to Sydney—shook with the ecstatic energy of jubilant traders and brokers jumping up and down and side to side celebrating my victory. P.S.—As my first official act I added another criterion to the pre-existing membership rules: All Band members must not only love ice-cream but also absolutely hate STINKER or anyone who closely even resembles his ugly, dehydrated, burning rubber face. They must hate him more than N.D. Tiwari hates a paternity test.

After our midnight discussion at the BSE, Ramesh had convened the meeting of the band at my Lonavala farmhouse this morning. Hence here I was, close to noon, awaiting the ensemble of loud, drunk, misfits I've come to know as my good friends.

The rumbling continued. At first I thought it was my stomach establishing dominion over the world's food products and signaling this intent to my brain by growling its walls. Even Ramesh standing next to me thought the same thing and looked at my stomach suspiciously. 'It's not me dude!' I exclaimed but for some reason he wasn't convinced.

The rumbling got louder. The ground started to quake, the air heated up like Pokhran after India's nuclear tests. Ramesh and I looked at each other trying to maintain our balance. The ground really was shaking!

'AAH! Earthquake! Earthquake!' I yelled looking for cover.

'Just calm down man, it's not an earthquake!' an off kilter Ramesh screamed.

'Well then, why is the ground quaking, genius?'

'LOOK, I don't believe that the earth's tectonic plates bridging the earth's crust are actually shaking. This seems to be a pointed surface vibration limited to our current position only.'

'WELL, WHO THE HELL MADE YOU A QUALIFIED GEOPHYSICIST?'

Before he could answer, the rumbling got even louder. Something was approaching from just beyond the horizon and the ground despite Ramesh's insights was still quaking.

AND THEN... It got even louder. I could see a metal pipe from where I was standing. The pipe was moving closer by the second. Ramesh and I looked at each other as we vibrated like mobile phones...ready to break out in a run at any instant.

As my bodyguards prepared to whisk me away, I caught a glimpse of the pipe. HOLY SHIT! IT wasn't just a pipe. It was the barrel of a gun! It was the long, tubular firing gun of a full-fledged army tank that was approaching towards us and was now less than 500 metres away!

One of my bodyguards immediately latched onto me and began whisking me away. Through the noise he cried aloud, 'SIR, we have to move you inside. I believe we are under attack.'

'Aaaaaaah! I KNEW IT! THE GOVERNMENT HAS DECIDED TO ATTACK ME BECAUSE I AM TOO AWESOME!' I uttered as the guard tried to pull me into the farmhouse.

'SHUT UP JHUN!' Ramesh uttered. 'I think it's them. I can see Subhash on the bike.'

'WHAA!'

The tank started to grind to a halt. I could now see a bit more clearly through the curtain of dust. A dozen BMW X98878 bikes revved up from behind the tank and were headed towards me. I recognized Subhash immediately. Ramesh was right! More familiar faces emerged.

Two more tanks rolled on from behind the other one. They were flanking the giant metal Abrams M1 Tank. Gobsmacked, Ramesh and I stood on the pavement as the entire procession marched towards us like a herd of angry elephants on steroids.

It was unbelievable! About 6 fighter jets scrambled in the cloudless blue sky above.

Behind the tanks was an envoy of dark green army trucks. I didn't know what the hell was going on! Absolutely perplexed, Ramesh and I stood by the side of the road overlooking the farmhouse. The slumbering street dogs had been awakened and were barking at the tanks. I was reminded of Bhanu Pratap (the court puppy) and decided I must send him an email and seek advice from him on investing in the pedigree dog food company.

The tanks and the trucks rolled on. The bikers in black helmets and black biker jackets cut away from the pack and screeched towards us. Ramesh and I waved at them.

Seconds later, the bikes screeched to a halt just in front of us. Subhash alighted and immediately started to yammer. The 35-year-old thin, usually clean-shaven fund manager had grown a stubble peppered with streaks of grey. Clad in a leather biker jacket, a white shirt, and a pair of blue jeans, he moved over to Ramesh and started talking. Ramesh signaled to tell him that we couldn't hear anything because of the rolling tanks.

Soon the tanks and the trucks pulled up and switched their engines off. Phew! The decibel level was finally back to acceptable levels.

'WTF is this! What are you fellows doing with these tanks? What the hell is going on with these trucks and bikes and why are there fighter jets doing sorties in the sky!' I thundered.

Subhash growled with jubilation as I surveyed the scene, 'BANDMASTER! I am so happy to see you! Please hug me! Aapko dekhne ke liye aankhen taras rahi thi when Ramesh Sir called.'

'First tell me what all this heavy artillery is doing outside my house! Mere farmhouse ko Republic Day parade banake rakha hai!'

'Arre Sir! Lekin aapne hi to bola tha ki we are going to war. That's why we have arranged all this. Come and look at the guns.'

'Guns?!'

'Yes, guns. All new stuff. Please come and see no Bandmaster!'

Subhash clasped my shoulder and forcefully nudged me towards the space behind the tanks. I waddled along slapping high fives to the band members who were delighted to see their fearless leader. Subhash led me to one of the trucks in the back. Iqbal and Vishal from my office, also band members, lowered the back door of the truck and raised me up as I heavily landed with a thud on the truck. As Subhash stepped inside, I screamed.

'DUDE! WHAT THE HELL IS THIS? THERE ARE ENOUGH GUNS IN HERE TO START WORLD WAR 3!'

'Arre Sirji! When you said there was going to be a war against this Notco fellow, I personally arranged these guns and bombs. Look at the stuff here. We have everything! We have it all. I've had to personally call up every known arms dealer, gun smuggler, bomb maker, and terrorist organization for these! And look at the quality. We have everything here—rifles, shotguns, pistols, revolvers, hand grenades, flamethrowers, stab daggers, trip wires, landmines, IEDs, stunners, buzzers, and even bazookas!'

'BAZOOKAS!'

'Yes Sirji, bazookas,' Subhash reassured and picked up a bazooka. 'These bastards will blow away and burn the enemy till not even traces of his DNA remains. TOTAL VAAT LAGA DENGE. So Mahabaharat kab ladni hai? WE ARE READY!'

The band screamed in chorus, 'WE ARE READY!'

'I didn't mean an actual war, dude!' I explained flabbergasted. 'I mean, it's a war but we will do it without any guns and shit!'

'Whaaat! You mean I have to get rid of all this?' whined Subhash unhappily.

'Yes!'

'DUDE! WHAT THE HELL IS THIS? THERE ARE ENOUGH GUNS IN HERE TO START WORLD WAR 3!'

'But Sirji! Getting all this at such short notice was so much of a hassle. Do you know how many Somali pirates and Lashkar -e-Toiba fellows we had to rob to get this stuff?'

'I don't care! Just get rid of it dammit!!'

'Can't we at least keep the tanks?' Subhash pleaded.

'We'll see.'

'Sirji! Please don't be angry, no! We will do anything for you! Your word is everything Sirji! You just give us the word Sirji. The band is ready. Even now we can actually go to war. There are Navy ships standing off the coast of Vizag ready to await your order, dear Bandmaster! Just give the word!'

Moved by his words I said, 'I appreciate your loyalty and friendship, Subhash. Without you and the band, this whole thing would take a hell of a lot longer. I deeply appreciate it!'

'Don't say that Sirji!' Subhash insisted as he pointed the Bazooka at me. 'Hamare aankhon mein aaason ki baarish ho jayegi!'

'OYE! Keep that thing aside before you hurt somebody,' I instructed as Subhash hastily placed the bazooka on the floor of the truck.

'Come let us hug!' I said loudly as we got out of the truck. The ardent devotees thronged me. I hugged them and thanked them all. Soon we entered the farmhouse and had a grand feast. Notco was going down.

THE PLAN

Shortly after lunch, we gathered in the multi-acre, air-conditioned and Dolby woofer surround sound powered auditorium in the underground car park of my farmhouse. By now you would hardly be surprised that a guy who has his own whale-shaped submarine, the Batmobile, the Optimus Prime Transformer truck, jetpacks, Aston Martins, limousines, limousines made out of Aston Martins (*Limoustines*), and most importantly Nitro powered auto rickshaws also has his own auditorium…in his car park…underground…in his farmhouse…in a secret chamber… underneath the swimming pool. I'm not boasting. I'm only describing my recreational farmhouse.

We seated ourselves around the giant kilometre-long dining table. This thing is so long, there are traffic signals every 50 metres to regulate the movement of the dishes which run on tracks placed upon the table. The signals were placed after a fruit salad had smashed into ice-cream. It was a dish best served cold.

The long table helps when you need to dine in style and even more to conduct business in an orderly manner. The dining table often turns into a conference table post lunch, like today. We sat around the table, many chewing paan like yokels and ready to collapse from food induced coma but kept awake by the burning desire to bring Notco down.

As the tanks, bikes, and battle trucks nestled in the hot sun outside, I puffed on a Gurkha and began the briefing of the war plan.

'Dear band members, we are gathered here today to plot and execute the downfall of one Ramakant Shastri, currently Chairman of Notco industries, pioneer of the Nothing market and most importantly, a third-rate-snot-covered-pimp-dressing-funnel–wearing-ass-clown-punk who thinks he is God.'

Ratmalani immediately banged his fist on the table and yelled 'OBJECTION BANDMASTER SIRJI! But he cannot think he is God. Only you can think you are God. This is blasphemy!'

The guys applauded as Ratmalani looked around patting his own back as if he had made a winning argument in court. Ramesh motioned to him to keep quiet.

I continued with my game face on. 'A few months ago I met this demure little man in my office. Since then I have witnessed his transformation from aspiring entrepreneur to complete jackass. This is a guy who has sold millions of empty boxes to very willing, naive, stupid, and easily manipulated customers. In the process he's become a billionaire.'

The room shuddered.

'He's even richer than all of you guys!' I said.

Subhash yelled, 'O SIRJI! You give me the order right now and I will punch him in his underground area. I will punch him so hard his man-bags will split!'

The room shuddered even more.

I looked disapprovingly at Subhash who had a grimacing *'So when do I get to split this guy's man-bags?'* look.

Taking a deep breath, I circled my gaze around the eager faces seated all around the table and proclaimed, 'A little over a day ago he lied in court and directly implicated me in patent fraud. Today, we find ourselves at the threshold of a breaking point. On Monday morning the markets will open at 9 am. The most important sentiment, one which overwhelms all logic, all rationale, and mathematical equations, will be in short supply…especially in those companies I have put my money in. This sentiment folks is confidence.

'An emperor under a cloud of darkness, wrongdoing and cheating does not enjoy the favour of his citizens for long. Your emperor's empire is under threat. I have now accepted that by Monday afternoon my investments will be down by at least 15–20%. They have already fallen by 2–3% after I was marched off to jail on Friday in the closing hour of the session.

In overall numerical terms, I'm looking at a probable loss of billions of dollars which will ultimately put the entire economy in peril. This cannot be tolerated under any circumstance. I am Sir Sri Jhunjhunwala. The World needs me.'

An air of silence meandered through the room. Hapless, anxiety-filled faces looked at each other. I continued. I was the General leading the troops into war and on the eve of the Mahabharata, this was the war cry. THIS WAS SPARTA!

'When you become a trader and an investor, you must be prepared to lose money *only* because of bad economic decisions made by pinhead economists, ministers, bureaucrats, and bankers who have no clue as to how stock markets work… NOT because of lying, manipulative, fraudster wannabes like Ramakant Shastri. *He gives hardworking, fully legit, taxpaying, and tax hating billionaires like me a bad name!'*

The crowd rose to their feet and exploded into an applause.

Soaking the thunder of applause in, I motioned to the guys to sit down and let me speak. Obediently and in awe of my fearsome oration, they sat back down and listened. I thundered on, 'Even though I forecast a fall in my investments because of negativity and rumour mongering, *I am confident that the lack of confidence in my skills or ethics among devotees who buy the same companies I do will not last long.* Moreover making money has never been difficult for me. It's as easy as snapping my fingers. Whatever I lose, I will make ten times as much ten times sooner. As Shah Rukh Khan once said in the Ganesh Jain produced, Abbas–Mustan directed, Eros Labs distributed, United 7 creations released and Anu Malik musicated film *Baazigar—haar kar jeetne walon ko baazigar kehte hain.'*

Cheers of 'Bravo! Bravo' and 'sign my bra, sign my bra' from female bandmates erupted from the aisles. I motioned once again to the crowd to quiet down. The energy in my words was more than enough to overcome the stupor of the grand meal I had thrown for them.

'YOU MAY NOW ADDRESS ME AS GENERAL!' I roared. 'I even got this fancy green army hat made with the word 'GENERAL' embossed in size 48 Palatino font to indicate my badass cutthroat attitude. It is time to fight, my dear band of brothers and sisters who are in a minority here because the world of finance is more male-dominated. *And as you fight, remember we must strip away Ramakant Shastri at the end of this war, the man who has christened himself but not earned the title of "Emperor". It is time we showed the people the truth about this pseudo emperor and his new clothes.* So I ask you…ARE YOU READY?'

BOOM! The applause and mad cheering tore the roof off. Shouts of 'YES!', ' HELL YEAH!', ' BRING IT ON! ', 'LET'S DO IT!', 'THROW ANGRY BIRDS AT HIM!', 'WE'LL BURN HIS HOUSE DOWN IF PETROL IS AFFORDABLE!' and other phrases indicating unequivocal readiness ending in an exclamation mark were showered gratuitously. Subhash yelled, 'LET'S DRESS HIM UP LIKE A 15-YEAR-OLD GIRL AND SEND HIM TO GODMAN ASARAM'S ASHRAM!' The sound was deafening but hey, this was the band. Don't expect us to be quiet!

I basked in the glory of the thundering rapture of applause. After letting it resonate for a minute, I raised my hand. The band laid down their instruments and listened attentively to their effervescent general cum bandmaster.

'Does anyone have anything to say?' I asked.

Subhash spoke first. I've always thought that even by my standards Subhash is clearly nuts. The only place for a man of his madness is either the world of finance or politics. He's chosen the former. He works as a fund manager. This means that every time you are putting your cash in a mutual fund run by the Tatas or Birlas, you are pretty much leaving it in the hands of Subhash. Be warned!

'Don't worry, General Sirji,' he said. 'Hum aapke liye apni jaan tak de denge aur jaan tak le lenge. Just give us the word. Bahar truck mein chain gun aur machine gun pade hain. We will go to his house right now and put so many holes inside him, saala doodh ki chalni jaise dikhne lagega!'

'Subhash, have you been taking your medicine?'

'Of course General! I am fit and fine! My paranoid schizophrenia is now normal schizophrenia.'

'We are not going to put holes in him. That will raise eyebrows,' I said.

'Then let's shave off his eyebrows,' he retorted.

'No!'

'What I suggest is we take him and snip, snip...' he said moving his index and middle finger in a scissor motion.

'Give him a haircut?' I asked.

'Arre no Sirji. Nasbandi kar dete hain uski! By snip snip, I meant let us kidnap him in the middle of the night and give him a vasectomy. A south Indian version of that *Vicky Donor* film called *Balasubramanium Donor* is also releasing soon. I am sure around this time there will be an enhanced demand in the spermatozoa market. Obviously having realized that his product is worth a hell of a lot less because of the vasectomy, he will feel demoralized. We would have broken him emotionally. We can imprison him in an isolated labyrinth, videotape him and watch him lead the rest of his sterile life. That will be the perfect revenge...'

'Dude!' I exclaimed. 'I don't think the schizophrenia has reduced and now I am paranoid you will give me a vasectomy when I am asleep! STAY AWAY FROM ME!'

Ratmalani interrupted as Subhash looked at me in surprise. 'Sirji, just give me the word. I will file so many cases against him he will lead the rest of his life in court itself. Aisa halat kar doonga uski susu karne ke liye bhi high court se order lena padega…'

'Ratmalani! I am not listening to you. The last time I left you to handle things, you put a puppy in my hands. This time only god knows which animal you will stick me in there with.'

I rotated my gaze around the engaged group. Subhash once again sounded off convincingly 'I still say let's give him a vasectomy…'

Before I blew my lid and punched him in the face, he interjected.

'Sir, we need a plan. Ramakant Shastri ka fake encounter kar dete hain! I know at least four to five cops who will readily agree to encounter his ass. We'll abduct him and then 'BANG, BANG' …over…maamla khatam. Notco = no more. Problem solved. Whiskey party at night…okay?'

'Dude! What the hell is wrong with you! I don't want to kill him. I want to teach him a lesson he will never forget! Now shut up and listen to me. Especially you Subhash! And no more talk about vasectomies or fake encounters! Jeez!'

'Calm down JHUN! Warna something else will burst like your appendix,' Ramesh said as I sat down and drank water.

Rehydrated with fresh water, I cleared my throat, adjusted my glasses, stood back up and laid my hands on the table.

'Pay attention folks. I do not just want Notco gone, I don't just want Ramakant Shastri gone, I want to destroy this very idea of NOTHING. I want this entire concept uprooted and thrown into the trash,' I said as I warned Subhash with my eyes to not open his mouth.

'Okay so how do we do this?' asked Nandini.

'This brings me to the plan,' I replied. 'Dear Band, our success depends on the execution of this plan. Now I came up with this last night and it is more complicated than advanced calculus and molecular biology combined. Even Einstein would have required years to come up with something as brilliant as this, but me being intellectually superior, I have managed this in just a few minutes and that too because my pen was physically unable to withstand the speed with which I was jotting down my ideas, otherwise I would have come up with this in seconds.

I flashed a big brownish yellow envelope the size of a telephone directory with the words: *'Jhunjhunwala's Grand Awesome Master Plan To Destroy Notco Without Causing Anyone Else Harm* or JGAMPTDNWCAEH'

Waving it around I said, 'Folks this is *not* just a plan, it is a *grand masterplan*'

Anticipation palpitated off the room. I was holding the Ten Commandments in my hands and the faithful bowed in reverence and adulation.

'I will now explain the grand awesome masterplan, so listen up carefully.'

A quiet hush blanketed upon the room. Everyone was concentrating hard save Subhash who once again mouthed 'snip, snip' menacingly and did the scissoring action with his fingers as I looked around the room once again.

'This plan will be stage by stage and step by step,' I began.

Ramesh added, 'Now remember the longer the false news that Jhun directed Shastri to claim the patent as his own is allowed to circulate, the worse it's going to hurt Jhun.

'As Jhun said, we know that the immediate damage is unavoidable. Many people will believe that all of this is Jhun's fault and not Ramakant's. They will sell shares in companies he has big stakes in believing he has engaged in unethical practices in them as well. This is a blot on his reputation. We cannot help this in the short-term. But in the long-term it is something we can not only repair but also restore and enhance.

'Our immediate goal is to therefore contain the damage. The PR firm will do this in the media and by managing perceptions. But what they do down at the level of the street will be useless unless we take charge.'

Pleased with his description, I declared as the band furiously scribbled down notes:

'Therefore, this is the breakdown.

'Stage 1—On Monday morning, we will assemble every trader and broker and start selling Notco shares on the market. Sell every single Notco share you get your hands on. It doesn't matter who you talk to or where you get it from. *Just sell.*

'Ramakant thinks he is invincible. What he does not realize yet is that his company is a listed entity. Key word—*listed.* He's playing ball in my playground. If a company is listed on a stock exchange anywhere in the world, I can find a way of destroying it.

'Once the selling occurs, people will add to the panic by abandoning ship. They will be led to believe on TV and the news that the patent case is causing all this negativity and that's why Notco investors are selling. While this will be true in part, what they won't know is that for the large part the band is the one selling shares and driving down the value.'

Nandini interjected abruptly as she looked at me, 'If I may point out Sir, we won't be able to sell that many shares without the bear cartel knowing.'

'Don't worry about that for now. I will handle that.'

'How?' asked Ramesh agreeing with Nandini.

'Don't worry about it boys and girls. I will take care of that,' I replied as the Band whispered. Nandini's important observation about the bear cartel had sparked off a debate.

'What I am worried about Sir,' she continued, 'is that average common people who have put their savings into Notco after buying into the hype will lose their hard earned money if we drive the price of Notco down. They value of their investments will be worth a lot less overnight if we do this.'

'True. This, however, dear Nandini is not the entire plan. It's only a part of the plan, rest assured,' I replied.

Reading from the JGAMPTDNWCAEH, I paused and continued.

'Notco's shareholding is divided as follows:

'One: Ramakant is the major promoter; he owns 55% of this company in shares.

'Two: I own another 15%.

'Three: Out of the remaining 30%, only 5% is held by small investors and individuals.

'And finally: The other 25% is held by mutual funds, foreign investors, government companies like LIC and banks, and such.

'We will target this 25%. We are gonna be spending much of today and tomorrow calling up every single one of these medium and big financial institutions, and offering them a backroom deal to buy their shares out. It's like a hostile takeover. These guys won't agree at first, but after stage two they'll be begging to sell.'

'Sirji! My head is hurting,' Subhash interrupted sueezing his forehead and whined, 'This is getting too complicated. Can't we just shoot the guy and be done with it?'

'No!'

'Let's give him a vasectomy first and then shoot him... where he just had a vasectomy. Then lets shave off his eyebrows and shoot him there also...'

'NO!' Ramesh shouted.

I resumed as Subhash looked on, massaging his temples.

'Stage 2: Around 10 am, an hour after trading begins, news is going to break that a government report has discovered that Nothing causes cancer. *Not just Notco Nothing but Nothing in general.* The substance or rather lack of it in itself is inherently harmful.'

'What?!!' Iqbal said astonished as the echoes picked up. It seemed he had uttered the word with the exact same sentiment that was going through everybody's mind after hearing Stage 2.

Calmly, I explained as I read out from the JGAMPTDN-WCAEH, 'There's a small government affiliated lab in Kozhikode which tests bug spray. They've been wanting a tennis court on their campus for a long time. So I've made sure that those guys get a tennis court in return for which they will issue a report saying these exact words *"Preliminary testing under diluted conditions suggests samples of a wide variety of pure Nothing in loose state likely to display probably produced cancer-related symptoms in individuals showing tendencies of inclination toward the same by virtue of chromosomal anomalies susceptible to carcinogenic neoplasms".'*

'What the hell does that even mean!' an exasperated Ramesh yelled.

'It doesn't matter what it means!' I replied emphatically. 'It's not a lie. It basically says people with cancer when exposed to Nothing will still have cancer.'

Huh?

'What matters is how the media will read it. Put together the words "government", "cancer", "nothing", and "causes" and every TV channel will run with the headline "GOVERNMENT LAB CONFIRMS NOTHING CAUSES CANCER".'

'But is this even a government lab? Where did you find this thing?' Ramesh enquired.

'It's a government affiliate meaning it sometimes tests samples for the government when the government's own lab is too busy. Anyway it doesn't matter. This news needs to break and be active. Now as long as India does not win a World Cup or Kareena does not divorce Saif on the same day, I am sure this news will keep running on loop on the TV. Can't wait to watch Goswami's 9 pm debate then!

'With this, the pace of selling will be a lot more. Most of the 25% with whom we've spoken will get back to us and take up the offer. They will sell their stake to us and we can bargain for a lower price. Standard vegetable price haggling.

'By the time the market closes at 3.30, Notco will be significantly down.'

Nandini squeaked with the spark of understanding, 'Hmm… And the average investor is a small-scale investor. When a big mutual fund comes along and starts selling its holding, its order will take precedence over that of the smaller investor with the smaller stake. His stake will remain unsold. Conversely no one is going to buy Notco in an environment where only selling activity is predominant and if they still do then well…'

'Well, that's when we begin stage 3,' I said peering into her eyes. The band was stirring.

'Stage 3: This selling will keep on occurring over the course of a week i.e. from Monday to Friday. Every hour on the hour. Session after session there will be only selling. Ramakant will find that his company's value is down by a hell of a lot. The banks which keep his cash flow rolling will start strangling him. Investors will begin cursing him. He's going to be under a lot of pressure. That's when he's going to find a light in the dark.

'An Oman-based company will offer to buy Notco. But guess what? That company is gonna be owned by us!'

The band started screaming raucously! Untethered and off the chain like racehorses on a green pasture!

'Listen, listen,' I pleaded loudly over the sound of the band cheering again. 'I know this plan is just too awesome but let me explain it fully…Ramakant will not know that this company will be owned by us. In fact no one will. This company will be a shell just like his product. Pretty packaging, looks real, feels good but underneath no real substance and no real use. This company does not exist. This is where he gets conned.

'This company will approach him and say they want to buy at least a 95% stake in his company. He can't help but accept because the value of his company is falling any way. He's gonna then make an open offer (when a company goes to its shareholders and agrees to pay for their stake as well so it can increase its ownership majority control, sort of like a buyback program) to the shareholders of Notco.

'Every average investor bothered by the rumours and the fact that Notco's value is plummeting everyday will move to save his cash. He or she will put in his shares and take back his cash. This is our way of ensuring they get fair compensation for their investment. I am sure some will hold out but most will sell, especially considering how the PR firm is going to be feeding the media with stories of how Nothing causes tons and tons of cancer,' I said looking at Nandini who smiled and blinked in approval.

Ramesh surmised, 'Accha...Ramakant has only two options now. One, he either sells his existing company assets like his Rikhitpur factory to obtain the cash needed for the open offer...'

'Or Two...' I added, glad he had grasped on along with the rest, 'he pledges his 55% shares with a bank as collateral. No one will buy assets from him. His factories are all located in areas which he himself has proudly described as the middle of nowhere. The real estate value of even the land here is negligible. Even small farmers like Robert Vadra are uninterested in those.

'Shastri collects the 95% of his shares via the open offer. Even I will tender my 15% stake in the open offer. He's gonna have a 100% of the company left. 95% he believes the Omani company will buy from him and 5% they allowed him to retain control of as the founder after the sale.'

'This is when the Omani company will disappear without a trace. He's left high and dry without as much as an inkling. Gone into thin air!' Vishal injected as he and the band coyly exchanged glances delighted with the simple yet sinister plan that had poured from their leader.

'Stage 5—' I resumed as the Band leaned forward with anticipation waiting for me to explain the final few pieces of the puzzle. 'Shastri realizes he's left with a 100% of his company BUT NO BUYER. *He's got nowhere to go with nothing to sell and a loan borrowed from a bank against collateral which is now worthless!'*

'Stage 6—We release another government report from some fancy name like *The Indian Virology Institute of Higher Bacterial Studies* or something like that which will say in very uncertain terms what has already been said before—that Nothing causes cancer. The media will once again run with it. They will now say three different reports from three different government-backed laboratories indicate that Nothing is indeed cancerous and the government doesn't care, it's ignoring its citizens, death of democracy, and stuff like that.

'Forced to intervene, the government will move in a manner to save its own ass. It needs to be seen as quick and decisive and not as slow and useless. Most likely it will direct the Ministry of Corporate Affairs to shut down Notco.

'Ramakant now has two options. First—accept the government's notice and shut down his company. Second—go to court and fight the cases against him and his company. If he chooses the second he will be operating in an environment where he hardly finds new investors, fails to find new buyers, and fails to woo back the old investors. He has to work in a hostile atmosphere where there's gonna be such a tidal wave of backlashes at him that he's pretty much gonna be screwed.'

As I finished, Ramesh deduced loudly, 'Whichever option he chooses one thing is for certain. Notco will never rise again. No one will back a company without a legitimate business or a business model WITHOUT the hype. No one else will bother to replicate Ramakant's company and 'sell' Nothing because we've now established that it causes cancer. As time progresses even those who want to buy Nothing will no longer buy it because they will either believe it causes cancer or because they've lost interest.'

Placing the JGAMPTDNWCAEH back into the envelope I arose and thundered. The roar was a battle cry as the Band sensing the moment stood up. Chairs creaked vociferously as I growled with ferocity, 'Now, are you ready?'

'YES! YES! YES!' shouted back the Band.

'This plan will ensure total catastrophe for Shastri! His entire operation will become FULL BEDA GARAG!'

The band looked at each other, thrusting their fists into the air, and burst into ground shattering applause as the room echoed with the electrified energy of a raring army. I smiled at Ramesh and lit another Gurkha.

'Are you ready my brothers and sisters?' I asked again over the earth shattering mingle of applause and war cries.

'YES SIR!' Subhash shouted. 'We will do anything for you! We will lay down our lives for you! I still don't understand the grand master awesome plan But I will do anything. I am ready to even suicide bomb myself for you!'

The band cheered on as Subhash tore away his shirt…to reveal a freakin' suicide vest underneath. They quickly quietened down as I yelled.

'DUDE! WHAT THE HELL IS WRONG WITH YOU? First the guns and tanks, now a suicide vest. Is that thing ready to blow?!!!!!'

'No sir. Its wired with C4 explosive which will blast only when I press this button,' Subhash replied pulling out a remote from his trouser pocket and moving his thumb towards the red button…

'YOU IDIOT! Don't press it! You wanna blow us all up or what?!'

'Arre relax Sirji, iss remote mein battery nahin hai. See,' he said mischievously as he opened the back of the remote. Most of the band now hiding under the table came out heaving sighs of relief.

'Dude! You're crazy!' Ramesh shouted at Subhash as he snatched the remote from his hand.

'Arre Sirji! This is proof we are all willing to do anything for you. In your name we will blast all the infidels who troll your name.'

'What's that on the vest? Looks like writing!'

'It's an autograph, Sirji. Osama bin Laden personally autographed this suicide vest before I bought it.'

'DUDE! WHAT THE HELL—AND I ASK FOR THE UMPTEENTH TIME—IS WRONG WITH YOU? YOU

HAVE A SUICIDE VEST SIGNED BY BIN LADEN? WHEN DID YOU EVEN MEET THAT GUY!'

'I never met him Sirji. I bought this vest from some beggar at a traffic signal. He said that he was the #1 distributor of Bin Laden related memorabilia in Asia. Now that Bin Laden's dead, I am sure I can sell it for a pretty good price.'

'DUDE! I REPEAT…you're crazy. You seriously need help.'

'Arre Sirji, in the words of Dr Sheldon Cooper "I'm not crazy. My mother had me tested!".'

THE SULTAN OF OMAN

Upon a gleamy, sun-baked strip, cutoff from the Indian subcontinent and heralding the gateway into the middle-east, my private jet skid onto the runway of the airport in Dubai.

Since addressing the band 24 hours ago, two things had happened:

1. I had worked tirelessly running the phones all night long with everyone at the farmhouse base of operations. Together we had dialed hundreds of numbers and generated more revenue for Bharat Sanchar Nigam Limited, Lonavala division in 1 day than an entire year—getting every single interested party on the phone like telemarketers and hammering them. I personally ~~issued death threats~~ spoke persuasively to hundreds upon hundreds of investment bankers, mutual fund guys, corporate financers, NBFC's—basically anyone who made up the 25% we were targeting.
2. Subhash was injected with animal tranquillizer because ordinary human sedatives were found to have no effect on him. After five glasses of whiskey and finding two batteries, he had rushed off in one of the tanks towards Mumbai, wanting to explode Notco Towers with his vest. Luckily Nandini had found him screaming 'DEATH TO RAMAKANT THE

INFIDEL!' just as he boarded a Tank and was about to exit the area and immediately alerted the others. He was now handcuffed to one leg of the conference/dining table and had passed out.

Some shareholders readily agreed to sell their shares to us the first thing the market opened tomorrow. Many, like I predicted, were reluctant, inquisitive, and befuddled.

It was our prerogative to make sure that the media had not gotten wind of our activities. They needed to be kept busy. Subhash had dug a 20-foot hole in the ground and was intent on throwing a 2-year-old toddler inside in order to distract the media from our activities. However, plans changed when that first glass of whiskey led him to a set of batteries.

The PR guys I had hired were hyping news of a marriage-less honeymoon getaway between a leading actress and her new manager/boyfriend/boytoy/booty call/mature adult partner/relationship enabler/true love/romantic interest/on again off again on again consort/possible spouse at a beach resort in Mauritius. Clearly this was of tremendous national importance and way more attractive for the media to focus on compared to a humble, multi-billionaire tycoon's nefarious billion dollar con aimed as revenge for having been conned in the first place. So with the media at bay clicking bikini pictures and then debating at primetime if clicking bikini pictures was invasive paparazzo culture or intense investigative journalism, the band felt relatively safe that our activities would avoid scrutiny at least for a day or two and quietly went to work.

At around 2 pm, I had flown out of the farmhouse on the jet leaving Ramesh to handle stage 1 and 2. Armed with Princy in one hand and Bhanu Pratap, the golden retriever puppy, in the other, the Big Bull and 2 little mutts along with Iqbal and Vishal departed for Dubai. Stage 3 was underway. We were making preparations to open a shell company operated from Oman.

A shell company was important in bringing Notco down. A shell is also known as a *benami holding* and the man who would help me in this regard would be the Sultan of Oman.

Imagine a corporate entity which looks real from the outside, boasts a lot of numbers, employees, profits, growth, and blah blah but on the inside is totally empty. It's an attractive layer of lies hiding a hard, inconvenient truth.

It's only a name operating under the guise of a commercial enterprise and only the name exists, *nothing else*. I was still unsure if this would work but having been a gambler all my life, the risk was no stranger despite the consequences. The key thing was that in my plan, Ramakant had to be convinced that the company was a real one, only then would he accept the offer from such a company to buy Notco. Of course back home stage 1 and 2 would need to go off without too many hitches for stage 3 to become relevant. Nonetheless preparations needed to be made.

Slightly after 4 pm, we alighted into the desert city of Dubai. Even though it was well past noon, that trademark Emirate sun was ruthlessly beating down on the city. The wind was slow, flat and sandy. I popped on a pair of black goggles, said tata, bye bye to Captain Topinath and promised to return in a few hours. He looked sad, so I gave him a hug and a 10% increase in salary.

With the dogs in my hands, we strode into a black Cadillac waiting for us a few metres from where the jet had landed on the runway. A chauffeur held a placard with the words ' Sir Sir Sri Sri Sri Sheikh Keshra Wala Nujh Nujh'. I waved to him as we got in and started off to the hotel.

As we made ourselves comfortable inside the car, Iqbal said with a worried tone and a forlorn look, 'Sir, I think there's been a mistake. The placard said "Sheikh" and had your name all jumbled up.'

'No mistake Iqbal. As part of the grand awesome master plan, it is imperative we keep our names and identities secret. That's why, as long as we are here you will only address me as your Excellency Sheikh Keshra Wala Nujh Nujh. This is my alias.'

'OKAY...' he accepted reluctantly as his confusion began to fade 'I was wondering about the dogs. I mean I know Princy is your dog and she travels with you but what about the puppy? Have you adopted this pup also?'

'This puppy my dear friend is the key to our success in stage 3.You will realize this when we meet the Sultan soon. Make sure all the papers are in order.'

'Yes Sir! Checked and double checked. Being here with you is so exciting!' Iqbal said as his forlorn expression changed into a grin of delight. Vishal acknowledged Iqbal's sentiment with a similar grin.

Princy and Bhanu Pratap were both tired and were sleeping on the opposite seat. Poor Bhanu Pratap, this was his first flight. So much burden at such a young age for the poor pup—a modeling career, a dog–food specialist, Ratmalani's witness, and now a cross-country traveler all at the tender age of 3 months! Poor dog!

Iqbal started going through the papers as Vishal looked impatiently at his watch.

I smiled humbly as I tore open a packet of Gutkha. The driver peering from the rear view mirror appeared miffed.

'Sheikh, you cannot consume gutkha or tobacco products in our country,' he warned.

'OYE! This is not gutkha. It is medicine. I am suffering from severe awesomitis,' I retorted.

'Oh. Sorry to hear that but gutkha is banned.'

'This is not gutkha my friend. It is just powdered mouth freshener.'

'Errr... what is that smell I am getting? Smells like tobacco!'

'Haha! Tobacco? Me? I never smoke. And I definitely don't drink alcohol. God promise! This is special mouth freshener. It contains aloe vera. Thats what you must have smelt.'

'Hello what?'

'Not hello. Aloe.'

'A...l...o...e...' he repeated each syllable like a Chinese guy learning Bhojpuri while simultaneously turning the steering wheel.

'Yes aloe. Now you may chalo,' I said.

Iqbal and Vishal smiled mischievously. They were marveling at my BADASSNESS. Here I was in another country breaking the law by consuming banned products with little regard for myself or the law. I'm a rebel and a renegade. A handsome hunk of a rule-shattering God.

We traversed the busy streets of Dubai looking at hawkers, turbaned Arab folk, women in burqas, and little kids in smart salwars. The roads were crowded and beaming with life.

The car began to slow down. Soon, we arrived at the big ship—the Burj al Arab hotel.

A masterpiece of architecture, a concrete sailboat on a manmade isle in the middle of a blue lagoon. The world's costliest hotel. They charge you thousands of dollars just to look at the damn thing from 10 feet away.

I had booked the penthouse conference room. We were ushered in by eager hotel employees. I've been to the Burj al Arab a few times before. I once played tennis with Roger Federer on the roof. He said I was the greatest tennis player he had ever known and thanked God that I was a legendary investor by profession and not a tennis player.

I retired with the dogs to my penthouse suite and readied myself for the meeting. It was shortly past 6. The sun had not yet gone down though it was cooler now. I quickly made a call to the wife first and then Ramesh to check how things were going. The dogs had woken up. The hotel staff had planted doggie bowls and the two mutts were busy treating themselves to some fine desert produce.

I picked them up and headed to the conference hall at the end of the corridor. Vishal and Iqbal were waiting outside its glass doors. I could see the Sultan looking at a painting with his back turned to me.

Pushing across the door, I headed in. The sound of the door alerted the Sultan who immediately turned around and smiled. I gave the dogs to Iqbal and proceeded towards the Sultan.

'Welcome! Welcome my friend!' he greeted warmly. The Sultan swayed elegantly in his golden yellow rich silky robe. His white beard stood pristine on his jaw as his wrinkly 65-year-old face flashed his pearly white teeth at me in a warm smile. His belly protruded under the robe as he took two steps forward and smiled some more.

'Thank you, O great ruler of the Sultanate of Oman!' I replied as I went to hug him.

Before I could close the gap, he said anticipating an embrace, 'Normally I would hug you my friend, but off late I've developed a disease called OCD. Rich people tend to suffer from it and it prevents us from touching others for fear of germ contamination.'

'I do not have germs. I am squeaky clean,' I clarified. 'I bathe myself with Lifebuoy soap and drink Dettol liquid. In addition, I use Notco germ powder which kills 99.99% germs.'

'You really drink Dettol liquid!' he said aghast as we moved to the big rectangular table at the centre of the room. The entire room was like a glass house. Toughened glass panels enveloped the room instead of cement walls. We were looking down on giant skyscrapers below and because the Burj itself was so damn high, they looked like little shanties.

Pulling up a chair and seating myself down at the nearest corner of the table, I replied, 'Well, it's actually whiskey in a Dettol bottle. They're both the same colour. Don't tell my wife!'

The Sheikh sat down across from me and obliged, 'Okay and you please don't tell any of my 27 wives that I suffer from OCD.'

'But I want to hug you! You didn't even come to Davos this year!'

'Accept my greetings without the touch my friend! I am always happy to see your fa...I mean illustriously flubber encased roly-poly fertile figure!'

'I demand that you touch me right now, Sheikh!' I said vehemently.

'NO!'

'Touch me dammit!'

'NO!'

'I came all the way from India and you won't even touch me!'

'I know Jhunjhun but OCD is a killer disease. I don't want to take chances. I am just being safe. Please don't mind!'

'Hmm... If I didn't need something illegal done from you I would totally protest and launch a satyagraha!'

'Arre! Please don't do that bhai!' he pleaded. 'As it is the way these middle-eastern countries are tumbling one after the other after that Egypt Tahrir square mess; Allah only knows how long the Sultanate will remain a monarchy and not become a true democracy...the type ruled by figureheads controlled by American puppet masters.'

'Fine!' I conceded. 'I will allow you to not touch me this time only because I know how sick you are. I have also not been well off late. I am suffering from awesomitis.'

The Sheikh, looking perturbed, whined, 'Oh! The horror! Why is the good lord giving us rich so much sickness! The Shah of Bahrain recently died after mistakenly choking on his ruby ring while sleeping.'

'I heard. Such a tragedy. We billionaires are becoming extinct by the day. Now only 679 of us are left in the wild. There are more tigers than us. Can you imagine?'

'Ya Allah!'

We both sighed our miseries. Vishal and Iqbal seated themselves next to me at the table. Princy was at the Burj's dog spa getting her nails painted and her coat brushed. Little Bhanu Pratap, docile and innocent, yelped sleepily.

'Why don't you eat something?' the Sheikh suggested. 'I've had the kitchen prepare a meal for us. Nothing too fancy... just a little fried boa constrictor and a mountain Goat-head with an apple in its mouth. I wanted to eat roast Panda babies but the bloody Chinese have become very vigilant about panda exports so we will have to settle for some ordinary winged albatross breast!'

Shocked with the menu, I gasped, 'I don't eat all this! And why are you eating this? I have told you not to eat animals. Be a vegetarian like me...Or an alcoholic like me!'

'I tried my friend! And I really love animals. I eat all kinds. Here have at least some world famous dates from home which I brought myself and just for you along with the Burj al Arab's swiss ice-cream!' he said as he pushed a small brown paper bag towards me from his side.

'YAY! I scream for ice-cream!' I rejoiced.

The thought of eating a creepy snake grossed everyone but the Sheikh out. He seemed to enjoy taunting me. Vishal and Iqbal looked like they were about to puke.

'These are my colleagues. This is Vishal and this is Iqbal and that pup in his hand is Bhanu Pratap,' I pointed toward them rapidly thereby eliminating their snake-induced nausea.

'Asalam waleykum my brothers and little doggie. If you want any oil fields or beautiful women, do let me know!' the Sheikh said as he looked at them.

'Thats a generous offer Sheikh!' Vishal said in delight. 'Thank you very much. The way fuel prices are rising back home we might actually have to take you up on that offer.'

'Any time my friends. I have so much oil it's getting a little boring. If you open the tap in any of my houses you get only oil not water.'

'Wow!' Iqbal squealed.

The Sheikh scratched his beard and nonchalantly remarked, 'I have so much oil I don't even drink water anymore. I only drink oil... My mileage has been consistently improving. I now give 50 kilometres/litre.'

The Shah and I sighed some more. The guys kept silent. When King Kong meets Godzilla, everyone else just watches.

After a few more sighs and a few more offers to have sauted Antelope brains, duck-billed platypus chow, and deep fried rhino, the Sheikh asked, 'So Jhunjhun my friend. How can I help you? You seem to be asking for a lot.'

'I am asking for a lot but it's not that much Sheikh.'

'You even made me fly out to Dubai! Why?! We could have had this meeting at my son's palace in Muscat. There's even a viewing gallery in the backyard. We could have watched a few journalists get beheaded from there while eating African Elephant Kababs!'

'Yuck!' I uttered in disgust and remarked, 'Oh! the son must be coming off age! You must be happy.'

'I want to retire soon and handover the reigns to him before he deposes me off in a coup. I have 104 children and I can't trust bloody any of them!'

'Don't worry Sheikh.' I said comfortingly. 'You can always come and stay with me in Mumbai. I'll give you my Malabar Hills home in case you need to escape execution… but no more eating snakes and panda!'

'Thank you my friend! But I don't think he will have me executed like the Shah of Iran's son did to his father to usurp the kingdom. He is a good boy that way!' he said thanking Allah for small mercies.

'Great,' I acknowledged. 'I am happy for you and thank you for meeting me here in Dubai. I wanted a quiet place with an international appeal but conveniently located away from Europe and India to do business in.'

'I'm happy we do business in the Burj al Arab. Last time you were here you beat that Swiss tennis fellow too.'

'Yes. He sends me 15% of his winnings on the ATP tour to me every month. I use that to run the Tennis Federation of India. We will finally unearth an Indian singles player who will win a grand slam.'

We sighed some more as Vishal and Iqbal pitied the problems of us humble billionaires.

After a few seconds of silence, I pushed forward, 'Now about my request. I was hoping we could seal the deal. As a fellow billionaire and honorary band member, it is your duty to help me out Sheikh.'

'I don't know Jhunjhun. What you're saying is that I open a shell company in Oman which is run by your trader friends in India while we hire my fellows to pretend to be company officials who are very interested in buying a company which makes Nothing and is now in dire straits over two separate lawsuits. Sounds complicated. Can't you just shoot the guy and be done with it?'

'A friend suggested the same thing.'

'Well, where is he now?'

'He's chained to a table leg and is unconscious after being injected with mass amounts of very potent animal tranquilizer.'

'WHAT!'

'Long story. Don't ask.'

Still perplexed, the Sheikh said, 'Think about it, I know a good assassin who has done a few assassinations for me. He now freelances for the Taliban. I recommended him to them. I even wrote his reference letter. The Taliban's hiring practices have become very stringent ever since the Americans killed Osama. "No reference, no jihad" is their HR motto these days.'

'I don't want this guy to die. I just want to teach him and everyone around him a lesson,' I said reiterating my stringent opposition to everyone wanting to kill Shastri.

'Hmm…' the Sheikh pondered loudly and insisted, 'I still say just shoot the bastard and be done with it. If you don't like the assassin, let's go meet the underworld guys. Most of the bhai log are here in Dubai only anyway! Two or three of them even placed some bets on my behalf in the IPL. Unfortunately I didn't know any of the team owners so I lost a little money…but no matter. Next year I will join the International Cricket body itself as head of the anti-corruption bureau. Even their head office is here in Dubai! I wonder why all these criminal enterprises have their headquarters in Dubai. The city doesn't seem so criminal to me!'

'Hmm…'

Scratching his beard a little more, the Sheikh explained, 'Anyway, look even if I arrange for everything...Get the government licenses, process the paperwork in 1-2 days...Rush the whole thing...Get guys to act like they are company officials ...Get the brochures and sales reports printed...Get my guys to call the guy and make the buyout offer... Put on the entire show and everything, people are going to track the money...They'll know it was me.'

I sipped some water, looked at Iqbal seated to my right, and proceeded to untangle the Sultan's queries.

'I know. Obviously the money trail is going to be a problem, but rest assured Sheikh. It won't be a hassle. Iqbal here has already opened an offshore bank account in a small private bank in Madagascar. Soon as we agree, a certain amount of money will be wired to this account from another account in Amsterdam. The money in the Amsterdam account came via a transfer from Dublin, Ireland. The Dublin account received the cash from a Paris account. The Paris account received it from a New York account which got it from a Sydney account which got it from a Honduran account which got it from ...'

'Okay! I get it,' the Sheikh conceded cutting me off abruptly. 'You're making sure the money keeps circulating every few hours. It never stays in the same place. So the cash keeps rotating around different accounts in the world?'

'Yes.'

'But there must be some bank receipts somewhere with a name.'

'Sure, but only for records sake with names like: "Flash Frozen Foods" , "Salem Utensils", " Broken Horse Entertainment", "Green Mushroom Cloud Software Inc.", "Le Femme Le Real Nail Polish", "Cook's Cooking Cookers", "Abhijit Enterprises", "Chunky Pandey school of Drama", " Force Marketing". Whatever!' I replied dismissively.

'So the names will be untraceable?' asked the Sheikh, his eyes squinting at me wondering if every hint of dubious wrongdoing would be copiously hidden.

'Yep, just like the money,' I declared.

'Hmm…'

'Sheikh, I wouldn't involve you in wrongdoing if there was a chance you would get caught. If I need someone to get caught for my wrongdoings, I usually set up the government! I look after my friends. Moreover, no one can even implicate you. You are the Sultan of Oman. No one is going to piss off the man who controls 15% of the world's oil supply. They can live with any level of fraud as long as petrol doesn't go upto $200/barrel. The Americans alone will have a fit! They'll have to make friends with Iran and Venezuela which they never will! It's like expecting Sushil Kumar Shinde to make friends with his brain or Mayawati to become friends with Mulayam Singh or Kissan tomato ketchup to become friends with Maggi tomato sauce. IT'LL NEVER HAPPEN!'

'It's anarchy! It's like Israel becoming friends with Palestine!'

'Exactly,' I said happy that the Sheikh had finally grasped my idea.

'Hmm.'

'I don't want to resort to this but the guy back home has forced my hand. I gave him an opportunity even after I had been cheated once. I trusted him and he made a mockery out of me in court. Now when the markets open tomorrow, every stock I own will be beaten down and people are already asking questions. *Yeh mere reputation ka sawaal hai!* And as that wonderful philosopher of our time and the natural enemy of silence—Navjot Singh Sidhu—has said, *"Nothing deflates faster than a punctured reputation"*. If I fight this guy in court, then my lawyer and his lawyer will debate matters till the world ends. All the while this guy will go on selling emptiness to people.'

The Sheikh looked a bit more sure now. Just to make sure he wasn't going to change his mind, Vishal added, 'As Jhunjhunwala Sir says the only way to stop a cheat is to cheat the cheat till the cheat can no longer cheat.'

'Correct. Thanks Vishal,' I said turning to him.

Vishal tried to smile as I turned to the other side and looked at the sleepy Bhanu Pratap in Iqbal's hands. Turning forward to the Sheikh I said cracking a smile, 'Sheikh, Also I got you a gift. I know you'll love this. You've been eyeing him since the time we walked in here! Iqbal, give the Sheikh Bhanu Pratap,' I instructed to Iqbal.

A happy smile burst on the Sheikh's face. Vishal got up and pulled back Iqbal's chair allowing him to stand up as he marched with the little pup in his hand. The Sheikh joyously accepted the little pup and held him close to his satin covered chest. Looking into Bhanu Pratap's eyes first, then nodding towards Iqbal, and then back into the puppy's eyes, the Sheikh of Oman bawled delightedly!

Emphatically he declared, 'You got it Jhunjhun! Boy you sure do know how to bribe a man who has everything. This puppy has turned the tide. I will direct my men and a few clandestine trusted officers with the setting up of your shell company.'

'Thank you Sheikh!' I said, relieved the deal had been sealed.

'And don't worry,' he added 'I will take care of this puppy like the king he is! '

'I know you will, O great Sultan!'

'I'm going to go back to Oman now with my new friend. What about you? Why don't you come with the family to the palace sometime. I'm also taking a 28th wife sometime later this year. Do come for the wedding.'

'I will. Let me just wrap up this mess first.'

'So what happens now?' he asked stroking Bhanu Pratap who had awoken to the warm touch of the Sheikh's hands.

'I hope you can have the company ready by Wednesday. Your guys should be able to make the offer on Thursday. We're gonna get Ramakant with his pants down by the end of next week,' I replied.

Hugging the pup and putting him at his cheek he proclaimed as he looked at me, 'We surely look forward to that, don't we Sheikh Bhanu! Don't worry Jhun. It will be done.'

I adjusted my glasses, pushed the chair back and stood up.

Adjusting his robes, the Sheikh moved forward as we met at the head of the table. Slowly he put out his hand with a grateful look and outstretched his hand forward as he remarked, 'One time only my friend… for the puppy!'

'Aye!' I said and clasped his hand.

One more goodbye wave and we were off towards the lobby. The Sheikh pinged me his Facebook status: 'Sheikh is now friends with Bhanu Pratap—Taliban likes this'

I smiled, collected Princy from the dog spa, and exited to the waiting black Cadillac outside. Iqbal seemed oddly blank. After entering the car I asked, 'Why so serious Iqbal? Don't be so sad, I'll gift you two bottles of Himani Navratan tel. Okay?'

'No Sir! Of course not,' he exclaimed. 'I was just wondering why a man like him with so many doubts would agree to help in this potentially risky activity. Why would he be so thrilled after receiving that puppy? I mean… '

'Love, my friend… Love,' I replied with an unequivocal, unflinching smile.

'Pardon Sir?'

'What do you gift a man who has everything like the Sultan of Oman? The Sheikh is a dog lover. It's only the other animals that he eats.'

'Oh! So that's why you brought the pup along!'

'Yep.'

I grinned with the satisfaction of a done deal. The Burj had disappeared from view. I began preparing for a tumultuous Monday opening.

THE EXECUTION

8.55 am, Monday morning, Dalal Street. After the return flight and another sleepless night, I addressed the band holding a loudspeaker megaphone to my mouth.

I was charged like a lightning bolt and raging like an angry bull. Standing on the shiny white floor of the Bombay Stock Exchange with the band in front of me, I thundered, 'SATTAR MINUTE! SATTAR MINUTE! For the next sattar minutes…but mostly till the end of 4 pm today my friends, trade with your hearts! Trade with your souls! Give everything you have for this day for this is the day we discover ourselves! Today we discover the meaning of life. Today is your chance at greatness! Fight for your life! Sattar minute, bitches! Sattar minute!'

'Dude! SHUT THE FU*K UP!' Ramesh yelled like a troll 'You're just giving that speech from that *Chak De India* film!'

'Eh! That was a good film. I invested in a Hockey stick company in Patiala before the film released and made a lot of profit after that film released. That film led to an overall increase of 350% in Hockey equipment manufacturing in India.'

Ramesh glared at me. The cold vibes gave me the jitters. Brrr.

Carefully averting my gaze from him, I stared forward and thundered again, 'Band walon, Aam Aadmi, Investoron aur trader

'SATTAR MINUTE! SATTAR MINUTE! For the next sattar minutes... but mostly till the end of 4pm today my friends, trade with your hearts! Trade with your souls! Give everything you have for this day for this is the day we discover ourselves!Today we discover the meaning of life. Today is your chance at greatness! Fight for your life! Sattar minute, bitches! Sattar minute!'

walon ko yeh dikhao ke aap unke bhai ho aur Ramakant ko yaad dilao ki tum uske baap ho!'

Immediately a voice screeched from the back 'Sirji! Kitne baap ho sakte hain ek aadmi ke?'

Unhappy I had been interrupted, I roared as the walls of the exchange echoed with the sound of my voice, 'OYE! NEXT TIME SOMEBODY INTERRUPTS WHEN I AM GIVING AN INSPIRATIONAL SPEECH THEN FORGET BAAP...MAA-BEHEN EK KARDOONGA... SAMJHE!'

Pin-drop silence remained as my echoes faded. Ramesh, who was probably the only person in the world who could interrupt that moment (apart from my wife) after such a direct order, scowled unflinching, 'OYE JHUN! Now you are delivering dialogues from that Sanjay Dutt film *Policegiri*! Bandh karo and get serious! Saala...have we come here to do a *shadayantra* or high school talent day par film dialogue bolne aaye hain?'

I continuing to blare on the megaphone, 'RAMESH! You are my best friend, iss liye I am leaving you warna if anyone else had spoken out against Sanjay Dutt or *Policegiri*, wahin zinda gaad deta usko!'

The band looked on impatiently. Ramesh was firing missiles upon missiles of cold, angry, icy stares. His lips grimaced as the moustache on his lips looked like the spikey back of a porcupine.

Lowering my voice but with the same intensity I uttered, 'Dear Band, thank you all for all your efforts through the last 2–3 days. This is a time of great crisis. I haven't slept in 2 days and you guys have overworked yourselves for me. I cannot express my gratefulness. Let's bring this home fellas! For today we begin the execution of the plan. We begin the execution of Notco!'

BOOM! The silence ruptured with their mad cheers. The boom was even louder than the ferocious cheer that had exploded in the farmhouse. It was hard to imagine these guys were sleep-deprived. They had more energy than a class of kindergarteners driving the teacher insane. Shouts of 'Hurrah! Hurrah', 'Oh hell yeah!' and

'THIS IS SPARTA...NO SORRY... STOCK EXCHANGE!' echoed off the halls of the Bombay Stock Exchange. The band was ready.

I had decided to attack Notco from the supreme headquarters: The Exchange—the centre of it all—the Bull's eye. *The J signal* atop the Bombay Stock Exchange had been lit. It's like the bat signal, a silhouette of light and shadow signifying that the superhero of the markets is at work and anyone going to mess with him would get their asses handed to them. The signal would have been lit last night itself but it hadn't been used in years... so had stopped working.

The guys from the Bombay Mahanagar Palika repaired it only this morning. Thus it had been on only for 30 minutes and not the 12 hours I had wished for because then it would be cool and super dramatic. Anyway, even with 30 minutes, word had spread that the Big Bull had taken charge. Every Exchange employee was on tenterhooks because the boss was in the building and none of them knew why. It was perhaps ironic or co-incidental that Shastri's Blue beam was also visible in the skyline considering how it was only turned on in the evenings. My 'J signal' rose over the exchange while the Notco Towers' blue laser beam flashed into the daytime Mumbai skyline. The faceoff had begun.

Sharp at 9, the exchange bell roared just the way it had rung for the last 135 years in Asia's oldest stock exchange. BAM! Like a gunshot. A war cry.

Excitement was in the air. I seated myself at a trading terminal to the left, next to Nandini with Ramesh behind me. The entire setup was like the control room of NASA or ISRO before the launch of a space shuttle. Anxious faces, dripping with anticipation like wax off a candle, blinked at the shifting numbers on their screens. Each second the prices changed and every time they did, it meant someone somewhere was buying and someone somewhere was selling.

NOTCO TOWERS
BSE

I looked at my screens. All 5 of them at my station. The one towards my utmost left was the prime objective. It was the Notco screen, the screen which showed the price of Notco. The next one was my portfolio of other stocks I've invested in. My stock portfolio is a work of art, like the Mona Lisa. It deserves to be put in the Louvre Museum and encased in bulletproof, bombproof cases and hung next to Da Vinci's Mona Lisa for all mankind to watch, enjoy, and revel in admiration at the brilliance of the two greatest artists of all time for generations to come.

Of the 3 other screens, one showed gold prices and the other the dollar–rupee prices. The last screen on the right was where I was checking my email and looking for funny pictures of cats wanting to eat *cheezburgerz* and R.R. Patil trying to talk and Cats eating cheezburgerz while watching RR Patil talk.

Right in front of us, the giant TV screen on the wall with the pretty little anchor on CNBC business started blaring—'BREAKING NEWS: Notco shares down 15% in market opening. Lawsuit effect?'

In a matter of minutes, a correspondent adjusting his earpiece, mic in hand, started yelling as though he was the Chairman of Notco.

'Good morning, folks. In a surprising shock development, Notco has fallen by 15% in opening trade. Trading analysts feel there is a lot of pressure on the Notco investor, especially after its eccentric chairman Ramakant Shastri accused legendary investor Jhunjhunwala of masterminding a plot to claim the funnel-sucking technology patent. Notco has also been sued by the Environment Ministry for causing cancer in the Rikhitpur region through its factory as you remember and if not then I am reminding you now because I need to say things to fill space till the time the pretty faced anchor who is sitting and smiling right now in the air conditioned studio takes a break which is when stupid advertisers will sell you shit and thanks to these breaks, I get my salary.'

I stared at my portfolio. The stocks were down by 5%. It was going to be a long day. Here I was, watching two screens. On one the collective basket of my fruits, hoping they would grow rich and ripe, juicy, succulent, and delicious when picked off their trees and on the other a rotten apple, worm-infested, planted by a bad gardener and toxic as hell. I needed to get rid of this rotten apple before it rotted out my entire basket.

An hour passed. Notco had recovered since its opening fall and was now partly up. The tide was shifting in Notco's favour. Not a good sign for me.

The band observed it too. All we were doing was blinking away at the screen watching the number indicating Notco's share price change...second by second. With every fall we cheered in our heads and with every rise we booed, cursing the ones who were still buying the damn thing.

Around 11 am the news read: 'Notco up 5% after initial 15% fall. Is the trend changing?'

S.P. Tulsi, my favourite market analyst, was discussing the state of affairs with the pretty anchor.

'You see, you should buy Notco because the odds are in its favour. It may have fallen today BUT it also rose. Sure it may fall again...Maybe even rise again... and then fall some more and then rise...then rise even more but the important thing is that the numbers are looking good. It has a good business and a strong distribution network, a growing customer base, and a hi beta cycle. You must be cautious...but hopeful...but careful...but alert... and look for profits as long as losses don't happen... which might. You must take risks also. The square root of pi is 22/7. I'm secretly a serial killer. It doesn't matter what I say now because people have already stopped listening. I like wearing women's clothing.'

Immediately the anchor chipped in, 'Remember folks, trading and investing are high-risk activities. Please consult a trained broker. Our experts offer financial advice based on past data. Neither the channel nor the company can be held responsible if you idiots listen to these jackasses we interview everyday and lose all your cash after listening to their advice… Stay tuned for more advice.'

The morning session was turning into a mixed bag. We had been unable to start a fire. We had only sparked off a mini-chaos. My plan was to convince shareholders that there was a disaster with Notco just like Ramakant had convinced people his product was actually useful to them.

If there is a significant drop in the price of a share, it is occurring because people are selling it faster than others are buying it. If more sell, the steeper the price goes down and at that time those still holding the shares have to make a choice—either to hold on till a time the price recovers which may take months or years or may not even happen at all or like the rest of the sellers, sell for what they can and escape the fall further.

What I needed was for Notco shareholders, of the 25% especially, to sell completely. The remaining would fall into place. It's like a domino effect.

For the moment, two scenarios were playing out: Notco had opened with a fall of 15% and then recovered 5% so it was totally down 10%. My other shares were down by 10% as well more or less.

The band looked worried. Their morale needed a boost. More selling on screen 1 had to happen.

Getting up, I walked to a quiet corner, harder to find in a crowded exchange than an empty seat on a rush hour Mumbai local.

I sent out a text and heard a figure creeping up eerily. Quickly I turned around and found Ramesh staring like a peacock at my head.

'Thanks for turning around fatso!' he chimed sarcastically. 'Thanks for letting me enjoy the hind view of your fat donkey brain! I thought you'd take forever to take a U-turn and get back to your station!'

'EH! DON'T CALL ME FAT. I'M NOT FAT. I'M JUST A VICTIM OF HORIZONTAL EXPANSION! ASSHOLE!' I retorted as I began walking back to the station.

'What the hell are you doing! You're supposed to be at your station! Are you sending death threats to Jayalalitha again?'

'I'm sending a text yes or rather just finished sending one and no, I did not send anything to Jayalalitha, ok!'

'Fine. Get back.'

'Oye! Who made you boss? This is my evil plan hatched for good purposes!'

'Dude, we better do something. Notco needs to fall faster,' he said, the sarcasm from a moment ago turning into genuine worry. 'You're the king of the markets, right? Kuch setting karo! Kaam khatam karo.'

'Hmm.'

I walked back to the station, pulled out the megaphone again and screamed!

"OYE! Everyone. Listen up. HURRY THE HELL UP! Pick up the pace…now! I want the exchange to be flooded with Notco shares. There should be an over abundance of shares. HURRY UP! GET THE HOLDERS TO DUMP NOTCO…NOW.'

KABLAM! Immediately the room exploded into a big bang. The pace picked up furiously. It was like a driver putting pedal to the metal and going from 20 kmph to 120 kmph in a matter of milliseconds. The general had given direct orders. The troops looking sullen just a moment ago tore through the room. Lightning had struck. A second wind was hurling through the exchange.

Things picked up even more when promptly at noon, news of the Kozhikode lab examining Nothing broke. Like a time-bomb it exploded, delivering the worst impact to Notco. *Nothing is more dangerous in the market than news based on rumour. Nothing.* All I needed was to plant a seed of doubt and the rest…panic would do. The Kozhikode report did exactly that. Even the regular news channels were now picking the story up.

My shares were now down 15% but Notco was now beginning to seriously decline. The band was delivering. The gang was in full flow hammering phones, furiously tapping away at the keyboards and exchanging notes. Even Subhash had shown up. The poor fellow, still groggy with a sedative hangover, was trying his best to match up with the others. I took a deep breath. Time to set another cat among the pigeons. I sent out another text, stood up with the megaphone and addressed the room.

'Folks. We are in the final lap of an F1 race now. It's time to take the checkered flag. In the next few minutes, a huge block of Notco shares will be sold. After that the selling is going to ripple like an atom bomb. There will be so many shares sold that SEBI will undoubtedly impose the ceiling limit. So focus...remember my sattar minute speech and SELL! SELL! SELL!'

Screaming with joy the band pumped their fists, high fiving and clapping. Instantly the celebration had to be cut. We needed to get some more selling done. It's like a team chasing in the second innings of a Test. We may have reached the opposition total but we still needed to get a good lead.

Notco was down 20%. I could sense the panic outside. Anticipation was rife. The channels showed media vans hovering at Notco Towers. Reporters were being held back by the guards as they tried to enter Notco Towers.

On every news channel the same words flashed as anchors debated with correspondents and analysts if 'The Notco story was over', 'If this was the beginning of the end', 'If the Notco Bubble had burst', 'If cancer was a life-ending tumour in the Notco story', and so on.

The slaughter had begun. My portfolio had recovered slightly; the fall was down to 12% but with Notco the drop was close to 25%.

SP Tulsi screamed, 'I had predicted that the investor must be cautious sometime back only. I had said that Notco was showing strong signs of cracking. Its fall does not surprise me at all. I recommend that all investors should exit the stock immediately. That said, I think you can also consider this a bargain... and maybe buy if you think it will rise...after falling...because earlier it had risen...and now it is falling...but it may rise again...just like Anil Kapoor who went from singing 1, 2 ka four in Subhash Ghai Film to being hero of Hollywood films like *Slumdog Millionaire* and *Mission Impossible: Ghost Protocol*...where Tom Cruise was supporting actor.'

The news was spreading successfully. Ramesh smiled in amazement. The adrenaline rush was exhilarating. Vishal ran to me with a big smile and said, 'Sir Congrats! SEBI has imposed a lower ceiling. Notco has closed 26% down!'

Whenever a company's share value falls by a certain predetermined percentage limit, SEBI automatically imposes something called a *ceiling limit*. If a share falls too drastically it immediately gets locked. No trade on that company is then possible. This is done to protect small investors from losing too much value in a day.

I smiled. Ramesh ordered tea from the chaiwallah outside. The room breathed a sigh of relief. Sipping tea from a little, white plastic cup I finally relaxed. Day 1 was over. It was 2 in the afternoon. The sun outside was heating the exchange like a gas stove.

Walking through the aisles congratulating everyone, I told them to disband and take time off for another session tomorrow. The major work had been accomplished today. The band had managed to successfully erode 26% in Notco's market value. This meant that for every 100 rupees you bet today on a Notco share, you'd now only be left with 74 bucks. I could imagine Ramakant Shastri throwing a hissy fit, prancing around in his fur coat and long boots. The bull had just run riot on his ass and the band had bajaoed him.

No more trading in Notco was going to happen today.

As I walked out with Ramesh sipping chai we discussed our strategy.

'Good day's work,' he said in contentment. His moustache had softened from the prickly porcupine at the start of the session into its regular toothbrush bristle cluster.

'Yep.'

'Shastri ki toh waat laga di.'

'He deserves it. Let him know what it feels like to cheat someone.'

'The media is going to be running this all day and night long. We've just reduced a company's value by almost 1/4th in just 4 hours.'

'I know,' I said as we passed the Bronze bull outside. 'This is a mafia hit. We targeted a stock and put a bullet in its head but it needed to be done.'

'How much is your portfolio down by?'

'12–15%. I've lost money, but the market will correct itself when people realize I had nothing to do with Shastri's patent.'

'You going home now?' he asked as we waited on Dalal Street at the foot of the BSE.

'Yeah. I'm a little tired. Haven't slept since the night in jail.'

'Three days.'

'Yeah.'

'Theek hai. Aap chalo bhai. Hum dekh lenge idhar.'

Smiling and grateful, I said with gratitude, 'Thanks yaar. Ganesha is kind for giving me a friend like you and the guys inside.'

We hugged as the Bentley pulled up. I looked at the bronze bull next to the stairs, adjusted my glasses, and headed home.

EXPLODE THINGS BEHIND ME, BITCHES!

Over the next two days, Notco started to disintegrate. The company began to collapse faster than a multi-storey in Mumbai hammered by the heavy monsoon. Like the builder of said building, Ramakant had gone underground.

On Tuesday, the band continued mauling Notco. We drove the price down by another 12% and today we had driven it down by a further 14%. In three trading days since the beginning of the week, we had driven the value of Notco stock by a comprehensive 50%. This meant in no uncertain terms that just after Monday, Tuesday, and Wednesday, the company was now worth less than half of what it was just a week ago!

Imagine an entire city of cash disappearing by half. Piles and piles of money erased…flushed…destroyed…gone…Just like that…

It reminded me a bit of how the city of Dwarka disappeared one night after Lord Krishna had left. Swallowed by the sea, now lying in ruins under tons of sea water, Notco was now a lot like the Titanic.

As I sat in my office that Wednesday evening smoking a cigarette, drinking whisktea (mixture of whiskey and tea), I reflected on what we had been able to pull off, Stage 1 and 2 had came together. We had triggered a collapse in Notco stock and had gotten the big guys, everyone from bond holders in Tokyo to Bankers in Europe and America who had bought Notco stock...to sell. Those few who had held out had also sold now, after my guys and the falling numbers had persuaded them.

The news of the Kozhikode lab report had proved to be better than expected. The government had directed the Environment Ministry to go after Notco with even more force this time. They had also unleashed the Ministry of Corporate Affairs on them. A 3-member committee had been formed, the formation of which had caused 3 retired judges to hang up their retirement boots, discard their plans of getting the newest AVIVA retirement life insurance policy, and return to duty as investigators of Notco's criminal culpability in causing cancer to the residents of Rikhitpur village. Basically...it was the beginning of the end.

I had been successful in creating an atmosphere of doubt. When so much pessimism and adverse sentiment surrounds a company, investors begin to abandon ship. A '*wait and watch*' approach and '*hope for the best*' attitude is replaced by a '*get out now*' approach. The risk of losing real money accelerates the process.

Now it was time to nail Ramakant's ass to the wall. I waited patiently for the Sheikh's call while watching the Notco story unfold on television. The pretty anchor had been replaced by a dorky looking goofball. I was sure from the way he was fidgeting on the chair, he was suffering from a severe piles problem. The TRPs for the channel would surely go down now that a goofball had replaced the maiden. Their problems were definitely piling up...HAHAHAHAHA!

20 minutes later my phone rang.

'Hello,' I said pressing the phone to my ear.

'Jhunjhun my friend! Greetings.'

'Who are you?'

'It is I, the Sheikh of Oman! Don't you recognize my voice Jhunjhun?'

'This line may be under surveillance. I know not the individual you are seeking. My name is Sheikh Wala Nujh Nujh.'

'IDIOT! Fine! Can I please speak with his Excellency, the Sheikh Keshra Wala Nujh Nujh?'

'Of course! Now that the proper sobriquet meant for suspicious activity has been rendered we may now formally begin this conversation.'

After waiting for a few seconds the Sheikh, who was probably pondering what 'sobriquet' meant during that time, said with a chirpy voice, 'You'll be happy to hear that the arrangements have been made. All papers processed. All appearances put on. The shell is ready.'

'Excellent!' I cried. 'Thank you so much Sheikh! I am indebted to you. Does the company have a website?'

'Of course! Nothing proves that a company exists like a good old website,' he asserted. 'Check your mail. Just sent the link…'

'Checking…checking…hold on please.'

I quickly scrambled the mouse and clicked onto the link.

The site popped up and stood out immediately with a flashy looking template. 'Oh wow! Nice. Looks real,' I said satisfied at the initial appearance.

Examining the homepage with a bit more detail, I muttered in confusion, 'The company is called "*Applied Services Integration—Total complete full solutions for completion of totally full needs*" what does that even mean?'

'Hey, you wanted a company which was ambiguous. This is it. It's set up to be a conglomerate based in the Sultanate with "*Multiple*", "*Varied*", "*Progressive*", and "*Diverse*" interests in various "*Life enhancing sectors*".

Not satisfied with the answer, I asked, 'What will you say if he asks what your main product is?'

'We'll say quantitive applications,' replied the Sheikh with a steady voice.

'Meaning?'

'Meaning...services are offered which when applied cause integration. Hence *Applied Services Integration*. ASI.'

'Glad you made that clear. I don't want it to be confused with the Archaeological Survey of India...Anyway, what is it supposed to do?'

'I don't know what it's supposed to do but it sounds real enough!'

After a few seconds of quiet pondering and silence pervading across both ends, I declared with hesitation, 'Agreed. *If the name is so confusing then the product must be twice as promising.*'

Breathing a satisfied sigh into the phone, the Sheikh remarked, 'So I'm gonna get my associates to contact him now.'

'Cool. I hope he bites. We have to get him to make an open offer first so he can buy back all the Notco shares.'

'Yes, I know. We will insist on that. Do not worry.'

'Thanks Sheikh,' I said in a tone of appreciation and went on to ask, 'How is Bhanu Pratap?'

'Sheikh Bhanu is fantastic!' he replied, exuberant at the very mention of the pup Ratmalani had stuck in my hands in a courtroom a little under a week ago. 'I've included him in my will. He will become a millionaire after I die.'

'That lucky son of a bitch!'

'Let me get to it now Jhunjhun...err...I mean SheikhWala Nujh Nujh. I will call you with an update,' the Sheikh said with a hint of urgency as we approached the finish line.

'Thanks a lot Sheikh. Just be convincing please!' I pleaded.

'Got it. Khuda hafiz.'

I sat by the phone smoking some more. Nandini and Vishal were busy talking to company directors about my portfolio, reassuring them that everything would be okay. Iqbal was working with Ramesh to tie up a few loose ends. The last act was drawing near.

I had directed the band to disperse. We had gathered and kicked ass successfully. We would celebrate like kings later if the plan came together.

From what I had heard, the bloodbath on the street had left Ramakant stunned. He hadn't come out of Notco towers in three whole days. The Rikhitpur factory had been shut for now. Sales had fallen. All plans for the future had been abandoned. It was the beginning of the end.

Of course, it wasn't going to be over till he fell for the last play. I had persuaded the Sheikh to put together a shell which would now approach Shastri and offer him one last hope.

This company would offer to buy Ramakant's company because they still saw *'potential'* in it. Ramakant would now have to make what we call a *'distress sale'*.

When a man's money is attacked, he doesn't have too many options. You can predict what he will do based on his track record of tackling difficulties. Ramakant would either a. Resort to fraud b. Make the deal with the Sheikh, or c. File for bankruptcy

At this stage, as that great maven of cricketing wisdom Ravi Shastri has observed so poignantly, 'All three results are possible.'

I waited by the phone and drank some more whisktea. Soon it rang again. It was the Sheikh. This was the call I had been waiting for.

'Congrats my friend. He has accepted.'

I smiled triumphantly.

Ten days later, Nandini walked into my office and said, 'Sir, Ramakant Shastri is here to see you.' The aversion in her voice for Shastri was very well-hidden.

'Well, well. Send him in,' I ordered, pleasantly surprised he was here.

During the last fortnight, news of an open offer launched by Ramakant Shastri had surprised the street. The Sheikh had come through. He had successfully managed to pull the strings, getting Ramakant to agree to sell his company to the Sheikh. Shastri had bargained to keep 10% of his company even after handing over the majority 90% to the shell which he did not know was a shell.

I didn't bother too much. SEBI had launched an investigation into the open offer because any company which loses 50% of its value, has two separate lawsuits hanging over it, and then launches a program to buy back shares from investors screams '*Daal mein kuch kaala hai*'.

SEBI would have to finally approve this open offer… but *I didn't need the shell to exist all the way to that stage*. The moment Ramakant made an offer to his customers to buy out their holdings, the shell's *use* was done. Like an egg shell it would crack… but andar na milegi yolk na banegi omelette.

Ramakant made the offer and eager investors, the common man, and the daily trader more than happily cashed their stocks in. To pay them, Ramakant pledged his shares as collateral to a set of banks who were ready to give out loans in the hope of earning interest.

Now armed with fresh cash from the bank loans, Shastri used it to pay his investors and bought back their shares. If SEBI decried the offer, he'd have to return the cash *but it didn't matter*.

That's when Applied Services Integration vanished just like Dawood Ibrahim after the 1992 bomb blasts. Poof!

Ramakant had no buyer, even the website was gone. Stuck with a worthless Notco company, still facing two lawsuits and owing the banks the money he had borrowed from them to pay those who tendered their holdings in the open offer, Shastri was done.

It was 4 pm that evening when Shastri came to see me. The market had just closed. My portfolio had recovered and the fall since Shastri's court fiasco was down to 8%. Notco on the other hand was flat on the charts.

No one was buying. This thing was flatter than a stone pillar's pulse. Trading had become inactive simply because the number of stocks in it had reduced after almost everyone had sold it back to him. No one else was buying and he wasn't interested in selling because he thought that the Omani company was going to buy it off him. There was no demand and no supply…NOTHING.

I hadn't seen him since the day in court. I wondered what coloured coat he'd walk into my office wearing.

I heard a slow, dragging knock on the door.

'Come in,' I said somberly.

Pushing aside the door, Shastri entered. For a moment I almost didn't recognize him. The crown was gone, so were the rings and the chains. Even the thud of the boots were gone! His face was shaved clean, no goatee, no moustache…nothing. A sign of familiarity prevailed, however, with him still wearing fur. This one was white.

Dressed in a pair of navy blue trousers and a white striped shirt underneath, he tried to wave at me. I instructed him to sit down. He sat across the table, removed the fur, folded it into a heavy ball and placing it onto his lap spoke up.

'Hello.'

'Whats up dude?'

'I came here to ask you something? I have a few questions for you.'

'Why? You want to play "Kaun Banega Crorepati" with me?'

Shastri blinked like a slow computer cursor. His face looked cold, dull, expressionless …tired.

'A few days ago a company from Oman approached me and offered to buy Notco. As you may very well know, the share value has fallen drastically, I still don't know why. I thought it was a good offer. One which would save my company, so I took it,' he said as his voice drooped.

'And?'

'They insisted on complete control and said it was a one-time only offer. They said if I sold Notco in full to them, they would allow me to keep 10% and I would continue heading the company as the CEO.'

'So problem kya hai?'

'That's why as you know I launched the open offer. Even you tendered your 15% shares in that.'

'Yeah, I remember,' I remarked trying to appear absolutely apathetic. 'Never been happier to get rid of a stock. It was a bad memory, your company, just like Sanjay Leela Bhansali's *Saawariya*. It still gives me nightmares.'

Ramakant hadn't moved since he had sat down. Not one bit. Looking plainly at me, he continued with a heavy, wooden voice.

'After the open offer succeeded, I tried to contact them but... they were gone. Disappeared. I've been tracking them for more than a week. They've just vanished...'

'Oh! That's not cool.'

'I even got a private agency to investigate the company in Oman...but...they said the company doesn't even exist. Even its registration addresses...tax receipts...website...sales reports... everything...is...false'

'So the company doesn't exist?'

'Yes.'

'Looks like you've been cheated,' I said staring into his drooping eyes.

'I...'

Sensing his loss for words, I swung my chair in an arc from left to right and said in an enquiring tone, 'Just to be clear you're telling me that a company which doesn't exist has managed to cheat a company which exists because it sells something which doesn't exist? Wow! I am replete with irony.'

Stirring slightly Shastri stammered, 'I...I...wanted to ask you if...'

'Yes...'

'If...If...you have a role to play in this. I was about to break the news to the media that Notco was being acquired by an Oman based conglomerate but before I could...it just...'

'Are you accusing me of something?'

'I want to know if you screwed me over Mr Jhunjhunwala...'

'ME! I'm just a fat man who drinks and smokes a lot. I've only been sitting here in my humble office being fat and drinking and smoking…a lot.'

'Hmm…'

'I swear! Ask anyone. Would you like to see my liquor, cigarette, and chair invoices for the past few days?'

'No.'

A few minutes passed silently. Shastri was searching for answers but it seemed like he didn't want to ask the questions. I continued to gaze at him patiently.

Sometime later he remarked, 'I was just thinking who it was who could have done this to me. I don't think anyone but you could have pulled this off. I mean open a benami in Oman, appear just in time after my stock gets beaten down. Lure me into a false sense of security, make me pledge my shares to raise money and then disappear just like that…In fact I think you are the one who cause my shares to fall in the first place. Only you could have caused a company to fall over 50% in just 3 days! Only you!'

'Whoa! Whoa! Whoa! Don't speculate…err comment without proof,' I said cheekily reminded of his earlier comment.

'You know proof is impossible to get. I've hired people in Interpol and the CIA. Even they can't track where the money is coming from or who these people are.'

'All I can say is that this entire…scheme could have been hatched and executed only by a genius.'

Shastri budged. His eyes flickered just a little with a tiny cold spark of realization. Looking hurt, he asked with a slight hint of condescension, 'You think you're very smart don't you?

'I don't think. I know,' I replied as a chill set into the room.

'You must be really happy boss. You've just cost so many people their jobs.'

'Since when do you care about jobs?' I questioned continuing to stare into his eyes which were now blinking faster. 'Ever since I've known you, all you seem to care about is money. As far as jobs go, I'm sure they will have no problem finding a job which actually makes them happy. One which doesn't involve simply packing air in boxes.'

'How could you do this to me?' he stirred with a hapless frown.

'I didn't do anything man,' I countered and rattled off, 'You've brought this on yourself. You shouldn't have:

A. forged my signature
B. tried to sell nothing to people
C. become a total jackass in the process
D. disrespect customers who actually gave a damn about your product
E. lied to me and the court about stealing the patent despite the fact that both you and Agarwal had come up with it.'

Shastri was now visibly a lot more animated. He growled, 'Please! Ajay and I were about to settle this out of court. We discussed it when the open offer was on. I would pay him and he could legally claim the patent as co-inventor. You would have also got off.'

'How convenient. Slime my name, my reputation, my career, my ethics, and then offer to exonerate me. Looks like someone did the same thing to you.'

'What are you talking about?' he asked. I could sense that he knew what had happened but wanted to hear me say it.

'Doesn't matter,' I said and added strongly, 'It brings me to F. Fitting letter because you truly tried to F me over.'

Looking forlorn, Shastri slowly said, 'I know my saying sorry won't help… but can you help me in some way?'

'Sure. I can give you the number of the nearest police station. You've been cheated. Law enforcement in our country is very serious. We have very fine officials who will make sure that the law will take its own course. Do you have a piece of paper?'

'Uh'

'Wait. I'll write it for you,' I said reaching for the notepad on my desk.

The colour had drained out from Shastri's face. A groggy pout stuck on his lips. I told Vishal to fetch me the number. As I handed it to him, the quivering skinny agarbatti seller pulled the thin yellow piece of paper stuck between my fingers and gently said, 'Can we at least still do business together?'

'You're kidding, right?'

'No.'

'Okay. The day the aliens come is the day we can do business. I watch *India TV* for news of regular alien sightings along with up to the minute information about *Bhoot-pret* and *punar-janam*. I will definitely be in the loop therefore. The moment the aliens land... we will restart our partnership.'

Shastri questioned frantically, 'What am I supposed to do now? My company was all I had...'

'Why are you asking me?' I howled, struck with the absurdity of the question. 'Do I look like your event planner? Go read a book. Watch a film. Fly a kite. Watch Ajit Agarkar's career highlights. I don't know! What happened to your wife, your kids...even Shruti Sharma...jaake uske mooh pe phir se chipak lo.'

'She left me,' he replied.

'Who? Your wife or Shruti?'

'My wife's still around...though I wish she had left. Shruti left me sometime back...'

'Sorry to hear that. So I guess the marriage is off. Hmm. Well, at least one good thing happened. You'll at least not die of sexually transmitted disease.'

Ramakant glared coldly.

'I'm serious. What should I do now? I've lost all I have. My company, my erstwhile best friend Ajay, Shruti, my wife, my kids, my...reputation...my...money...*everything*...'

Taking a deep breath I gazed at him. He was now visibly frustrated and sad. A hint of pity ran within. Measuring my words, I said, 'If you seriously want my advice... Seriously?'

'Yes. Please,' he said immediately jumping at my words.

'Start over,' I declared. 'Start honestly and earnestly. You can get everything back '

'Including the money?'

'Hahaha! Especially the money dude. Money will come and go always. Look... In 30 years, I've lost money more times than I've made it, but I'm rich today because when I made cash I made it big. Life will sort things out for you as well. Ganesha is great. The reason I am awesome...is not because I have this much cash...but because I never let it control me. *I am its master. Not the other way around. I hope you understand this. Family, friends, people... Life is more important than money.*'

I got up, put the phone in my shirt pocket, and called out to Iqbal.

'Take care dude. I wish you the best of luck,' I said heading towards the door with my hands tucked into my trouser pockets.

'Do you really mean that?' he asked with a hint of doubt. He wanted to believe me but just wasn't sure.

'Of course,' I replied without any fuss. 'I bear no ill will towards you dude. For the motives you adopted and the actions you took, you've gotten what was coming to you. You don't deserve more punishment. Pick yourself up, have a drink, clap your hands and get back to doing what you love. Maybe sell agarbattis again. Who knows?'

'I wish it was that easy...'

'Anyway. You should probably leave. Things are going to get very hot in here. This room is going to catch fire.'

Ramakant looked at me with a puzzled expression as though he had misheard what I had just said. Just then, Iqbal arrived.

'Iqbal. Get the explosives box,' I ordered standing near the door.

'Now Sir?'

'Yes. Now. We are doing the explosion drill so tell the staff and keep the fire extinguishers nearby. I'm heading home.'

'Yes Sir!' he said mischievously and ran off.

Ramakant got up and pushed his chair back. Standing to his feet he asked, 'Whats going on?'

'Do you watch action movies?'

'Yes...sometimes.'

'Do you notice how when the hero of the film wins in the end, he blows up the villain's entire operation and how he finally walks in a supercool, super stylish, slow motion walk as everything explodes behind him?'

'Yeah...'

'That's what is about to happen now. I'm going to walk out of here in slow motion with things exploding behind me.'

Ramakant was more puzzled. Unable to believe his ears he uttered in astonishment, 'But this is your office! Won't it catch fire?'

'Yes, it is my office but it won't catch fire. I have a habit of blowing things up and walking ahead of the flaming debris in slow motion. That's why my architect ensured that not only my cabin but the entire office is plastered with asbestos...because at the end of the day...THAT IS HOW BADASS I AM! I'M GONNA WALK OUT OF MY OWN OFFICE...IN SLOW MOTION... WITH THINGS EXPLODING BEHIND ME!'

Ramakant picked up the fur coat in sheer disbelief and trudged out of the door. He was so shocked that he had to be forcefully escorted by Nitin. Outside, the office boys and staff were ready with the fire extinguishers. Iqbal and Vishal lined up the explosives behind me and were ready to set them off with remotes.

Slowly Shastri climbed into the elevator. I looked at Vishal and Iqbal as the others covered their ears like little kids waiting for a just lit diwali bomb to explode.

I put on my shades, started walking in slow motion, and yelled 'EXPLODE THINGS BEHIND ME BITCHES!'

BOOOOOOOOOOOOOOOOOOOOOOOOOOOOOO OOOOOOOOOOOOOOOOOOOOOOM!

BOOM

THE END

To whoever is reading this,

My name is Ramakant Shastri. I am 45-years-old. For much of my life, I've been a bonded labourer in coat and tie, with a cellphone in my pocket, a car, a laptop and a house. I have a wife and 2 kids.

I'm supposed to be what people call a 'professional'. I'd much rather like to think of myself as a contractually bound salaried hostage.

I'm supposed to be happy, but the truth is far from it. I've never been happy for long and I have now resigned myself to the fact that I will indeed, never be happy. I will always be unhappy simply because what you need the most in life to be happy is—money. With money you can pretty much buy anything, even happiness.

You might have heard a lot of things about me recently. I've become quite rich over the last few months because I managed to successfully start a company called Notco.

People have had all sorts of reactions to what I have been selling. They've said it was hype, aggressive advertising, big spending, taking advantage of consumer boredom, fantastic publicity, unique placement, a trend, a fad, a fraud, and a whole bunch of other things.

Nobody, however, asked WHY I was selling Nothing. Even I could never have imagined anybody, let alone myself, could have obtained money for literally nothing! People were actually paying for box after box, packet after packet of freakin'... Nothing!

But these people cannot be blamed. I feel sorry for them, sorry that they haven't been able to open their eyes and realize the truth. Who knows, maybe they have but chosen to be in denial. Denial that they too are slaves. Slaves for money. As long as money is around...anybody can be controlled, bought, and sold. People are just like commodities. We've created a world where little bits of paper with names, numbers, and pictures on them have become more important than anything else including actual, real, living beings.

Nothing is more important than money and absolutely everything... EVERY DAMN THING, has a price. Even if you have to take a piss you have to pay to use the toilet. You do it for free and they arrest you for littering.

Only a species as cursed as ours would monetize even the act of urination. Only human beings.

Everything is about selling or buying. Everything costs money and everyone only wants to make money. All that matters is numbers, profits, and money. Even more than human relationships. Money is the most important thing in the world.

This is the world I was born in. This is the world I am a part of. A world where the pursuit of profit is paramount to anything else. Profit is the only way to make money, to keep the money you make, and to get MORE.

More because the money always runs out...it's never enough...no matter how much you save...no matter which bank, stock, jewellery, property, commercial enterprise, vehicle you put it into. IT ALWAYS RUNS OUT. IT'S NEVER ENOUGH...because just like you... others are also making money. They are making it by taking it from you.

If you want something from them, you have to give them money. If they want something from you then they have to give you money. This is a cycle which will never end.

I wanted to make money. I wanted to make lots of money. I wanted to make so much money I could literally soak myself in glue and roll around in 1000 rupee notes.

Guess what? I did make so much money. I was the fastest to become a billionaire. 7 billion people on this planet, and I ended up being the fastest and quite frankly…I deserved it.

I've been living in one rathole after another doing one crap job after another getting paid peanuts and working overtime like a donkey… all for what? Me work like a dog for crap while my bosses live like kings? Where is the fairness? Where is the justice?

After Notco spiked on the stock market, every single bank manager was kissing my ass to park my money in his or her bank. These same guys then showed up just minutes after Notco crashed and like vultures pulled out my embellishments. My crown…my rings…my chains… my boots…everything, till I was left with nothing.

They took my cars, my houses. They broke up my assets into little bits and auctioned them off as though they were pieces of meat at a butcher shop. This was everything I had earned and these bastards… sucked me dry like vampires.

But I guess that's the nature of this beast. One thing is however crystal clear… I can see it as clean as daybreak…I sold nothing…ME.

I got people to put their hard-earned money into my pockets and in return all they got was just emptiness in a box. I did that. Me.

But why did I choose to sell Nothing? I could have gotten rich off anything else. I could have sold underwear or shit as fertilizer and still made money but why did I sell Nothing? Why?

Because… When I decided to stop being a slave and go after the cash for the first time in my life implicitly, explicitly…I needed something which was so unbelievably fantastic that it would catch peoples' imagination. More importantly, I needed something not to sell unto them but actually use it to…punish them…

These people…these slaves…who horde cash and create this world needed to be punished. If I succeeded in getting even one single idiot to buy Nothing and give me their money in exchange, I would be a winner.

I believe that if you create something idiotic then some idiot somewhere will buy it to convince the other idiots around him that he is just as idiotic as the rest of them.

But this isn't about my victory... It's about my defeat.

A few days ago, the party ended. My company collapsed on the stock market. I tried to sell my enterprise to an interested buyer only to learn that the buyer did not exist. 3 reports from 3 labs said that my product was causing cancer. Ha! What a joke.

I am now penniless and broke in more ways than one. Everything I own has been taken away. I've lost all my possessions. I don't think even my family loves me. They only wanted money from me because that was supposed to be my 'job'. They wanted me to be a slave too. I am perhaps fittingly left at this moment with truly...nothing.

I am sick and tired of being a slave. I have lived like a king for the past few months of my life and for this I am grateful.

I have tasted the opulence and comfort that money can provide. I can no longer reconcile myself to any other life than the one I have become used to.

This is a world I am unable to accept and a world I am unwilling to change.

I will not go back to selling agarbattis. I will not go back to a life of slavery where all my time and all my efforts will go only in making some rich person even richer. I will not do something called a 'job' and pursue something called a 'career' when even I know... all I am doing is finding ways of selling something to someone for money and in the process making someone else richer.

My passions, my education and my interests are easily flushed down the drain. All that matters is how much I sell and if I can sell more than the other guy—that's 'success'.

Success is a constant, never–ending struggle for the next 'target'... the next 'quarterly projection'...the next 'topline growth'...the next 'new product'...the next 'sales forecast'...the next 'innovation'...the next 'game changer'...the next 'market'...on and on and on...till you die...when someone just like you will take your place and continue to do what you just did to reach the next 'next'.

And after you reach all the next's you realize there is still one more next...and one more...and one more...and one more...

You can enjoy your life with money only when you are buying someone else's next and saving so that you can buy more 'nexts'...the cycle never ends.

Even if I become a little rich by wetting my beak, it's a joke compared to how a true king lives. I may not be the king now but I refuse to be the slave anymore.

In this world of humans...Money isn't everything...It's the only thing.

And so... Money it will be for me.

I would like to apologize to Mr Jhunjhunwala for naming him in my patent case. He had nothing to do with the whole thing. I never wanted to involve him but at that time it seemed like the right choice. Perhaps, in hindsight it was the wrong decision. It was me along with Ajay who came up with that bullshit funnel sucking thing. We did it just for fun then. We were best friends. We thought it would be cool if we found a way to sell 'Nothing'. Of course Ajay never really cared and only conveniently showed up when I began making so much money. Maybe he thought he could escape slavery by securing his freedom with my money. Who knows?

I want to tell my wife that the first few years we were together were some of the truly happiest days of my life. Back when she didn't care about money. Back when she supported me and I supported her, before she became a total money-digging, angry, envious, ravenous bitch who drove me mad.

I want to tell my kids that I love them and that I am sorry I have not been around always to watch them grow up. I've been busy, my dear children, making money so you can lead a better life and not be slaves like your father.

To the rest of the world I want to say that I, the Czar of Nothing, King Nothing—Ramakant—may not have lived truly on his own terms but he sure as hell will die on his own terms.

By the time you read this you will find me hanging from the ceiling fan of room 614 of the Blue Jasmine Hotel.

I apologize to the hotel staff in advance for the trouble I am causing them. Luckily you can always charge a little extra for room service or a 'suicide fee' from your other guests to make up for this. Ha!

It is 2.30 am. All I hear is the heaviness of the a/c. The corridor outside is quiet. Even the street dogs outside are not barking. No soul in sight. No sound to hear. Nothing left but death and after that... nothing else.

Goodbye,
Ramakant Shastri

In the evening's afterglow, I sunk onto a corner sofa at Geoffrey's clutching Ramakant's letter. The sweat from my palms had soaked the white paper into a brownish, greasy dirty rag.

All day long I had been wondering if my attempt to derail Ramakant had cost him his life. In the last 2 hours I had read and reread the letter about 20 times. I didn't want the family around me. I was reeking of Black label whiskey through every pore in my body. I had drunk 4 bottles since 10 am and was on my fifth.

Ramesh had been with me since noon trying to get me to get up and go home.

'You should go home Jhun. Don't drink anymore,' Ramesh pleaded as I continued to stare at the white tabletop without bothering to raise my head or blinking an eyelid.

'Okay,' I replied and gulped down another glass of whiskey defiantly.

'What did I just tell you?!! You've been drinking since the morning. At this rate you'll need a liver transplant right here. Chalo bhai...utho.'

'No.'

'Will you get up? Do I have to get a crane to lift you up now? Go home, have a bath, and drink some coffee bhai. Aise rahoge toh what will the kids think?'

'What about Ramakant's kids?' I asked sadly muffling my voice and pressing my spectacles up the bridge of my nose. My head was still unable to believe that he was indeed…gone.

'Hmm…'my best friend sighed. I made no effort to look at him. 'I know you are upset but don't blame yourself. Ramakant made the decision to kill himself. *He and he alone is responsible for that. No one else.* You didn't drive him to that.'

'I shouldn't have gone after Notco that hard. Practically set him up…'

'Yes but you didn't force him to do anything. He chose to drive off the cliff…by hanging himself, so to say. Not you.'

'Poor guy even mentioned me in the letter…'

'Jhun. Listen to me,' Ramesh said. 'You've read that letter about a 100 times since the cops gave you that copy. Haven't you still realized?'

'What?' I said as I stirred to look at Ramesh. The bar was more or less empty save for a few regular patrons dispersed about haphazardly.

'Ramakant was way too attached to his money,' Ramesh said waving his index finger slowly in the air. 'The moment he learnt he had lost it he couldn't bear it. He was unwilling to work hard and straight. Who knows maybe one day he could have made ten times what he made with Notco. But, he just gave up. *He just didn't want to live without money.*'

'He said he was a slave that day I met him at Notco towers also…'

'He is a slave,' Ramesh brazenly declared setting his finger down on the table.

Ramesh paused as I crestfallen looked into his face.

'I mean he…was…' he corrected hesitantly. 'He was a slave… definitely…but not to his work or family or even his life. He was a slave to money. He couldn't live without it. That's why he killed himself.'

'Poor guy…I liked him…'

'Look. Go home, okay. Come with me. I'll drop you. You've been sitting here ever since you heard he was found hanging. You forced the owner to open Geoffrey's just for you at 10 in the morning. Even the cops took your statement here! Now get up. Bahut ho gaya. It's almost 8. Let's go home man.'

I drooped back and sunk further into the red cushioned chair. As I reached for the almost empty bottle staring at me from the table, Ramesh snatched it away. I was in no mood to put up a fight and dropped my outstretched hand like a ton of bricks by my side.

'Look who's here,' he said after snatching the bottle as I went back to staring at the tabletop in dejection.

'Huh?' I said perking up slightly.

'Turn around,' he said repeatedly pointing the finger he had just waved at me a few minutes back in the direction above my shoulder.

Slowly I turned my head over my left shoulder and sighed loudly.

'Oh crap. I am so not ready to talk to him of all people right now…' I said shaking my head and closing my eyes as I turned back.

As Ramesh looked on over my shoulder, I plucked the whiskey bottle out of his unguarded hands and before he could even utter a word, emptied it down my gullet.

'Dude, what the hell is wrong with you! That's 5 bottles of whiskey in one day! Something worse than appendicitis will happen at this rate!' he whined angrily darting his hand forward desperately to snatch the empty bottle still stuck in my hand.

'Bah!' I replied dismissively.

As I banged the empty bottle and asked the bartender to get another bottle, Stinker walked up.

'Well! Well! What the hell is this, fatso? Oh…crap! How much have you you drunk? You smell like a dead animal!' he immediately sounded off as he stood at the table with his hands in his pockets.

Immediately I yelled, waving my fist in the air 'SHUT UP STINK FACE! YOU SMELL LIKE YOU CRAWLED OUT OF A LATRINE! AND DON'T CALL ME FAT. ASSHOLE!'

'You are a fatass!'

'No! I'm not fat! I'm just voluptuous. You're just jealous because you have the appearance of a skeleton wrapped in cellotape!'

'Guys! Please,' Ramesh pleaded as Stinker got ready to fire back. 'Don't fight okay. It's been a sad and long day.'

Grunting apologetically, Stinker removed his hands from his pockets and resting them by his thighs said, 'Yo Jhunjhunwala. I'm sorry. I heard about your boy Ramakant. I wished he hadn't killed himself.'

'Thanks.'

'Ya. I wish you had killed yourself instead.'

'OH YEAH! I won't die till I drag that scraggly, itchy, witchy, stink-filled soul out of that commode you call a body and throw it into hell myself!!'

Ramesh frantically pleaded waving his arms around as Stinker and I continued to fume. 'GUYS, PLEASE! JESUS! CAN YOU PLEASE NOT FIGHT. Just for today? Someone has died very tragically. Please!'

Stinker looked at Ramesh as I poured some soda into the whiskey bottle he had left upon the table after snatching it from me a second time hoping to catch the last remnants of the alcohol albeit dissolved in soda.

'I came to talk to you,' Stinker said.

'About what?' I asked tilting my head as I emptied the soda from the whiskey bottle down my throat and placed it upon the table.

'Look I am sorry that Ramakant died. Anyway, you better live up to your end of the deal fatso!'

'I ALWAYS LIVE UP TO MY END OF THE DEAL! Now bugger off from here before I hit you so hard that you'll feel you've been punched by an asteroid!' I yelled.

'Fine,' Stinker accepted reluctantly. 'Next time fatso. Just don't forget our deal.'

'I told you I don't forget! Now get out of here. Next time I see you at Geoffrey's, I'm gonna have Subhash blow you up with his suicide vest. And don't call me fat!'

'Fu* k you fatso!'

'Fu* k you stinker!'

Stinker slowly stepped back continuing to stare into my eyes. After a few seconds, he turned around and headed back. I surveyed the scene at Geoffrey's for a second with puffy eyes and stared at the letter again which had now shrunk into the size of a tissue.

'What deal was he talking about?' Ramesh asked a bit confused as I turned my stare away from the walking Stinker and onto Ramesh.

'Kuch nahin,' I replied.

'What deal was he talking about? Tell me dammit!'

'Arre. Don't shout yaar!' I pleaded to Ramesh as I massaged my temples with my fingers. 'I have a headache and my appendix area is beginning to hurt as well...'

'Oh,' he said empathetically.

'I needed that stink face's help...no assistance...no business partnership...no... We couldn't have knocked the wind out of Notco without the bear cartel's assistance. He and his gang of idiots were needed especially to sell that Monday morning,' I reluctantly explained letting the bear out of the bag as I stopped massaging my temples and took a deep breath.

'Is he the one you were texting to at the exchange when we were all trading that day?' a surprised Stinker asked as the ends of his moustache stood up like Shikhar Dhawan's moustache.

'Yeah. I had called him up on Sunday and told him I was gonna go after Notco and that he should co-operate with us and bring the company down.'

'Unbelievable! But you two hate each other! Why did he agree to help you of all people?'

'Stinker wasn't helping me,' I replied as I clutched the letter which had by now shrunk even further. 'He was helping himself and the market.'

'Huh? I don't get it'

'No matter what our differences are, we both believe that the market at the end of the day is supreme. I am its guardian and he is a stupid stinkface, but we are both part of it. If companies like Notco are allowed to exist then it sets a bad precedent…for all of us.'

'I still don't get why he helped you?'

'He was only bothered about me profiting from Notco. Even he knows how stupid the idea of selling Nothing is. He thought Notco was rising because I had something to do with it. *Once he learnt I had nothing to do with Nothing, he calmed down and we agreed it needed to be done as long as I wouldn't profit from it.*'

'But you did profit bhai! You tendered your 15% in the open offer remember? That's worth crores even after the fall.'

'Yeah but I'm not keeping the cash,' I added immediately and taking a breath slowly declared, 'That cash will be divided for other purposes.'

'Like what?'

'First we will pay all the Notco employees a compensation. Second, you and I are going to Rikhitpur next week.'

'Why?'

Angrily I gritted my teeth and announced, 'That village has been underdeveloped for years! I am going to build a cancer hospital in that area and develop that place. Whatever money is left I will distribute to the people of Rikhitpur.'

'Your wife is going to be happy to hear that you will be doing that instead of buying another helicopter or a whale shaped sub or a jetpack or the Olympic torch…or alcohol…or more alcohol. Aren't you worried the government will stop you?'

'From what?'

'I mean they'll want to take credit. They'll say it's their job not yours.'

Outraged, I said waving my fist in the air, 'Since when do I need their permission to help people? If they try to interfere or scam the money I'll bloody hold the RBI itself hostage!'

'Arre don't do that bhai,' he immediately interjected. 'As it is they need your cash to keep GDP growth up.'

'Exactly. They won't interfere,' I affirmed as I calmed down. Looking at the letter in my left hand one more time, I said with sadness in my voice, 'I'm also going to make a donation with this money...'

'To whom?'

'Ramakant's family. Afterall this is his money...in a way. Let his wife use it to educate the kids. Let them all live in peace. I hope they will one day be happy again. I think Shastri would have wanted that.'

As I placed the letter now no more than a wet and dirty scrap on the table, the sound of a squeaky weep cut through the air. I lifted my head to find Ramesh rubbing his eyes.

'Dude! Are you crying?!' I asked surprised.

'No...no...no' he said ashamed that he had been discovered.

'Shut up! You are crying. What happened now?'

'Nothing...I'm just happy yaar.'

'Why? A man has just killed himself.'

'Yes...but at least a few people like you are still around.'

Taking a deep breath, I stroked my chin and, proclaimed 'Enough...please don't praise me...I can do that myself.'

'Of course! We all know that.'

Getting ready to finally leave, I said humbly, 'I still wish there was some way this whole thing could have been avoided. Maybe if I hadn't got awesomitis... I wouldn't have gone away...Shastri wouldn't have forged my signature... We could have prevented all this.'

'So what are you gonna do now?' Ramesh said helping my drunken, stupor-induced heavyweight body from the sofa.

'I think we've all learnt something very important,' I said resting my massive hand across his puny shoulders as he heaved me through towards the door.

'What's that?' he said curling his eyebrows as we took a step forward.

'Awesomitis is a very dangerous disease,' I declared breathing heavily. 'Look how much trouble my awesomeness has caused. All this happened because I am too awesome. Oh! For humanity's sake! Why am I so awesome God? Why? WHY? WHY!'

'Shut up!' he cried trying to mask his amusement as we exited Geoffrey's.

ACKNOWLEDGEMENTS

A foray into literature with a humour novel has been a baptism by fire and a book like this has only come about because of the kindness and effort of a few, and the support of a few more.

A big thank you to my Mom for supporting me, encouraging me, and taking care of me all these years despite all the nonsense I have put her through.

Death has taken them away, and I wish they could be here to see me at this time. Thank you for being here. I keep you in my heart and will forever do so.

Distance and time have separated us. Impressions remain. Thank you for them.

Thank you to my literary heroes—R.K. Narayan, René Goscinny and Albert Uderzo, Roald Dahl, Jerome K. Jerome, Agatha Christie, Tolkien, Arthur Conan Doyle, Premchand, J.K. Rowling, Charles Dickens, Stan Lee, Masashi Kishimoto, Oscar Wilde, Mark Twain, and countless others.

My agent Kanishka Gupta whose help, guidance and support have gone a long way in making this book a reality. I am grateful to you for the professional help and the personal friendship—thank you.

My publisher Random House for giving me the opportunity to realize a lifelong dream of becoming an author. I have wanted to do nothing else my entire life but to write and be read. Thank you for making it happen.

My sincerest gratitude to my editor Gurveen Chadha whose meticulous eye for detail, flair for improvement, and tenacity for doing the legwork on this book have all been reasons the final presentation has improved. Undoubtedly, this book has become more enjoyable thanks to her dedicated effort. I've troubled her so much yet she's been patient, focused, and incredibly tolerant with me. Thank you Gurveen and sorry for all the times I've bugged you!

A big thank you to Milee Ashwarya for signing me, overlooking each stage of the creative process, and guiding me through the grind with her kindness and experience. I'm sorry for bugging you too with my incessant queries and phone calls and thank you for being indulgent with me.

Anukriti Sharma—who stepped up when the last minute beckoned. Thank you Anukriti for your wonderful work on the sketches and for illustrating the ideas so well in such a short time!

Mr Balraj K.N.—thank you for your awesome work on the cover and initial sketches, dear sir. I am very grateful to you.

To all the RH personnel from sales, legal, marketing, and every other department—a huge thank you.

To the technical personnel who have worked on this book—Saanvi Graphics and Replika Press. The proofreaders and typesetters, your imprint will forever be a part of this—thank you profusely.

Mr Rakesh Jhunjhunwala—your sporting attitude has been a boon dear sir. You have allowed me to borrow traits from your personality to make a lovable fictional character and for this—thank you.

Mr Mark Fidelman—a chance encounter in 2007 has been the seed of all this. Thank you for creating the 'Jhunjhunwala' parody. Thank you for your support and friendship.

Thank you to Stupid Nitish and, apologies.

Sruthijith KK—a few hours in 2012 has played a huge role in this. Thank you for your help and friendship, macha.

Thank you to Atmaram uncle for the friendship and help through the years.

Thank you to the hundreds who read the blog and the thousands who read the tweets. Dear people of twitter—you are more than just 'social media' to me. If not for you, I wouldn't be here.

And finally, the big guy upstairs for making all the above and more come together in the way it has. Irrespective of where this road leads—thank you.

A NOTE ON THE AUTHOR

Aditya Magal is 28, lives in Bangalore, grew up in Bombay and calls this awesome, mad place called India his home. Writing is the only thing he has wanted to do but bills force him to trade stocks and do other things. He is addicted to pizza, pav bhaji, dosa, and other junk foods. His ambition in life is to eat, sleep, and watch TV. He can also be found blogging at www.rakeshjhunjhunwala.in and tweeting as @jhunjhunwala on http://twitter.com/jhunjhunwala

This is his first book.